MICHIGAN

STATE and NATIONAL PARKS

— *A Complete Guide* —

Third Edition
Revised

by
Tom Powers

Friede Publications

MICHIGAN STATE AND NATIONAL PARKS
A Complete Guide
Revised Third Edition

Copyright, 2001, by Tom Powers

This book may not be reproduced in whole or part
by mimeograph or any other means without permission

Friede Publications
P.O. Box 217
Davison, MI 48423-0217

514 Waukazoo Avenue
Petoskey, MI 49770-2759

Printed in the United States of America

First Printing, March 1989
Second Printing, November 1989
Third Printing, December 1991

Second Edition First Printing, April 1993
Second Edition Second Printing, June 1994
Second Edition Third Printing, July 1995

Third Edition First Printing, May 1997
Revised Third Edition First Printing, May 2001

FOR BARB
Who made it all possible and makes it worth doing

Maps: Gary W. Barfknecht

Photos by Tom and Barb Powers
(except where otherwise indicated)

Front cover photo: Warren Woods
Back cover photo: Straits State Park

OTHER GUIDEBOOKS BY FRIEDE PUBLICATIONS

Natural Michigan
A Guide to 199 Michigan Waterfalls
Canoeing Michigan Rivers
A Traveler's Guide to 116 Michigan Lighthouses
A Traveler's Guide to 100 Eastern Great Lakes Lighthouses
A Traveler's Guide to 116 Western Great Lakes Lighthouses
Ultimate Michigan Adventures
Fish Michigan—100 Southern Michigan Lakes
Fish Michigan—100 Northern Michigan Lakes
Fish Michigan—100 Upper Peninsula Lakes
Fish Michigan—50 Rivers
Fish Michigan—50 More Rivers
Fish Michigan—100 Great Lakes Hotspots

Port Crescent State Park

Foreword

I've had an ongoing love affair with Michigan's state parks for over 40 years. That doesn't mean I've always been completely faithful. State parks other than Michigan's have beckoned and, yes, the allure often proved too powerful to ignore. And Michigan's parks have not always returned unconditional love. I've nearly frozen to death at Indian Lake State Park and been all but eaten alive by stable flies at the Porcupine Mountains.

But in over four decades of camping throughout a significant chunk of America I've found nothing that can compare to the array of beauty, scenic wonder, and opportunities for enjoying or worshipping the out-of-doors that Michigan's state park system has to offer.

In the course of this 40-year relationship there was a period when Michigan's state parks began to show their age like a proud but impoverished dowager. The natural setting were still magnificent, but facilities became worn and ragged, parks were understaffed, nature and interpretive programs were scratched, and even basic services like garbage pickup suffered. This era of stagnation was ending about the time the first edition of this book was published in the late 1980s.

Improvements slowly bloomed in state parks from Warren Dunes in the south to Fort Wilkins in the north. Old parks got new campgrounds, maintenance improved, and services were overhauled. The passage of Proposal P in 1994 signaled a 17% annual increase in operating funds and the rate of change intensified.

The improvements begun in the mid 1990s have continued into the new century. Interpretive programs as well as hands-on environmental activities have been reinstituted at many parks. New restroom facilities are being built throughout the park system, and most campground electrical facilities are now a match for today's RVs. Two state parks (Hartwick Pines and Holland) offer campers full hookups including water and sewer and have sites that can accommodate big rigs.

In the last few years the number of sites has been reduced in many campgrounds. This not only makes camping less crowded, but also protects fragile habitats and allows ground cover and grass to re-establish themselves on worn sites. Sterling State Park is scheduled to close in 2002 for complete remodeling of the campground.

Six years ago the park system made big news when it was announced you could pick up a telephone and make a campground reservation. Today you can make that same reservation over the Internet and even — for the first time — reserve a specific site. That favorite spot that sits right on the beach at Wilderness State Park and is shaded by towering pines is now only mouse clicks away — to you and the other 1,000 people who also consider it the best camping spot in the state.

The old dowager has become tech savvy while reclaiming dignity and prestige, and so my love affair continues.

Tom Powers
April 2001

Introduction

Since 1917 the people of Michigan have had (and continue to have) the generosity and foresight to set aside parcels of their state's prime recreation land for public use and enjoyment.

Those priceless gifts to past, current and future generations today total more than half a million acres, divided among 96 state and four national parks. The unique treasures protect and preserve not only valuable scenic and recreational resources — such as sand dunes, forests, lakes, wave-lapped Great Lakes shoreline, ancient mountains, rare flowers, waterfalls and endangered wildlife — but also some irreplaceable pieces of the state's history. They also put them within both physical and fiscal reach of just about all residents as well as out-of-staters. For a $20 bill, you get unlimited entry for a year to almost all 90-plus parks, which are spread along four coastlines and scattered throughout the interior of both peninsulas. No matter where you are in Michigan, you're rarely more than an hour from at least one, most often several.

An incredible number of people take advantage of the opportunity. In an average year, more than 25 million visitors pass through the entrances of Michigan's state parks. Five million stay overnight, in everything from 40-year-old army surplus tents to $200,000 motor homes.

As a lifelong camper and lover of the outdoors, I have often been counted among them. And while researching this book, I had the rare and distinct pleasure of visiting just about every state park and national park in Michigan.

I took in thousands of unforgettable sights, from spectacular, overpowering vistas of our inland seas' coastlines to delicate wildflowers nearly hidden underfoot. It's possible to frame many of the scenes through a vehicle window; others come through binoculars or from under the brim of a sweat-stained hat during a hard day of hiking. Natural beauty is as close as Maybury State Park, Proud Lake Recreation Area, and other oases at the fringes of urban sprawl, or as distant as a long drive, followed by a six-hour boat ride to Isle Royale National Park.

The tremendous diversity of scenery impressed and delighted me, but what surprised me most during my visits was the variety and number of things to do. The list of opportunities is almost unlimited and includes not only the traditional — camping, hiking, fishing, biking, horseback riding, swimming, picnicking, hunting, skiing, birdwatching, to name a few — but also the unexpected and unusual, such as skeet shooting, sailboarding, hot-air ballooning, hang gliding, overnighting in a frontier-type cabin or Indian-style tipi, riding a self-propelled raft or a dune buggy, and strolling through a ghost town or a working farm. No matter what outdoor activity you enjoy most, chances are you can enjoy it in a Michigan state or national park.

Each park is a unique blend of often-unmatched scenery and opportunities for solitude or activity. Each presents a different way to relax, renew your body and spirit ... to just plain get away from it all.

The following pages describe in detail the wheres and whats so that you can best match them to your own hows. Whether you're an occasional state-park visitor or a lifelong user who's settled on a favorite, you'll find years' worth of new places you'll want to try.

And if by chance you have never visited a Michigan state or national park, when you open this book you will also open a door to a lifetime of pleasure.

Symbols

Map/Text

  BIKE TRAILS OR PATHS

  BIRDWATCHING

  BOAT LAUNCH, generally a well constructed, large ramp that will accommodate most fishing and pleasure boats.

  BRIDLE TRAILS

  CROSS-COUNTRY SKIING

  DUMP STATION

  EQUESTRIAN CAMPGROUND

 FISHING. Convenient fishing access to lakes, rivers, streams and other water bodies within the park or that form the park's boundaries.

 FISHING. Fishing access sites within the park. These vary in character and size from park to park and include shorefishing areas, piers, docks, and small launch areas that will accommodate cartop-size craft.

 FOOT TRAIL

 GRAVEL OR DIRT ROAD

  HIKING

  HISTORICAL ATTRACTION

Map/Text

  HUNTING

  MINI-CABIN (See *Preface* for details.)

  MODERN CAMPGROUND. Usually indicates electrical hookups and modern restrooms with showers.

———— PAVED ROAD

  PICNIC AREA

 RIFLE, SKEET OR ARCHERY RANGE

RUSTIC CABIN (See *Preface* for details.)

RUSTIC CAMPGROUND. Usually indicates pit toilets and no showers or electricity.

SCENIC ATTRACTION

S SHOWER

SNOWMOBILING

SWIMMING

T TOILET

W WATER

WATERFALL

Preface

FEES

State Parks

A motor-vehicle permit is required to enter all state parks. A daily permit costs $4 and is good for the date of purchase only. A $20 annual sticker allows the vehicle to which it is affixed and its occupants unlimited entry into any and all state parks during the calendar year it is issued.

Fort Mackinac, Old Mill Creek and Fort Michilimackinac have separate entrance fees as detailed in their descriptions.

Campground fees in state parks range from $6 to $15 per night depending on the services available.

National Parks

Sleeping Bear Dunes National Lakeshore charges $7 per day per car to enter the park or $15 for an annual permit.

Pictured Rocks National Lakeshore charges $15 for a backpacking permit for groups of 6 or less and $30 for larger groups.

Isle Royale National Park charges a $4 per person per day user fee. A season pass can be obtained for $50.

SCHEDULE

Except for those indicated in the individual descriptions, parks are open year round from 8 a.m. to 10 p.m. daily.

Campgrounds are also open year round, unless otherwise noted in the descriptions. However, between October 15 and May 15, water systems at some parks may be turned off.

RESERVATIONS

The Department of Natural Resources provides two easy ways to reserve camping sites at state parks. You can call 800-44PARKS (447-2757) or go online to www.michigandnr.com

You can currently reserve specific sites at 63 state park campgrounds and soon should be able to do so at all.

Reservations are only accepted 6 months or less in advance. No more than 80 percent of a park's campsites are reserveable; remaining sites are available on a first-come, first-served basis.

A non-refundable $5 reservation fee is charged, and you must secure your reservation with either Mastercard or Visa. You may cancel your reservation before 3 p.m. on the day of check-in, but you will be charged a $5 cancellation fee in addition to forfeiting the reservation fee.

Sites at Lower Peninsula parks must be reserved for a minimum of two nights. Upper Peninsula parks will accept one-night reservations. The maximum reservation time and site occupancy at all parks is 15 days.

There are several advantages for making reservations via the Internet. You can make online reservations 24 hours a day, seven days a week. The web site also contains campground maps for 16 of the park's campgrounds, with the sites numbered and keyed to indicate whether they are lakefront, shaded, or sunny. By 2002 site-specific maps should be available for all campgrounds. Web users can also determine which sites are available on any given date.

You can make reservations by telephone year round Monday through Friday from 8 a.m. to 8 p.m. and on weekends from 9 a.m. to 5 p.m. Most calls are received on Mondays and Tuesdays from morning until late afternoon. The fewest are received Wednesday through Sunday.

RENT-A-TENT

Although the Rent-A-Tent program is rapidly being phased out in favor of mini cabins, there are still a few state parks where you can rent a wall tent or an Indian-style tipi. The tents and tipis are set up and equipped with bunk beds and sleeping pads. All other camping equipment must be supplied by the camper.

Parks that have tents or tipis are Cheboygan, Indian Lake, Interlochen, Wilson, and Warren Dunes. If you are interested in renting a tent or tipi, you should call the parks before progressing too far with your travel plans because the status of this service is rapidly changing. The rental fee varies from $18 to $20 per night.

PICNIC SHELTERS

If you're planning a group outing and want to make sure you're not rained out, you can rent picnic shelters at parks that have them. The rental fee is approximately $40 a day. When the shelters are not reserved or rented they're available — first-come, first-served — at no cost to anyone who wants to use them.

RUSTIC CABINS

For a unique overnight state-park experience, you can rent one of five dozen-plus rustic cabins that are scattered among 20 different parks. An added plus to the rather rustic and spartan charm of the cabins is the fact that they nearly always sit in splendid isolation, well away from the park's other facilities.

Though they vary greatly in sleeping capacity — anywhere from four to 24 — all cabins are essentially the same: near primitive. Construction is basic — a single room with finished

log walls and a cement floor. Furnishings are spartan: twin-size beds or bunks with foam-rubber pads, a small table with chairs, a broom, and a pot-belly stove, with an axe and a stack of firewood provided for heat when needed. You have to fetch your own water at outside hand pumps, and bathroom facilities consist of vault toilets.

You must provide all other necessities and amenities — bedding, cookware, tableware, hand saw, lantern, flashlight, portable cooking stove, and first-aid kit, for examples. But you don't have to lug it all in on your back. Though almost all cabins are located at quiet, secluded sites (many overlooking water) you can drive your vehicle right up to most of them, even in the winter.

Reservations are a must and as far in advance as possible; even more than a year is acceptable. Make your reservations directly, preferably by phone, with the park at which you wish to stay. Parks that have rustic cabins are Bald Mountain, Brighton, Brimley, Cheboygan, Craig Lake, Fort Custer, Hartwick Pines, Highland, Holly, Island Lake, McLain, Ortonville, Porcupine Mountains, Rifle River, Van Riper, Warren Dunes, Waterloo, Wells, Wilderness and Yankee Springs.

The rental rate is $25-65 per night.

MINI-CABINS

A step down from the plush luxury of the rustic cabins are the nearly five dozen mini-cabins available at 35 parks. The small, bare-bones structures measure 12 feet square, sleep four (six if you put the kids to bed on the floor), and are equipped with electric lights, one electrical outlet, a small table for eating if the weather is too bad to dine outside on the picnic table. A few of the mini-cabins in the Upper Peninsula come equipped with electric heat. All mini-cabins are located on a campsite within the park's campground. Although the mini-cabins have no indoor plumbing, the campgrounds' modern restroom buildings are never more than a short walk away. No pets are allowed in the cabins, which rent for $32 per night.

Contents

State
PARKS

Wilderness
STATE PARK

More than 26 miles of coastline shapes Wilderness State Park, a finger of land that points into Lake Michigan at the western edge of the Straits of Mackinac. Most of the shore is a broad band of blinding white sand that stretches away to distant headlands. You can wander nearly deserted beaches for days without crossing the same sand twice, or you can wear a single path to and from the water at a favorite spot. Along the string of uninhabited islands that form the finger's tip, picturesque rock outcroppings, not sand, mark the transition from lake to land.

Away from the water, dense forest blankets one of the Lower Peninsula's largest tracts of wilderness. The area shelters deer, black bear, bobcats and small game, as well as birds and wildflowers.

The park's bird checklist numbers more than 100, and a similar guide to wild-flowers, with bloom dates, includes several rare and endangered species. A good way to see them all is along more than 16 miles of trails, which range from leisurely walks to strenuous hikes.

At Wilderness State Park you also have the opportunity for a real change of pace in overnight accommodations: rustic rental cabins. Six of the one-room trail-side cabins, which sleep four to eight, are set in private, exceptionally scenic surroundings. All but one are on their own stretch of beach. The log cabins are furnished with only the bare necessities: a wood stove, bunks with mattresses, a table and chairs, outdoor vault toilets, a hand water pump and unsplit firewood. You have to bring cooking utensils, a cooler, lanterns, an axe, bed-

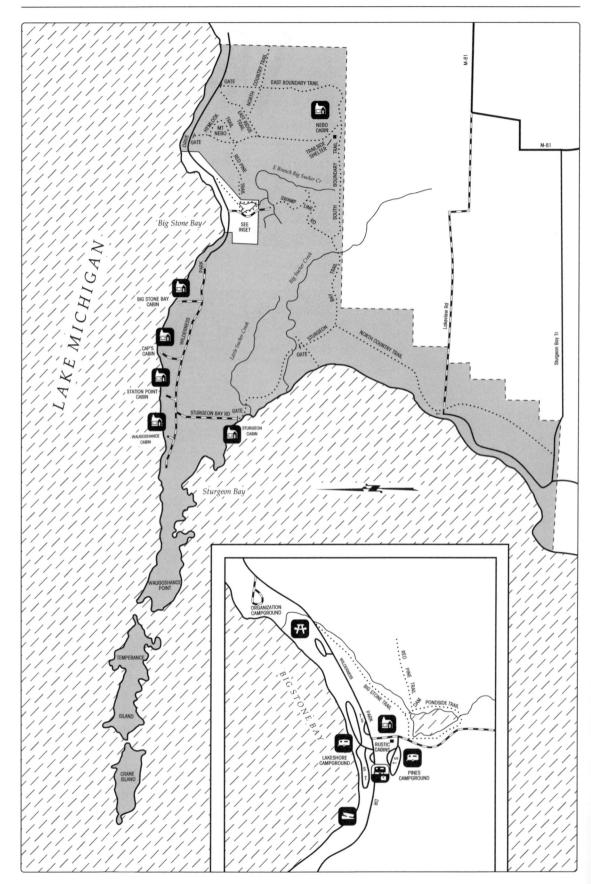

ding and any other comforts. Three larger frontier cabins, which sleep up to 24, are grouped together near the campgrounds.

All cabins rent for $50-65 a night, for up to a 14-night maximum stay, year round. Snowmobilers — although not allowed in the frontier cabin or Nebo Trail area — do, along with cross-country skiers, make heavy use of the trail-side cabins. The cabins, in fact, usually rent approximately a year and a half in advance, so reservations are a must.

Most overnighters stay at one of the park's two completely modern campgrounds, which also are heavily used throughout the summer. It's best to make a reservation, but park personnel say that, because of a high daily turnover, you have a good chance of finding a vacancy if you arrive before noon except on summer weekends.

A total of 250 sites are split into two areas by the park entrance road. Inland on a wooded bluff, lots 151-250 make up the Pines Campground, which features asphalt pads, good shade, plenty of space and a thick carpet of grass. It's only a short walk across the road to the camper's beach plus beautiful views of the Straits from the fine, soft sand that lines Big Stone Bay.

And it's that view and the waterfront sites that attract overnighters to the park's second camping area, 150 lots in the Lakeshore Campground. Campers there give up the grass and spaciousness of the Pines for sandy, well-worn, shady and usually smaller campsites that line the shore four rows deep. Relatively few sites are directly on the beach, and they are in high demand.

About halfway between the campgrounds and the park entrance, the day-use picnic area and swimming beach also stretch along Big Stone Bay. Tables and grills are scattered among pines and cedars, and you can usually claim a large, private parcel of the wide, sandy beach that extends on both sides of the picnic area. If you want more seclusion, walk west along the miles of shoreline that rings the park until you find a spot where you can play Robinson Crusoe.

You can also stretch your legs inland on more than 16 miles of trails that range from a leisurely stroll to a day-long tramp through wild, remote backcountry. The park's shortest path, the Pondside Trail, circles a small pond created by the damming of Big Stone Creek. The Pondside Trail is only a short walk from either campground. On the north side of the dam the Big Stone Trail leaves the Pondside Trail to follow the meandering creek to its end at Lake Michigan. Just a few yards south of the dam, the Red Pine Trail splits off and, a mile later, connects with the Hemlock Trail for a 3.5-mile round-trip nature tour guided by a brochure available at park headquarters. If you really want to test your stamina and resistance to blisters, or simply enjoy being alone in beautiful wilderness, take one of the well-marked 8-, 10- or 11-mile routes that loop from the park road through the vastness of the park's wild backcountry.

Day sailors, fishermen, and power boaters make heavy use of the boat launching ramp west of the campground. The sheltered waters of Big Stone Bay are a summer playground for water skiers and sailboarders, and in June and July the area surrounding Waugoshance Point is ripe with smallmouth bass.

In the winter, cross-country skiers and snowmobilers use the extensive trail system.

Much of the park is also open to hunting in season. Deer are plentiful, but park rangers say it's a hard area to hunt. Bear, rabbits, woodcock and partridge are also taken.

Other facilities/attractions

COUNTY: Emmet

CITY: Mackinaw City

CAMPING SITES: 250, all modern, plus six trail-side and three frontier rental cabins.

DIRECTIONS: Go 12 miles west of Mackinaw City on Wilderness Park Drive.

FURTHER INFORMATION: Wilderness State Park, Carp Lake, MI 49718; (231) 436-5381.

$\mathbf{P}$etoskey
STATE PARK

You can have the best of two worlds at Petoskey State Park. If you want to recharge your batteries in a setting of great natural beauty, you can relax on glistening sand that edges the blue waters of Little Traverse Bay or climb soaring, heavily wooded dunes. On the other hand, if and when relaxation flirts with boredom or you want to temper your dune walks with a stroll through two of northern Michigan's most attractive and popular tourist communities, you can make the short drive to Petoskey or Harbor Springs.

The park's shoreline, which punctuates the east tip of Little Traverse Bay, certainly holds its own when compared to the many other great beaches along Lake Michigan. The broad expanse of blinding white sand gently arcs a total of nearly a mile around both sides of the U-shaped bay. There's plenty of room for solitary sunbathing or beachcombing in sand so fine and soft you'll sink up to your ankles. The ends of the park beach point west to distant views of Harbor Springs, on the north side of the bay, and Petoskey on the south. Just a step away from the sand, between the two wings of the day-use parking lot, is a large, modern bathhouse and concession stand.

Nestled in a low hollow a short distance back from the beach parking lots, is a picnic area sheltered by a line of low dunes and canopied by large pines. Be prepared, however, to share your table and maybe your lunch with inquisitive chipmunks and begging seagulls.

The park's two campgrounds are among the finest in the Lower Peninsula. All 170 lots have electrical hookups and access to modern restrooms and, all things considered, there isn't a bad site among them. Not surprisingly, the campgrounds are heavily used, but park officials say that you can occasionally find a vacancy on summer weekdays.

The original 70-site unit, over the dunes behind the beach, is especially appealing because of the natural privacy. Lots wedged between the high-rising dunes at their base are often nearly surrounded by walls of sand, and some sites are so confined that only small trailers or tents can squeeze into them. Retaining walls around other lots keep the dunes from completely engulfing them. Away from the foot of the dunes, trees and shrubs divide sites into secluded, wooded enclaves. It's a sharp climb over the dunes, or a half-mile drive to the beach/day-use area.

Farther south, 100 lots (91-170), divided into four short loops, make up the park's newest campground. Nestled in a stand of mature pines and hardwoods, the grass-covered sites here are fairly private, well shaded, and larger than those in the older unit. Paved slips at each lot make for easy setup of trailers and RVs, and it's just a short walk to a section of beautiful beach well away from the crowded day-use area.

Inland, a palisade of high dunes along the east border cuts the 305-acre park off from the sights and sounds of busy highway M-119. You can get to the top of one of the mountains of sand by taking the Old Baldy Trail. The short route, which starts directly opposite the campers-registration station, is a climb up a series of stairs and steep paths that will literally leave you breathless as you take in the panoramic view of the bay through the trees. Other marked routes skirt the base of the dunes — their height and steepness hidden under a blanket of trees — and swing close to the beach.

 Two and a half of the park's three miles of trails are maintained in the winter for use by cross-country skiers.

Only minutes away by car, almost equal distances from the park along the north and south shore of the bay are fine restaurants, expensive boutiques, unique gift shops, art galleries, and streets lined with Victorian summer cottages in the small resort towns of Harbor Springs and Petoskey. Both have served as summer playgrounds for the rich and famous since before the turn of the century, and you can easily spend a day and a month's salary in either.

 Other facilities/attractions

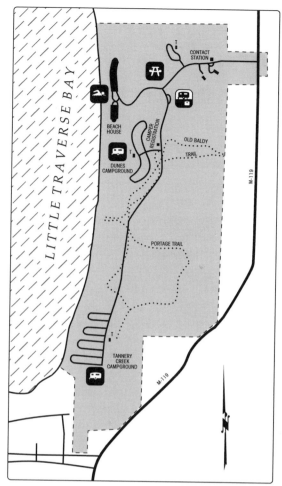

COUNTY: Emmet

CITY: Petoskey

CAMPING SITES: 168, all modern, plus two mini-cabins.

DIRECTIONS: Drive north from Petoskey on US-31 approximately 3 miles to M-119. Turn north (left) onto M-119 and go about 1.5 miles to the park entrance.

FURTHER INFORMATION: Petoskey State Park, 2475 Harbor Petoskey Rd., Petoskey, MI 49770; (231) 347-2311.

Burt Lake State Park

Burt Lake State Park is a perfect example of why Michigan is called a "water wonderland." The park spreads back from the south shore of Michigan's fourth-largest lake, a lake that is a magnet for both pleasure boaters and fishermen. Only minutes away by car are scores of other inland lakes, gentle serpentine rivers and boisterous streams. And an easy half-hour drive in any of three directions leads to the special character, mood and beauty of the great waters of lakes Huron and Michigan and the Straits of Mackinac.

But most important, Burt is one in a chain of lakes and rivers that make up the Inland Waterway, a 40-mile route across the northern tip of the Lower Peninsula that many claim is one of the most beautiful boat trips anywhere in the country. Boaters can travel any or all of the waterway, which connects Lake Huron at Cheboygan — inland through Mullet, Burt, and Crooked lakes and the Indian, Cheboygan and Crooked rivers — to Conway, only three air miles from Lake Michigan.

At Burt Lake State Park, which just about marks the halfway point of the route, you can launch your boat or canoe, then head out on the unique water highway in either direction. If you don't own your craft, you can rent a rowboat, canoe, power boat, pontoon boat, and even a small houseboat from marinas along the Inland Waterway. (For a detailed description of the entire Inland Waterway, see *Ultimate Michigan Adventures*, Friede Publications.)

You don't have to go any farther than Burt Lake's 17,000 acres of water for fine fishing, however. The popular, heavily fished lake is rated one of the Midwest's best for walleyes, and it also consistently yields impressive catches of large and smallmouth bass, plus rock bass, plenty of perch, brown and rainbow trout and some northern pike.

The park campground is more a refuge and respite from a busy day afloat or afield than a place to practice the finer points of lethargy. The grounds are large, and in recent years the number of campsites were reduced from 375 to 307 to give campers more elbow room in what used to be a very crowded campground with little privacy. Plans call for a further reduction in the number of sites to ensure that everyone has a quality camping experience. Nearly all sites are shaded by a dense leafy canopy, and all are close to the beach. Reservations are almost mandatory to ensure a space on a July or August weekend, but you can usually find a vacancy in midweek if you arrive early in the day.

North of the campground, tables and grills mix with widely spaced, mature hardwoods and cedars on a large picnic grounds that overlooks the lake. Conveniently located less than a mile from I-75, this picnic area is a pleasant rest stop for expressway travelers.

An excellent swimming beach with a modern bathhouse stretches nearly the entire length of the park's sandy shoreline.

Other facilities/attractions

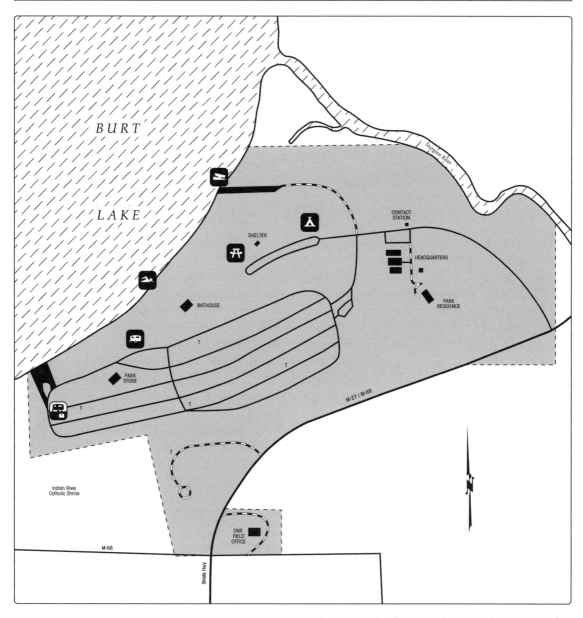

COUNTY: Cheboygan

CITY: Indian River

CAMPING SITES: 307, all modern and a mini-cabin.

SCHEDULE: The park closes from about December 1 to mid-April. Call for exact opening and closing dates.

DIRECTIONS: From I-75 take the Indian River exit (310) and go west 0.5 miles on M-68 to Old US-27. Turn left (south) and follow M-27/M-68 less than a mile.

FURTHER INFORMATION: Burt Lake State Park, 6635 State Park Dr., Indian River, MI 49749; (231) 238-9392.

Young
STATE PARK

A pleasing mixture of the unexpected and the presumed, Young State Park is easy to like.

For instance, with a mile-plus shoreline on Lake Charlevoix, Michigan's fourth-largest inland lake, you would expect a beautiful beach. But after you enter the park, you wonder if you will ever see *any* water. You wind through almost a mile of thick, lush woods just to get to the contact station, where the forested landscape still hides any sight of the lake. Not until you reach one of the three campgrounds or the day-use area do you catch a glimpse of the water through the trees.

Then finally, at the picnic area your presumption is verified — you get a close-up look at one of the finest beaches on any inland lake in the state. The wide, sandy strip approaches the water at such a slight angle that the lake appears undecided as to just where it should leave off and land begin. The flat, long expanse of sand often holds shallow pools, left after an overconfident encroachment by waves or from rain that couldn't find its way to the lake without the help of a more-precipitous slope. And there's an added plus: unlike at most parks, where you have to lug cooler and basket seemingly forever before arriving at a table, the parking lot here is conveniently close.

Overnighters are spread among 240 sites at three completely modern campgrounds. Use is heavy throughout the summer months, and an overnight stay, even in midweek from early July to mid-August, is chancy without a reservation.

The best sites — with shade, some privacy,

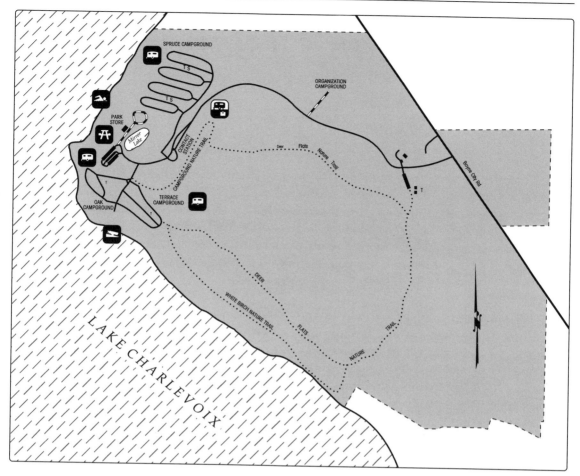

and views of the water from most — are in two adjoining campgrounds, Oak and Terrace, located south of the picnic area. These two campgrounds offer the only lakeside camping sites in the park. The 147 grass-covered lots at the Spruce Campground, north of the picnic area, are spread in four loops over an open meadow and offer some shade and privacy. Though there are no lakeside lots, it's just a short walk to the beach.

Stretching inland from the rear of the campgrounds are acres of forest that are overlooked or just plain forgotten by most visitors, who focus on the beautiful beach and lake. Casual hikers or those with a purpose such as mushroom hunting, birdwatching or wildflower gazing have their choice of the short White Birch or longer Deer Flats nature trails, which loop through the deep, quiet woods.

 Cross-country skiers crease the same six miles of trails when the snow flies.

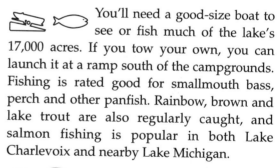 You'll need a good-size boat to see or fish much of the lake's 17,000 acres. If you tow your own, you can launch it at a ramp south of the campgrounds. Fishing is rated good for smallmouth bass, perch and other panfish. Rainbow, brown and lake trout are also regularly caught, and salmon fishing is popular in both Lake Charlevoix and nearby Lake Michigan.

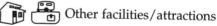 Other facilities/attractions

County: Charlevoix

City: Boyne City

Camping Sites: 240, all modern, plus two mini-cabins.

Schedule: Open May 1 through December 1.

Directions: Go 2.5 miles northwest of Boyne City on Boyne City Road.

Further Information: Young State Park, 02280 Boyne City Rd., Boyne City, MI 49712; (231) 582-7523.

Fisherman's Island
State Park

Shhh! Don't tell anyone else, but if you'd like to have miles of superb Lake Michigan shoreline and over 2,000 acres of unspoiled wilderness virtually to yourself, go to Fisherman's Island State Park. Compared to other nearby state parks this undiscovered gem is all but ignored by vacationers. Its beautiful 81-site campground is lightly used, even during peak summer months. And when you wander its miles of scenic beach in solitude, it's not hard to imagine you're alone on a deserted island.

It's also not hard to figure out why attendance is so low — services and facilities are minimal. The southern half of the park isn't developed at all, and facilities in the northern section are rustic, approaching primitive.

The park's main, partially paved road closely parallels Lake Michigan for almost two miles through the northern parcel.

A few tables at the southern end of the road make up the park's only picnic area,

You can park in a small lot at either end of the road and wander down the beach. Or you can pull off onto the shoulder just about anywhere along the route and enjoy the view, beachcomb or swim, though there's no bathhouse. The shoreline alternates between soft sand and piles of gravel created by centuries-long pounding of waves on low, exposed outcroppings of soft sedimentary rock. In other places huge boulders poke out of the lake near shore or rest right at the water's edge.

The scenic dirt road also connects the two widely separated loops of the park's rustic (pit toilets are the only facility) campground. Most of the 81 spacious, secluded sites are set on the inland side of the road in the shade of heavy woods. The half dozen or so widely spaced lots that do line the shore are among the most-scenic camping spots in the Lower Peninsula. At any of the other lots,

though, you're never more than a few steps from the beach as well as hundreds of acres of seldom-trod woods.

The only posted trail slips into the quiet woods near the park entrance and parallels the park road for three miles before emerging from the woods at the southern end of the road. If you're not up to walking the entire distance, you can take either of two short spurs — which cut the trail into three loops of about equal length — back out to the park road. Several other unmapped and unmarked paths also penetrate the pine-, cedar-, and hardwood-blanketed terrain. Most of the park is open to hunting, with deer, grouse and rabbits the game most pursued.

The park's nearly six miles of Lake Michigan coastline is neatly split at its midpoint by a mile of private property. Park land south of that partition is completely undeveloped — no restrooms, picnic tables, campgrounds, not even a sign; nothing except unsurpassed natural beauty few people take the trouble to discover.

It's not easy, but it sure is worth the effort. The only way into the area is on a rutted, pothole infested two-track that begins behind the Norwood Township Park in the village of Norwood, then leads north along the shore. First, check on the condition of the road at park headquarters. Then, if you're adventurous or have a four-wheel-drive vehicle, travel 2.3

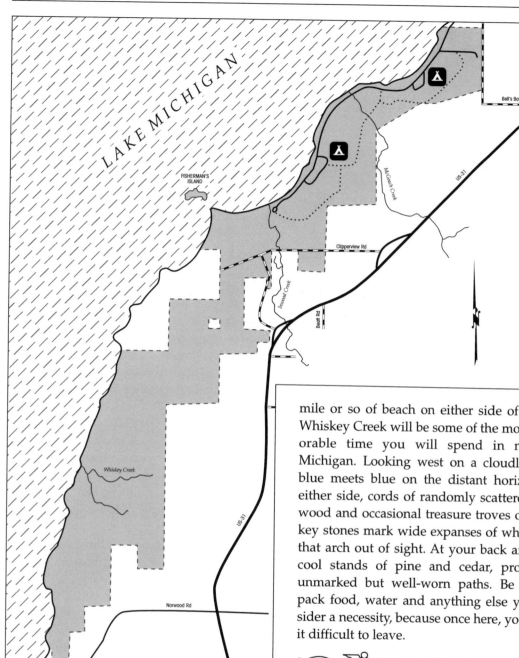

mile or so of beach on either side of Whiskey Creek will be some of the most memorable time you will spend in northern Michigan. Looking west on a cloudless day, blue meets blue on the distant horizon. On either side, cords of randomly scattered driftwood and occasional treasure troves of Petoskey stones mark wide expanses of white sand that arch out of sight. At your back are thick, cool stands of pine and cedar, probed by unmarked but well-worn paths. Be sure to pack food, water and anything else you consider a necessity, because once here, you'll find it difficult to leave.

Other facilities/attractions

miles north along the beach until the road ends at Whiskey Creek. Or to be a little more prudent and cautious, drive up the road until ruts and potholes force you into a turnoff, then hike the rest of the way.

No matter how you get there, get there. Part or all of any day walking down the

COUNTY: Charlevoix

CITY: Charlevoix

CAMPING SITES: 81, all rustic.

SCHEDULE: Open early April (weather permitting) to December 1.

DIRECTIONS: From Charlevoix, drive 5 miles south on US-31 to Bell's Bay Road. Turn right (west) onto Bells' Bay and go 2.5 miles.

FURTHER INFORMATION: Fisherman's Island State Park, P.O. Box 456, Bells Bay Rd., Charlevoix, MI 49720; (231) 547-6641.

Leelanau
State Park

Perched like a crown on top of the peninsula from which it takes its name, Leelanau State Park royally welcomes you with scenic views of Grand Traverse Bay and Lake Michigan, rugged shoreline, untouched woods, a picturesque lighthouse, a grassy picnic area, and a small, secluded campground.

The "crown" is the smaller of the park's two parcels, which total 1,253 acres and are separated by a section of private land. Almost all of the park's facilities have been developed around an historic lighthouse that stands at the edge of that 250-acre tip's rocky shore. The solid, white two-story structure, currently being restored by the Grand Traverse Lighthouse Foundation, was built in 1858 as the last in a series of beacons that guided ships into Grand Traverse Bay from the site since 1852. Tours of the lighthouse are available during the summer.

A few hundred feet away, well back from and out of sight of the water, picnic tables, grills and playground equipment are scattered across a large, open, grassy meadow.

In a dense grove of pine and cedar just east of the lighthouse, a 52-site rustic campground lines one of the few rocky stretches of shoreline along the entire eastern Lake Michigan coast. A combination of few sites and great beauty and seclusion add up to a full campground on most summer weekends, so reservations are a must if you plan to stay here.

All sites are large, deeply shaded and private, and great views of the lake come from most, even those not right on the beach. No matter which site, you won't have far to drag your lawn chair to the rock-strewn beach to sit and gaze at the water, soak up some sun, or read in the exceptionally quiet, peaceful surroundings. Because of the rocks, however, it's a less-than-desirable spot to swim or even wade.

A long stretch of wide, sandy beach does line the shore where the park's larger, south section, presses against Lake Michigan. But to get to it you have to hike almost a half mile from the parking area at the end of Dinsmore Road that intersects with CR-629 about four miles south of the campground entrance.

From the beach, the 1,000-acre-plus tract sprawls inland and in one small area comes close to bridging the narrow strip referred to as the Lower Peninsula mitten's "little finger." Eight miles of hiking and cross-country ski trails loop through dunes, marsh areas, interdunal wetlands, and deep, cool woods. Branching from the loops are three short spurs that lead to the beach, a magnificent overlook of Lake Michigan from atop a dune, and to the shoreline of Mud Lake. You probably won't bump into other hikers, but you may have to share your path with deer, raccoons, rabbits, fox, porcupines and other small mammals that are sheltered and fed by the diverse habitat. This section of the park is open to hunting in season.

Because of its location, Leelanau State Park is excellent for birding. Migrating raptors and songbirds resist crossing open water as long as possible. So in spring, as the migrants move north along the Lake Michigan shoreline, the peninsula acts like a giant funnel and its tip becomes a natural resting place. Raptors begin moving through the area in early spring and songbird migration usually

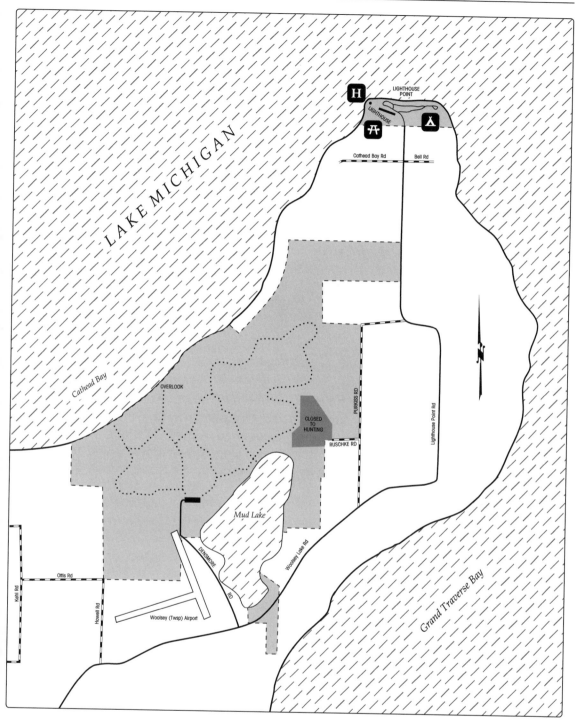

hits its peak in the first two weeks of May. The dense woods and varied habitat of the park's south section also attract many summer nesting species.

 Other facilities/attractions

County: Leelanau

City: Northport

Camping Sites: 52, all rustic, and two mini-cabins.

Directions: Go approximately 8 miles north of Northport on CR-629.

Further Information: Leelanau State Park, 15310 N. Lighthouse Point Rd., Northport, MI 49670; (231) 386-5422.

Traverse City
State Park

You don't go to Traverse City State Park to escape into the peace and quiet of Michigan's northern woods. The 47-acre parcel borders busy US-31 in the middle of probably one of the most-expensive zones of commercial real estate in northern Michigan. Restaurants, condominiums, million-dollar homes, a shopping center, expensive gift shops, motels, and at least three elaborate putt-putt golf courses all share a 2- to 3-mile stretch of highway with the park. Campsites, 343 of them, have been squeezed into every available inch of park property, including even an old parking lot. In short, Traverse City State Park is small, crowded and noisy.

You should avoid it, then, at all costs ... right? A quarter-million-plus annual visitors say otherwise. The campground is always full, with a daily lineup of inquirers hoping for rare vacancies. The only sure way to get a camping spot any time during the summer is to reserve one well in advance.

Why is this park — in as urban a setting as any in the state — so popular? Because it is one of the least expensive places from which to enjoy one of Michigan's most-attractive vacation areas. To most campers Traverse City State Park is an inexpensive outdoor resort in the middle of a good time.

Not far west of the park is great shopping, fine dining, a zoo, a museum, and countless other attractions and activities at Traverse City. Ringing the urban area are vineyards, cherry orchards, and ubiquitous roadside stands that sell mouth-watering fresh fruit, vegetables and homemade baked goods. Both arms of Grand Traverse Bay and other beautiful scenery is almost always in view, and M-37 — which branches off US-31 less than a mile from the park and runs up to the tip of Old Mission Peninsula — is one of the prettiest drives in the state.

Further afield, Sleeping Bear Dunes National Lakeshore is less than an hour's drive, and the quaint towns and scenic vistas of the Leelanau Peninsula add up to a memorable day trip.

The park does have a few attractive facilities of its own. Just across the highway from the campground via a pedestrian overpass is a long, narrow strip of land along the east arm of Grand Traverse Bay that makes up a day-use area. A sandy swimming beach, with a modern bathhouse, edges the bay at the east end, and picnic tables and grills overlook the blue-green water at the west end.

Immediately south of the camper's playground the Reffitt Nature Trail winds through nearly a mile of mixed hardwoods and pines and presents hikers with views of most northern Michigan ecosystems. If you want to stretch your legs on a longer hike or bike trip, the Traverse Area Recreational Trail is accessible from the southeast corner of the campground. That trail generally parallels the railroad tracks and allows bikers to pedal the three miles to downtown Traverse City without having to ride on any major highways.

Other facilities/attractions

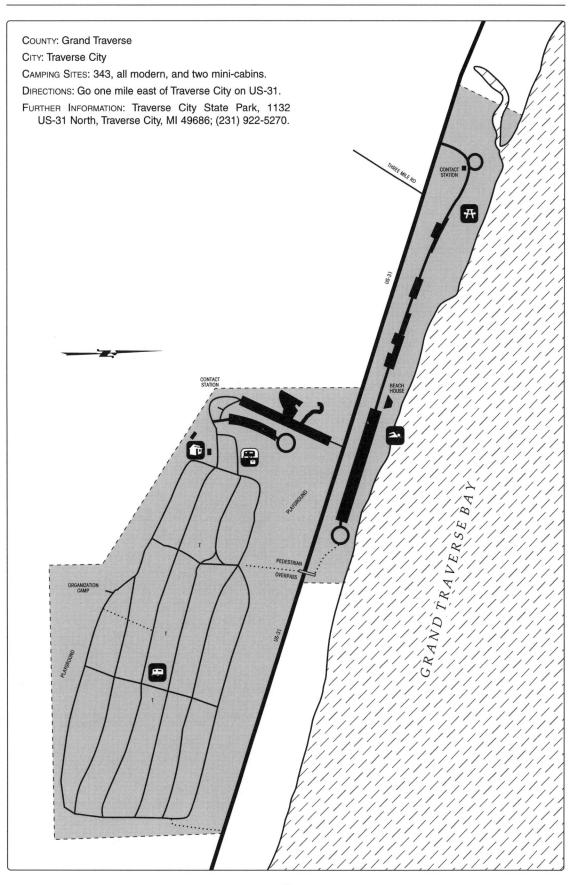

COUNTY: Grand Traverse

CITY: Traverse City

CAMPING SITES: 343, all modern, and two mini-cabins.

DIRECTIONS: Go one mile east of Traverse City on US-31.

FURTHER INFORMATION: Traverse City State Park, 1132 US-31 North, Traverse City, MI 49686; (231) 922-5270.

THREE MILE RD

CONTACT STATION

US-31

CONTACT STATION

BEACH HOUSE

PLAYGROUND

PEDESTRIAN OVERPASS

ORGANIZATION CAMP

US-31

PLAYGROUND

T

T

T

GRAND TRAVERSE BAY

Interlochen State Park

A stay at Interlochen State Park has the feeling of an old-time Chautauqua vacation* that emphasizes the fine arts. Most of the park's quarter-million annual visitors set up tents, trailers and RV's at the state-park system's largest campground, then flock to soak up some culture directly across the highway. There, among the pines in this rural, off-the-beaten-track corner of Michigan is the world-renowned Interlochen Center for the Arts. You can tour the complex, which includes the National Music Camp and year-round Arts Academy, and attend daily plays, exhibitions and, under the curving amphitheater of the sky, public concerts performed by both students and visiting guest artists.

Strains of music also drift on the wind through the campgrounds, which opened in 1917 as the first in the Michigan state-park system. They may be old, but they've kept pace. Four hundred twenty-eight of the 498 sites are completely modern, with electrical hookups and access to flush toilets, hot water and showers.

Those modern lots are divided into two wings that sprawl along the west shore of Duck Lake. The spots are generally small, grassy, and deeply shaded by stately, old trees, but most lack privacy. Both wings are laid out like large subdivisions, and it's easy for small children to get lost in the bewildering number of loops that cut through the deep woods. Older youngsters, on the other hand, dodge cars as they whiz along the paved, ready-made race tracks on their bikes.

Sandwiched between the two wings is a wide, sandy beach, backed by a broad meadow. Picnic tables and grills dot the grassy area and also hide in the surrounding deep woods. Other facilities include a bathhouse, a store and boat rentals.

*Victorian-era summer encampments — which began at Chautauqua, New York, and quickly spread over the East — where vacationing families were entertained by fine music and educational lectures.

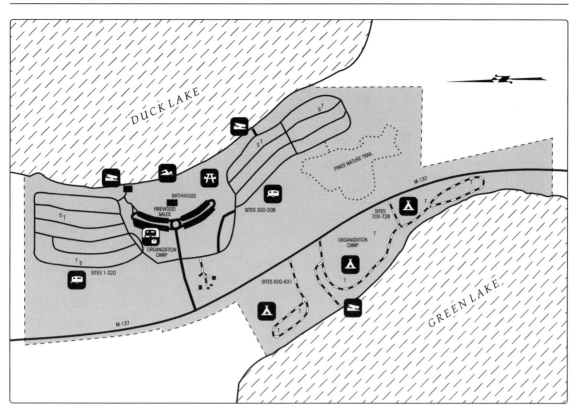

Across M-137 and slightly south of the modern campground/day-use area is a small, rustic (no flush toilets or electricity) overnight area. Sixty spacious, fairly private sites there are widely spaced in the shade of heavy woods on a low bluff overlooking Green Lake.

All 498 sites (more than any other state park) at the three camping areas fill on most weekends in July and August. Spots usually open up in the middle of the week, but if you're planning to vacation here, make reservations.

Though most visitors won't rate the scenery or outdoor activities as their number-one reason for camping at Interlochen, there are natural attractions to fill time between concerts. Several short paths, including a self-guided nature trail, wind through the few of the park's 187 acres that aren't developed. The most-awe-inspiring are walks in the shadow of 300-year-old virgin white pines that make up one of the last remaining stands in the state. You can also burn off enough calories on a walk to Interlochen, about a mile north of the park on M-137, to indulge in a guilt-free ice

cream cone at a roadside stand in the small village.

Fishermen wet lines in both Green and Duck lakes, which sandwich the park. Good catches of large and smallmouth bass, panfish, splake, cisco, walleyes, northern pike, and brook, brown, rainbow, and lake trout are pulled from both lakes and surrounding rivers and streams.

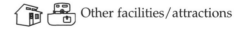 Boat access comes from a pair of launch sites on Duck Lake and one on Green Lake.

Other facilities/attractions

County: Grand Traverse

City: Interlochen

Camping Sites: 498 (428 modern, 60 rustic), including four rent-a-tents, one tipi, two mini-cabins and 3 organization sites.

Schedule: The park is open all year, but the modern restrooms are closed during the winter.

Directions: Drive approximately 14 miles southwest from Traverse City on US-31 to M-137. Turn south onto M-137 and go about 1.5 miles.

Further Information: Interlochen State Park, M-137, Interlochen, MI 49643; (231) 276-9511.

Otsego Lake
STATE PARK

If your idea of a great vacation is to set up camp in quiet surroundings, then do little more than plop into a comfortable chair and tend a campfire within view of a beautiful lake, Otsego Lake State Park is ready made for you.

There are no hiking trails and few distractions in this 62-acre park, one of the smallest in northern Michigan. If you do get the urge to move, a first-rate beach and picnic area are close at hand.

The park's half-mile-plus of Otsego Lake shoreline includes a large, triangular peninsula that projects into the water near the center. There, nearly surrounded by water and sand, picnickers have their choice of widely spaced tables and grills right at the water's edge or nestled in a quiet, secluded stand of mature red and white pine just a few yards back. Good views or at least glimpses of the water come from almost anywhere on the grass-covered area, and another plus is the convenient parking area at the base of the peninsula. On the landward side of that lot is a more-open, grassy picnic area with a large adjacent playground. On the north edge of the triangle, a wide, sandy beach and large swimming area front a park store and picnic shelter.

The nearly 5-mile-long, narrow lake is popular with both pleasure boaters and fishermen, who go after perch, pike and tiger muskies. Otsego Lake is also rated the best in the area for smallmouth bass. The park's boat ramp is located on the south edge of the peninsula. A new fishing pier pokes out into the lake only a few steps to the west of the ramp.

Strung out behind and to the sides of the peninsula is the park's completely modern campground, with 155 mostly shaded, well-worn sites divided into north and south loops. Lots 1-99, on a tree-covered bluff overlooking the lake, make up the north loop. Several scattered sets of stairs lead from that unit down to the water's edge and a playground there. The smaller south loop is closer to the water and, in fact, lots 100-104, 106, 108, 111, 113-116, 127 and even-numbered lots 120-126 are right on the shore. Because of Otsego Lake State Park's convenient location in the center of the northern half of the Lower Peninsula, its campground fills almost every weekend from early July to mid-August.

 Other facilities/attractions

---

COUNTY: Otsego

CITY: Gaylord

CAMPING SITES: 155, all modern, plus one mini-cabin.

SCHEDULE: The park is open year round, but camping is only available from late April to December 1.

DIRECTIONS: From I-75 take exit 270 (Waters) and go west less than half a mile to Old US-27. Turn right (north) onto Old 27 and drive about 3 miles.

FURTHER INFORMATION: Otsego Lake State Park, 7136 Old US-27 South, Gaylord, MI 49735; (989) 732-5485.

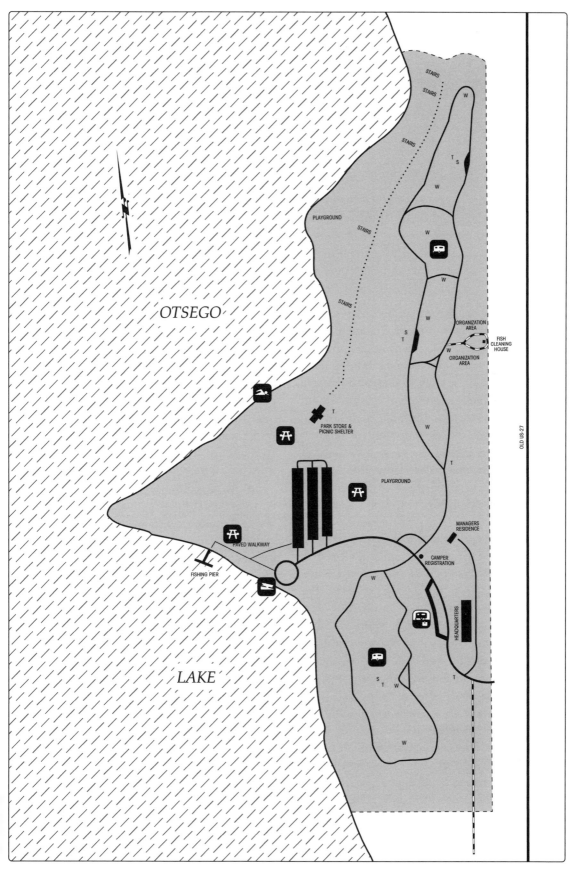

OTSEGO

LAKE

PLAYGROUND

STAIRS
STAIRS
STAIRS
STAIRS
STAIRS
STAIRS

W
T
S
W
W
W
W
S
T
W

ORGANIZATION
AREA

FISH
CLEANING
HOUSE

ORGANIZATION
AREA

W

W

T

T

PARK STORE &
PICNIC SHELTER

PLAYGROUND

MANAGERS
RESIDENCE

PAVED WALKWAY

FISHING PIER

CAMPER
REGISTRATION

W

W

S
T
W

W

HEADQUARTERS

T

OLD US-27

Hartwick Pines
State Park

A hundred years ago, you could have walked just about anywhere and everywhere in the northern regions of our state through magnificent white-pine forests. But by the turn of the century, 160 billion board feet of the timber had been harvested, a near clear-cutting that yielded more wealth than all the gold mined in California but left us with little more than the lore and legends of lumberjacks and logging camps. That colorful, bygone way of life, plus an awesome glimpse at what northern Michigan looked like before it fell to axes and saws are both preserved at Hartwick Pines State Park.

Be sure to begin your visit at the Michigan Forest Visitor Center, a 1,500-square-foot exhibit hall filled with hands-on exhibits, dioramas, and even a talking tree. Together they tell the story of the natural origin of Michigan's once magnificent forests, recount the colorful history of the state's lumbering era, and explain the development of modern forest management. A 14-minute, nine-projector, multi-image slide program continuously showing in a 105-seat auditorium complements and expands on the lessons learned in the exhibit hall.

From the rear door of the Center a paved trail winds through the spiritual heart of the park: a 49-acre tract of old growth white pine and an adjacent lumbering museum. The path, named the Old Growth Forest Foot Trail, is one of the most memorable short walks in the state. In the shadows of the towering old pines, voices are hushed and no one rushes. (The loop is about a mile long, but plan to spend a minimum of an hour and a half.) You can't help but pause — often to contemplate, almost in spiritual awe — the beauty, grace and noble bearing of these relics of Michigan's past, some of which are well over 300 years old and approach 150 feet in height.

From the pines the route gently winds to a logging museum that includes replicas of a bunkhouse, mess hall, camp-store, and blacksmith shop, which re-create the atmos-

phere of an authentic old-time logging camp. You don't have to spend much time at the complex to get the feeling that cutting lumber from sunup to sundown, six months a year, for a dollar a day plus room and board wasn't a glamorous job. Scattered around the grounds near the museum are some large tools of the trade, such as a steam-powered sawmill and 10-foot-high logging wheels used to drag cut trees out of the woods.

To fully enjoy and appreciate the Old Growth Forest Foot Trail, join one of the regularly scheduled tours led by park interpreters or pick up a detailed, self-guiding pamphlet at the visitor center.

Three other pamphlet-guided trails loop through areas near the pine tract. South of the grove is the 2-mile-long Mertz Grade Trail, an hour route along the roadbed of a narrow-gauge railroad that once hauled logs out of the area. The 3-mile Au Sable Trail swings north over high, rolling hills blanketed with a variety of forest types, and makes two crossings of the East Branch of the Au Sable River. Both trails begin at the day-use parking lot.

Other miles of footpaths that web the rest of the 9,672-acre park reward hikers with solitude and excellent views of two cedar swamps, vast pine plantations, a stand of old-growth hemlock, several near-pocket-size lakes, and the Au Sable River. Bright & Glory Nature Trail, the

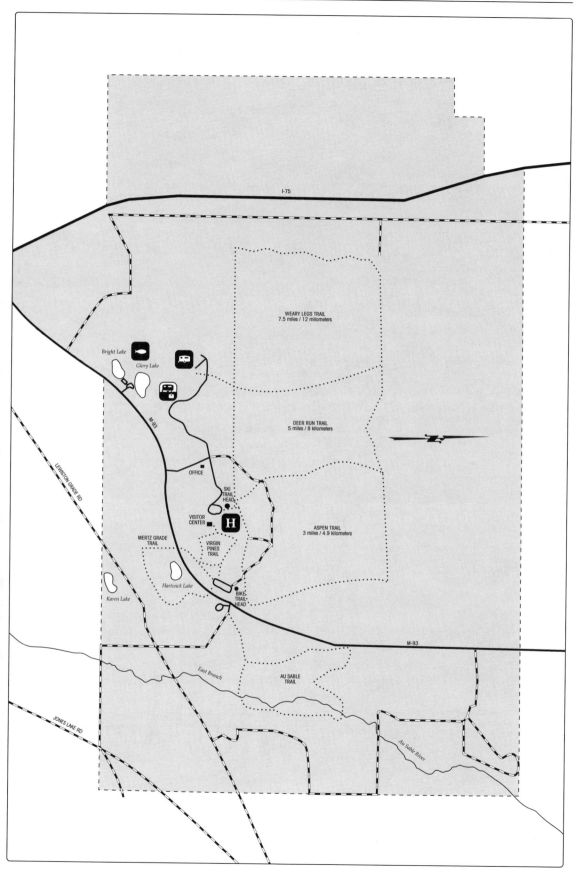

I-75

WEARY LEGS TRAIL
7.5 miles / 12 kilometers

Bright Lake

Glory Lake

DEER RUN TRAIL
5 miles / 8 kilometers

M-93

LEWISTON GRADE RD

OFFICE

SKI
TRAIL
HEAD

VISITOR
CENTER

H

ASPEN TRAIL
3 miles / 4.9 kilometers

MERTZ GRADE
TRAIL

VIRGIN
PINES
TRAIL

Hartwick Lake

Karen Lake

BIKE
TRAIL
HEAD

M-93

East Branch

AU SABLE
TRAIL

JONES LAKE RD

Au Sable River

shortest of the self-guided trails, departs from the park's campground and gives a lesson in botany and natural history as it leads to the two lakes bearing the trail's name.

Wildflowers, berries and mushrooms all sprout throughout the park in their growing seasons, and miles of the trails are open to cross-country skiers and mountain bikers. Hartwick Pines is designated non-motorized, except for a portion of the 6-mile Lewis Grade Snowmobile Trail that cuts through the park.

Deer, bear, grouse, rabbits, woodcock and other wildlife are rife in the park, and hunting in season is allowed outside the virgin pines and developed areas. The park area is a popular with deer hunters, some of whom use the campground as their base.

Fishermen can break out fly rods and test their skill and luck on two designated trout lakes, Bright and Glory, as well as nearly three miles of river. Bright and Glory lakes each have handicapped accessible fishing piers.

The park's fully modern campground is nestled in quiet woods, and most all of the 100 sites are open and sunny, though also fairly close together. All sites have electrical hook-ups, 36 offer full hook-ups, and there are even a few pull-through sites.

From the campground it's just a short walk to the trout fishing at Bright and Glory lakes, and a trailhead for the complex of cross-country skiing/mountain bike trails is just outside the campground entrance.

Though the day-use area has remained in the same location, the route to it has changed. Instead of turning off M-93 immediately into the day-use parking lot, you now follow a scenic mile-long drive from the park entrance to the grills and picnic tables scattered under a stand of mature pines.

Other facilities/attractions

COUNTY: Crawford

CITY: Grayling

CAMPING SITES: 100, all modern, including 36 with full hook-ups; one rustic rental cabin.

SCHEDULE: The park is open 8 a.m. to 10 p.m. year round.

The Michigan Forest Visitor Center is open weekends, 9 a.m. to 4 p.m., from November 15 through April 15; six days a week (closed Mondays), 9 a.m. to 7 p.m., from April 15 to Memorial Day; and seven days a week, 9 a.m. to 7 p.m., from Memorial Day through Labor Day.

The Logging Museum is open 8 a.m. to 4:00 p.m. in May, September and October and 8 a.m. to 7 p.m. from Memorial Day through Labor Day. The museum is closed during the winter months.

DIRECTIONS: From I-75 take exit 259 and drive east on M-93 2 miles.

FURTHER INFORMATION: Hartwick Pines State Park, 4216 Ranger Rd., Grayling, MI 49738; (989) 348-7068.

North Higgins Lake
State Park

Fifteen hundred feet of frontage on the distinctive blue-green waters of Higgins Lake, a beautiful campground, outstanding beach and picnic areas, and miles of hiking trails past lakes and through seemingly boundless woods make North Higgins Lake State Park a near-perfect vacation spot.

It wasn't always that way.

Less than 100 years ago if you had visited here or just about anywhere else in northern Michigan, you would have faced scarred, barren land. Lumbermen had ravaged the forest that once blanketed the state, and the fires and erosion that followed the axes and saws created a bleak landscape.

In 1903, as a first step in reforesting the wind-swept plains, Michigan created its first forest nursery on land that is now part of the park. Thirty-some years later — during a unique period when young men came to

northern Michigan and planted more than 400 million trees, constructed 7,000 miles of fire roads, improved wildlife habitat, and built campgrounds, picnic areas and hiking trails — a large Civilian Conservation Corps (CCC) camp shared the nursery space.

Today, many restored nursery buildings, (including Michigan's first iron fire tower), a 1.5-mile self-guided nature trail through the nursery grounds, and a one-of-a-kind museum modeled after a 1930s CCC barracks all bring to life the story of the people who restored the state's grandeur and turned it into an immense outdoor playground. At the former Cone Barn, for instance, you can learn how 20-22 million seedlings were grown and shipped annually. Daily interpretive programs add more details to the story of forest fires, reforestation and forest management past and present.

For a close-at-hand look at the results of the great reforestation undertaking, take the 3.8-mile Bosom Pine Trail, the 6.5-mile Beaver Creek Trail, or other long paths that penetrate the 429-acre park's backcountry from the old nursery area. A 1.5-mile fitness loop, with 20 exercise stations, also starts and finishes at the parking lot next to the nursery.

Cross-country skiers can glide over the backcountry routes in the winter, and snowmobilers have 10 miles of swaths of their own through the park.

Across County Road 200 from the nursery/museum area, the focus is on

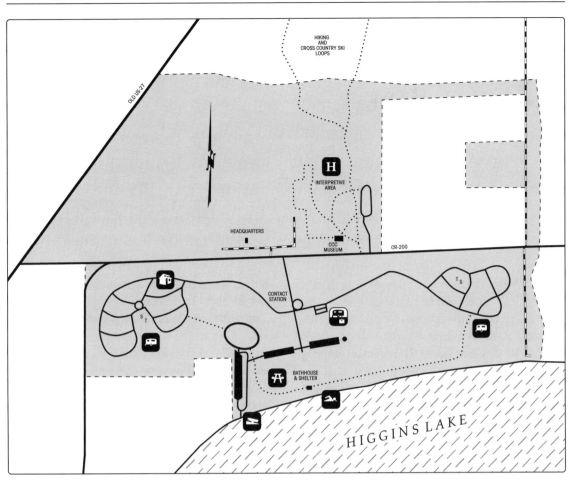

the crystal-clear waters of Higgins Lake and the park's 1,500 feet of sandy shoreline along it. The lake bottom slopes so gently that you have to wade out 50-100 feet just to get waist deep.

Close to the water on either side of a bathhouse and small picnic shelter, tables and grills dot the grass under a mature stand of red pines interrupted by an occasional hardwood.

Water skiers, fishermen, sailboaters and powerboaters all make waves after putting in at a ramp at the west end of the beach/picnic area, and scuba divers love to take the plunge into the deep, clear waters.

Short trails from the day-use area connect inland to each of the modern campground's two widely spaced wings. Many of the 175 lots are well worn, and most are roomy, shaded and fairly private. Generally, lots 101-182, which make up the east wing, are smaller and less private than those

(1-93) on the west wing. If you plan to stay here any time from Memorial Day through Labor Day, make a reservation, as the campground fills every summer weekend and is heavily used throughout the week.

During warm-weather months the entire park is almost always busy. But even when full it doesn't seem particularly crowded and is a nice alternative to its sister park on the south side of the lake.

 Other facilities/attractions

---

COUNTIES: Crawford and Roscommon

CITY: Roscommon

CAMPING SITES: 175, all modern, and two mini-cabins.

DIRECTIONS: From US-27 just south of its junction with I-75, take CR-200 a half mile east.

FURTHER INFORMATION: North Higgins Lake State Park, 11747 N. Higgins Lake Dr., Roscommon, MI 48653; (989) 821-6125.

South Higgins Lake
STATE PARK

Since its creation in 1924, South Higgins Lake State Park has been one of the most-popular vacation destinations in northern Michigan, and for good reason. Higgins is one of the most-beautiful inland lakes in Michigan. Its unusually blue, clear, spring-fed water is a magnet that draws nearly 350,000 outdoor lovers each year to its sandy south shore.

That's a lot of people, but there's a lot of beach and water. The 10,000-acre lake laps up against almost a mile of sandy park shoreline, almost half of which fronts the day-use area. The gently sloping lake bottom there makes for very shallow water far out into the lake, and tree-shaded grills, picnic tables and playground equipment creep right to the water's edge. Just a few steps away is a bathhouse and camp store, where you can buy ice cream, pop, snacks, some camping-grocery needs, and a plethora of typical "up-north" souvenirs.

West of the day-use beach, power boaters and fishermen can launch into a large, protected basin, troll out to the lake entrance, then weave past sailboarders into the open waters. Most fishermen go after perch. But lake and brown trout, which were introduced in the early 1970s, as well as smallmouth bass also provide good action. Rental rowboats, pontoons, sailboats, canoes and pedalboats are available at the store.

The boat basin and trailer parking lot behind it cut off the day-use area from the second-largest campground in the state-run system. Four hundred completely modern, heavily shaded sites are arranged in a series of long, narrow loops that point to the lake. You don't come to this campground, to enjoy peace, quiet and solitude.

None of the lots are especially small, but all are cheek by jowl with each other and you'll see (and be seen by) dozens of your neighbors. Lots in the older loops, are generally badly worn with only fallen leaves covering the bare earth. Lots in the newer loops, are grass covered (at least for now), and a scant few offer some privacy. None of the sites directly edge the water, so overnighters can swim from and sunbathe on nearly a half mile of uninterrupted, sandy campers-only beach.

The campground is not only one of Michigan's largest, but also one of its busiest. By the second week in February, park officials have handed out all reservations for the July 4th weekend. It is consistently full throughout the summer, and even though park policy allows only three-fourths of the sites to be reserved on any given day, your chances of claiming a vacant spot on or close to the weekend without a reservation are not good.

If you want to get away from all the people and activity, cross County Road 100 and hike all or part of 5.5 miles of trails that cut through a recently added undeveloped tract, which more than doubled the park's size to 1,000 acres. You can choose from 2.0-, 3.5- and 5.5-mile-long loops, the inner parts of which follow the shore of Marl Lake. The far end of the longest circuit, which nearly circles the small lake, reaches The Cut, a channel dug during the logging era to connect Higgins and Houghton lakes.

The trails are open during the winter for cross-country skiing, and the park land around Marl Lake is open to

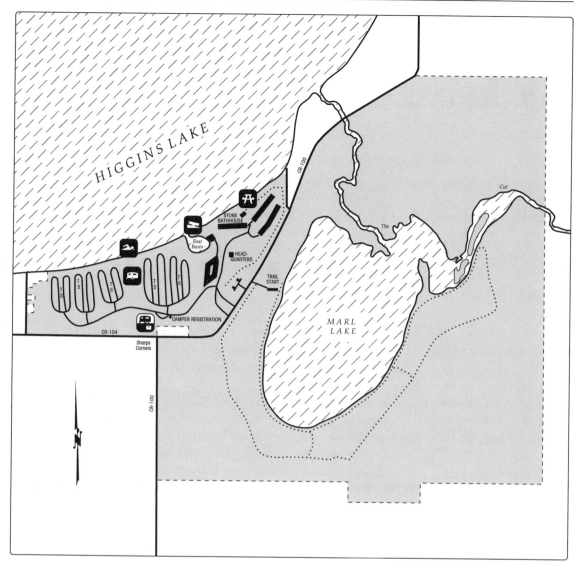

hunting, with ducks, squirrels, rabbit and deer all successfully taken.

  Other facilities/attractions

COUNTY: Roscommon

CITY: Roscommon

CAMPING SITES: 400, all modern, plus a mini-cabin.

DIRECTIONS: Go 6 miles east of US-27 on Higgins Lake Road.

FURTHER INFORMATION: South Higgins Lake State Park, 106 State Park Dr., Roscommon, MI 48653; (989) 821-6374.

$\mathbf{M}$*itchell* STATE PARK

If you like water or water sports, Mitchell State Park is an ideal vacation destination. The heart of the park covers a narrow isthmus that is nearly surrounded by water. Lake Cadillac laps at the park's east border and Lake Mitchell at the west. Connecting them along the north edge of the day-use and camping areas is a navigable 60-foot-wide canal, dug in the 1870s to move logs between the two lakes. A few campers, at sites that border the canal, have the rare opportunity in a Michigan state park to dock their boats practically next to their RV's or tents.

From the dock, a heavily used campers-only launch on Lake Cadillac near the canal mouth, or a day-use ramp on Lake Mitchell it's a short ride to fishing, water skiing, or just cruising on either of the two large lakes. On Lake Cadillac, for instance, you can motor past fine old homes that line the shore on your way right into downtown Cadillac at the east end. And on Lake Mitchell, which stretches several miles to the north and west, you can water ski in a straight line until your arms fall off.

Mitchell's large 215-site campground spreads south from the channel in four elongated loops whose eastern tips point to a campers-only playground and sandy beach on the shore of Lake Cadillac. The completely modern campground is usually filled to capacity during the summer, so reservations are a must to ensure a spot. Almost all sites are roomy and well shaded. If you have a boat, you'll want to try for the lots that back right up to a wood dock on the canal. There, you have the nearly unique opportunity in the state park system to tie up next to your campsite.

The long dock is also popular with shore fishermen, who go after pike, perch, bluegills, bass and walleyes in the channel. Walleyes are the number-one game fish in Lake Cadillac, and good catches of northern pike, perch and bluegills are also reported.

Lake Mitchell is best known for its largemouth bass but also walleyes and perch. Both lakes sprout icemen's shanty towns in the winter.

Across M-115 from the campground a day-use area takes up a few hundred yards of Lake Mitchell's shoreline. Within a few feet of the parking lot (and only yards from the sight and sound of busy M-115) huge, old pines stand like sentinels over scattered tables and grills. Sweeping views of the lake come from a narrow, sandy swimming beach that skirts the waterline in front of the small, grassy picnic grounds. Day-use boaters can launch their craft in Lake Mitchell from a ramp on the south side of the swimming beach.

On park property north of the canal is the Hunting and Fishing Visitor Center and the Heritage Fisheries and Wildlife Nature Study Area. Inside the center, dioramas, an aquarium, and other displays feature live and mounted Michigan wildlife plus a variety of other exhibits, including a multi-media slide show that outlines the history of hunting, fishing and conservation in Michigan. A store offers nature guides, T-shirts, wildlife art and other items.

A trail from the Center leads to the Heritage Fisheries and Wildlife Study Area, a 70-acre marsh encircled by a 2.5-mile-long path atop a dike. From the encircling dike,

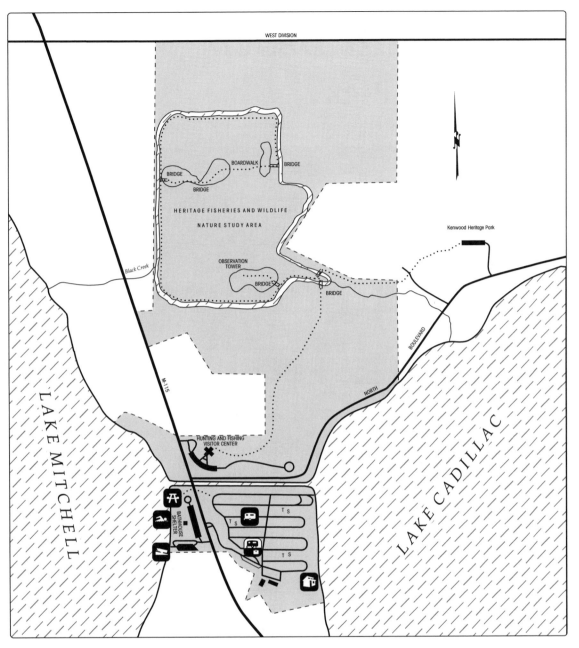

you have the option of cutting through the heart of the marsh — via an extensive system of boardwalks and bridges in the northern half of the marsh — or taking a shorter bridge across a pool on the southern edge of the marsh to an observation tower offering a panoramic view of the area. All of the trails pass through a profusion of wildflowers, and there's plenty of opportunity to spot waterfowl and marsh birds. You can walk through the area on your own or join guided hikes that leave from the center.

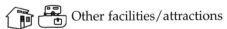 Other facilities/attractions

COUNTY: Wexford

CITY: Cadillac

SCHEDULE: The visitor center is open 10 a.m.-6 p.m. daily (except Mondays) from May through November, and Fridays, Saturdays and Sundays the rest of the year.

CAMPING SITES: 215, all modern, plus a mini-cabin.

DIRECTIONS: The park is located on M-I15, on the west side of the city of Cadillac.

FURTHER INFORMATION: Mitchell State Park, 6093 E. M-115, Cadillac, MI 49601; (231) 775-7911.

Orchard Beach
STATE PARK

Orchard Beach State Park perches on a high bluff that overlooks Lake Michigan, and the crow's-nest view from the edge is hard to beat. Beneath the arch of sky, distant freighters plow faint V's through the constantly shifting hues of blue and green. Closer to shore, smaller boats, too numerous to count, bob in the waves that sweep one of Michigan's favorite fishing spots.

Just behind the crest of the bluff, somewhat protected from strong offshore breezes, is the park's 167-site modern campground. Mature hardwoods and remnants of an old orchard also shelter and shade the large, level, grassy lots. Privacy, however, is minimal. This especially fine campground is extremely busy throughout the summer, filling every weekend then, so make a reservations if you plan to come anytime July through Labor Day. A long flight of stairs at the south end of the

campground drops from the bluff to the swimming beach. The strip of sand, though not very wide, edges the water for nearly 3,000 feet.

North of the beach and campground, picnic tables and grills spread over a large, grassy meadow atop the bluff.

Across M-110 from the picnic grounds, a half-mile self-guided nature trail and two additional miles of hiking trails, divided into three loops, wind through the 201-acre park's,

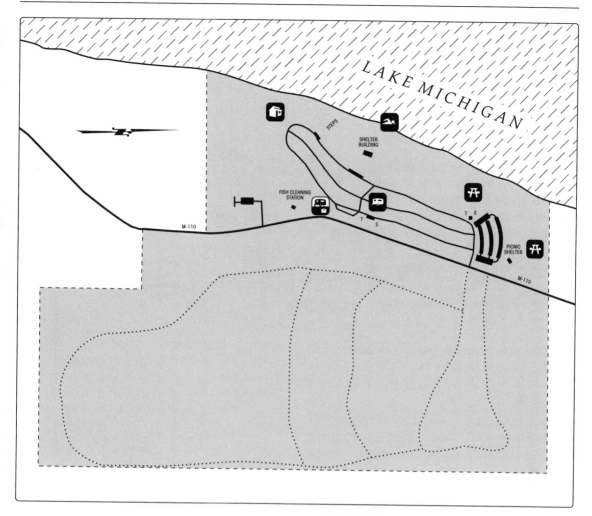

deer-rich backcountry. A trail guide, available from the contact station, describes the natural and geological history of the area traversed by the trails.

Though there is no boat access or good shorefishing within the park, prime angling comes from several ramps, charter boats and a pier in Manistee, just two miles south. Action on the big lake, Manistee Lake and from the pier can be heavy for king and coho salmon, lake and brown trout, and steelhead.

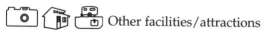 Other facilities/attractions

COUNTY: Manistee

CITY: Manistee

CAMPING SITES: 167, all modern plus a mini-cabin.

DIRECTIONS: Go 2 miles north of Manistee on M-110.

FURTHER INFORMATION: Orchard Beach State Park, 2064 Lakeshore Rd., Manistee, MI 49660; (231) 723-7422.

Ludington State Park

Don't be in a hurry to get to the heart of Ludington State Park. Drive slowly up M-116, which hugs Lake Michigan the last two miles to the entrance, to catch as many glimpses of the water and beach as you can through breaks in the curtain of low dunes. Or take advantage of the numerous opportunities to pull off the road, scramble over the dunes, and join campers from the park, locals and others who have lugged coolers, beach chairs and umbrellas to the magnificent beach. On summer weekends, you may have to parallel park in a line of vehicles at the edge of the highway, but even so, you'll find that the vast stretch of sand appears only lightly scattered with people.

When you do get to the end of M-116, you will have reached one of Michigan's finest outdoor playgrounds—5,308 acres of beautiful beaches, dunes and forests that wrap around picnic areas, hiking trails, three campgrounds, the Great Lakes Visitor Center, and fishing, hunting, canoeing and river-tubing opportunities .

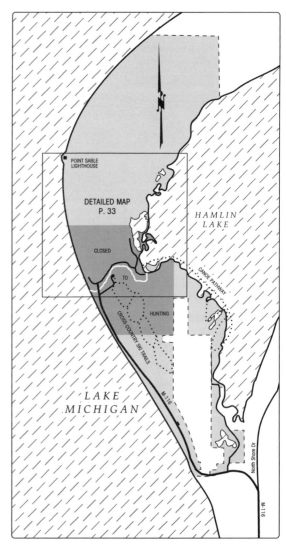

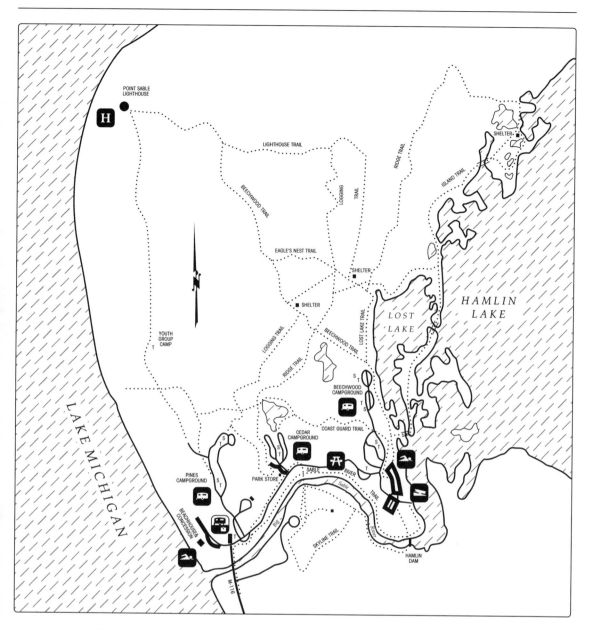

The park spreads over a wide strip of land between Lake Michigan and Hamlin Lake (Michigan's largest man-made lake), with the main facilities lining the Sable River, which connects them. Tube riders and canoeists float the stream, and cyclists pedal along a picturesque path that borders the river. Next to the river at close to the halfway point between the two lakes is a pleasant picnic area.

Near the Hamlin Lake end of the river a shaded picnic grounds closely borders a small, sandy strip of beach. South of the beach parking lot a historical plaque marks the site where the logging village of Hamlin stood before an earlier version of the present Hamlin Dam burst and swept the village's 40 homes, sawmill and a million board feet of lumber into Lake Michigan. The lake water there is warm, shallow, and only a step away from a concession stand and bathhouse. The Hamlin Lake beach also marks the starting point of a short canoe trail that edges the southeastern shore of the lake.

At the opposite, west end of the stream, a large bathhouse and a concession stand overlook a broad expanse of sand that gently slips into the crystal-blue waters of Lake Michigan. This beach — the park's most popular — and its small parking lot are often crowded.

North of the river, three heavily used, reservations-recommended campgrounds, with a total of 344 fully modern sites, are spaced along the road. Closest to Lake Michigan are the small, crowded, shaded lots that make up Pine Campground. Open, sunny lots at Cedar Campground are about halfway between lakes Michigan and Hamlin. Most sites there are roomy and grass covered and you're only a few steps from the park store. Farthest inland, the generally large, old, well-worn lots of Beechwood Campground are shaded by stately hardwoods, and a few line the shores of Hamlin and Lost lakes.

Eleven trails that lace the park's interior number among the finest foot paths in the Lower Peninsula. You can take a half-hour walk or an all-day outing on the 18-mile system, with loops and branches that reach north to the historic Point Sable Lighthouse, follow the jigsaw-puzzle-shaped shore of Hamlin Lake, climb forested dunes, and lead to the Lake Michigan shoreline. Three shelters are scattered along the remote sections of trail.

One short and especially scenic route, the Skyline Trail, forms a large loop around the Great Lakes Visitor Center on the south side of the Sable River. The trail climbs a long flight of stairs, then follows the crest of a towering wooded dune with sweeping views of both Lake Michigan and the low dunes that range inland. Inside the Center you can get a good overall picture of the Great Lakes' ecology and wildlife from live exhibits, slide shows, and other displays. You can reach the visitor center and Skyline Trail by car from M-116 or on footpaths from the campgrounds.

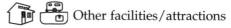 Cross-country skiers can set tracks on 16 miles of trails, and much of the park's acreage is also open to hunters in season.

Summer anglers launch at a ramp south of Beechwood Campground, then go after tiger muskies, northern pike, panfish, walleyes, and large and smallmouth bass over Hamlin Lake's 5,000 acres. Ice fishermen, too, pull out fine catches of pike and bluegill.

Other facilities/attractions

COUNTY: Mason

CITY: Ludington

CAMPING SITES: 344, all modern, plus three mini-cabins, one in each campground, all with electricity.

DIRECTIONS: Go 7 miles north of Ludington on M-116.

FURTHER INFORMATION: Ludington State Park, Box 709, Ludington, MI 49341; (231) 843-2423 or (231) 843-8671.

Charles Mears
State Park

If your definition of a fine park is, "a great beach," then an excellent synonym is "Mears State Park." More than 300,000 visitors a year leave footprints in the pillow-soft, white sand that covers almost all of the park's 50 acres, including the main attraction: a several-hundred-yard-long, over-50-yard-wide stretch along Lake Michigan.

Changing courts, restrooms and a concession stand separate that swimming area from a large day-use parking lot, and a few picnic tables are also widely scattered throughout the concession/parking area.

Most visitors also walk a few dozen yards south to a pier to watch pleasure and fishing boats that parade between Pentwater Lake and Lake Michigan. (The park has no launch facilities, but there are several ramps on Pentwater Lake in the nearby village of Pentwater.)

Fishermen also line the pier and in season pull salmon, steelhead, perch, lake trout and smelt from the channel.

If you're thinking about staying at the park's campground on any weekend during the warm-weather months, make a reservation well in advance because your chances of finding an empty campsite without one are only slightly better than hitting the Daily Three lottery game. The 180 relatively small sites are arranged very close together in several loops behind a low dune that separates and partially shelters the area from Lake Michigan. Each lot has an asphalt slip on which to park vehicles or set up trailers, as well as an electrical hookup and access to modern restroom facilities. Recently planted trees on many of the lots will shade them someday, but for now most heat up by midday in the open, sunny expanse of sand.

It doesn't seem to matter much. Most campers are on the beach, fishing, or exploring

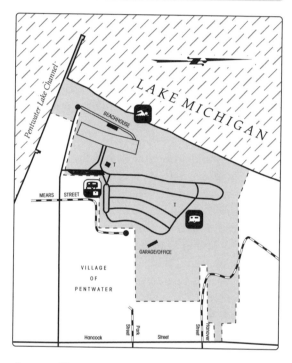

the small resort town of Pentwater, and use their tents, trailers and RVs just for sleeping or grabbing a bite to eat.

Other facilities/attractions

COUNTY: Oceana

CITY: Pentwater

CAMPING SITES: 180, all modern.

SCHEDULE: The park is open year round, but the campground is closed December 1-March 15.

DIRECTIONS: Go 4 blocks west of downtown Pentwater on Lowell Street.

FURTHER INFORMATION: Charles Mears State Park, P.O. Box 370, W. Lowell St., Pentwater, MI 49449; (231) 869-2051.

Silver Lake State Park

Don't come to Silver Lake State Park looking for rest and relaxation or expecting peace and quiet. Do come here if you'd like to spend time on an enormous, fun-filled sand pile that is surrounded by a virtual amusement park.

At Silver Lake you really can't separate the outside attractions from the park itself — the entire area is a huge playground. Within walking distance from the park are bumper boats and cars, arcades, one of the state's two commercial dune-buggy rides, sailboat and sailboard rentals, and slightly farther afield, riding stables and canoe rentals.

The main attraction within the park and covering half its 2,675 acres is sand, enormous mounds that separate Lake Michigan from Silver Lake. Except for the water, the treeless, wind-swept dunes are remindful of the Sahara Desert, and it's not hard to imagine that Beau Geste and the French Foreign Legion might march over the nearest crest.

Instead, what you're likely to see and hear are dune buggies and other off-road vehicles (ORVs). The northern quarter of the dune area has been set aside as a 450-acre Off Road Vehicle Area, the only such parcel in a Michigan state park. On summer weekends the park and surrounding area buzzes with dune-buggy traffic to and from the ORV dunes. The parking lot there is usually jammed full, and riders often wait a half hour or more just to get on the sand. If you want to give it a try but don't own your own ORV, you can rent one from a private concessionaire nearby.

If you'd rather hit the sand with both feet instead of four wheels you can hike and climb 750 acres of the dunes that are reserved for pedestrians. Access comes from a parking area just south of the ORV lot. If you'd like to combine a large expanse of sand with sun and water, head to the opposite (southern) edge of the park where a sand road leads to a small parking lot and access to a stretch of Lake Michigan beach guarded by the historic Little Point Sable Lighthouse.

Most of the park's developed facilities are compressed into a small parcel on the east shore of Silver Lake, out of sight and sound of the ORV hills. A small, sandy swimming beach there borders the warm, shallow waters of the lake, and a few picnic tables and trees ring a bathhouse and picnic shelter. The view across the lake is like no other in the state. Looking completely out of place, a wall of sand rises out of, towers over, and is the lake's west shore.

Just a short walk from the day-use area is the older of the park's two camping areas. Lots (1-84) in that unit are heavily shaded, well worn, and squeezed together, with very little privacy or room. The crowding is further aggravated by boats and ORVs that are jammed into almost every other campsite. Also heavily shaded but much roomier, more private, and less crowded are lots 101-236, which make up the newer camping area across the road. All campsites in both sections have electrical outlets and access to modern restrooms. The choice of sites doesn't matter much to most campers, who only return to eat, sleep and rest between activities. The campground is busy, filling to capacity every summer weekend, so reservations are a must.

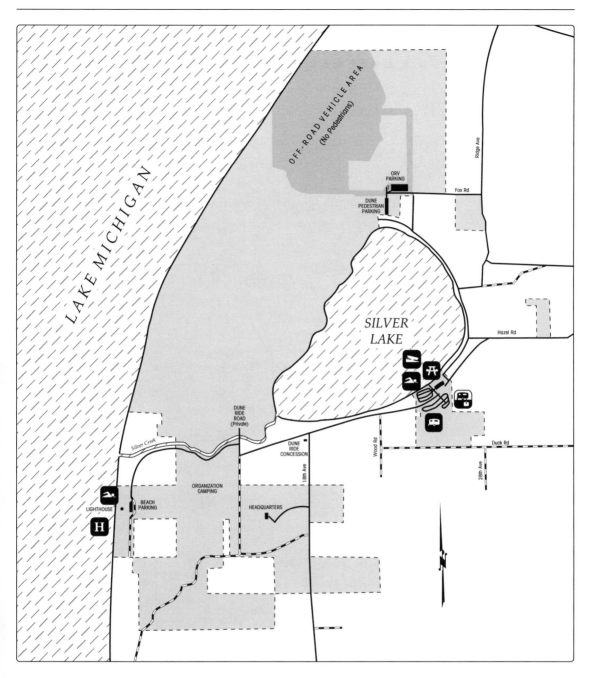

 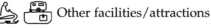 Boaters can put in at a launch on Silver Lakein the day-use area. Fishermen, who wet lines in both Silver Lake and Lake Michigan, go after walleyes, perch, large and smallmouth bass, brown trout, crappies and other panfish.

In the less-developed sections of the park, hunters try for deer, rabbits, raccoon, squirrels and grouse in season.

Other facilities/attractions

COUNTY: Oceana

CITY: Mears

CAMPING SITES: 198, all modern.

SCHEDULE: The park is open year round and campgrounds are open April-November, but modern restrooms are closed from October 15 to April 15.

DIRECTIONS: From US-31 about 35 miles north of Muskegon exit onto Shelby Road and go west 6 miles to Scenic Drive. Turn right (north) onto Scenic Drive and follow the road (which changes names several times) 4.5 miles.

FURTHER INFORMATION: Silver Lake State Park, 9679 W. State Park Rd., Mears, MI 49436; (231) 873-3083.

H*art-Montague Trail*
STATE PARK

The Hart-Montague Bicycle Trail was the first "rail-to-trail" state park in Michigan. A 10-foot-wide strip of asphalt that winds from Montague to Hart has replaced tracks that carried Chesapeake and Ohio trains along the route for nearly a hundred years.

The pathway is intended for use primarily by bicyclists, but hikers, cross-country skiers and snowmobilers are also welcome. The trail, which parallels US-31, passes through some of the finest scenery in western Michigan.

Although trail users encounter several small villages, most of the trail's 22 miles traverse open and uninhabited land. Woodlots, wetlands, open fields, picturesque streams, a few scattered picnic areas and scenic overlooks contribute to an ever-changing panorama. Mile markers are posted the entire length of the trail.

A detailed trail guide, available from the address below, lists all access points, private campgrounds adjacent to the trail, and restaurants and grocery stores found along its length.

A planned 10-mile-long extension will reach from Montague to Dalton, north of Muskegon.

COUNTY: Muskegon and Oceana

CITY: Hart and Montague

CAMPING SITES: None

DIRECTIONS: The Hart trailhead is in John Gurney Park, on the south shore of Hart Lake. The Montague trailhead is on Stanton Boulevard just off Business Route US-31 on the northeast side of town.

FURTHER INFORMATION: Hart-Montague Trail State Park, 9679 W. State Park Rd., Mears, MI 49436; (231) 873-3038.

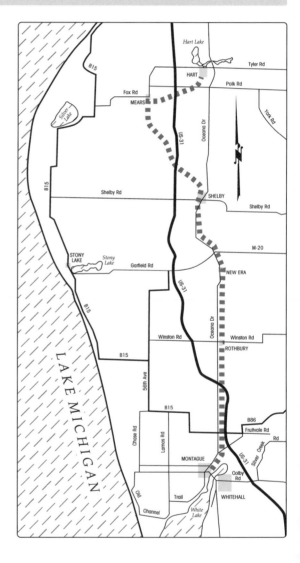

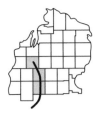

White Pine Trail
STATE PARK

The White Pine Trail State Park is not only the newest in Michigan's state system, but on completion will also be, by far, the longest. The gravel-surfaced route will eventually stretch from Cadillac to Grand Rapids, 92 miles to the south.

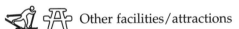 To date, 80 miles of the route — from Cadillac to Belmont, just north of Grand Rapids — is open, offering opportunity for some serious depletion of hikers' shoe leather or trail biker's tire rubber.

This "rails-to-trails" route follows the roadbed of the Michigan Northern Railroad and generally parallels US-131. Some 20 rivers and streams cross the trail, which parallels the Muskegon, Grand and Rouge rivers, each for significant distances. Some of the crossings offer attractive views, and plans call for the addition of boardwalks and viewing platforms.

The trail also runs through Paris County Park in Mecosta County, and camping is available within a mile of the route in or near Morley, Sand Lake and Reed City.

Other facilities/attractions

COUNTIES: Mecosta, Osceola, Wexford, Montcalm and Kent.

CITIES: Cadillac, Big Rapids and Reed City.

CAMPING SITES: None on the trail itself but camping is available in cities along the route.

DIRECTIONS: Plans call for this trail, when completed, to have the following 14 staging/parking areas: Kent County—Comstock Park, Belmont, Rockford, Russell Rd., Cedar Springs and Sand Lake; Montcalm County—Howard City; Mecosta County—Morley, Stanwood and Big Rapids; Osceola County—Reed City and Leroy; and Wexford County—Cadillac.

Currently, only three staging areas are open (Cadillac, Big Rapids and Sand Lake), and only the Cadillac site has been completely developed, including vault toilets.

To reach the Cadillac trailhead, from the junction of M-115 and US-131 drive northwest on M-115 a half mile to North 41 Road. Turn right (north) onto 41 Road and drive one mile to North 44 Road. Turn left (west) onto North 44 Road and drive approximately a half mile to the trailhead, on the left (south).

To reach the Big Rapids trailhead, from US-131 exit (139) onto M-20 and drive east about 3 miles to Maple St. Continue east on Maple for two blocks to a depot building on the right (south).

To reach the Sand Lake staging area, from US-131 take exit 110 and go east on Lake St. about 1.25 miles.

FURTHER INFORMATION: White Pine Trail State Park, 211 W. Upton Ave., Reed City, MI 49677; (231) 832-0794.

Newaygo State Park

Newaygo State Park is not the Club Med of Michigan state parks. Camping conditions are rustic, there's no swimming beach to speak of, no picnic area, no hiking trails, and no fancy facilities. So why come here? Well, if you're looking for a naturally beautiful place to get away from it all while staying at a campground where you're not crammed in elbow to elbow, this park rates four stars.

Newaygo State Park's 257 acres spread over a high bluff on the south side of a large impoundment of the Muskegon River called Hardy Dam Pond. "Pond," however, hardly seems the proper name for a body of water over a mile wide and six miles long. Canoeing is rated good along its wooded shore, and anglers go mainly after walleye, but also smallmouth bass, perch and pike. Boaters have easy access from a launch ramp (with a large boat-trailer parking lot) that dips through a break in the line of bluffs to a small cove between the campground's two wings.

The campground is rustic — meaning vault toilets and no electricity,

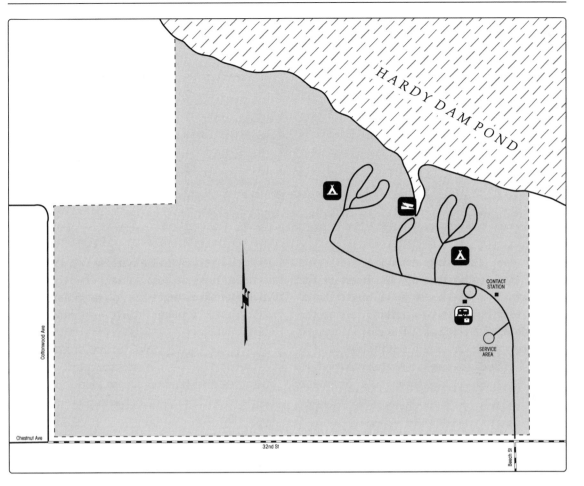

although water tanks of trailers and motor homes can be filled and holding tanks emptied at a sanitation station near the park entrance. The overnight area is exceptionally quiet and peaceful, but because of the lack of facilities is only moderately used and you can generally find a vacant space even on summer weekends.

Ninety-nine sites in two double-looped wings spread across the top of the bluff, with good views of the lake coming from some lots. The campsites are little more than small openings carved out of the thick woods that blanket the entire area, so you get a lot of privacy and deep shade. Each wing is equipped with a small playground for children.

Away from the camping area, the vast majority of the park property is completely undeveloped. The bluff meets the lake at a sharp angle and is heavily wooded to the water's edge, so there's no good place to swim in the park. It's just a short drive, how-

ever, to attractive beaches at township parks that ring the pond. No marked hiking trails cut through the thick forest of oak, large-tooth aspen and white pine. But it's easy to wander the woods and lakeshore in search of the many wildflowers and mushrooms that poke up in season. Park officials say that birdwatching can be excellent, especially for numerous waterfowl and shorebirds on the pond and warblers, thrush and other songbirds in the woods.

COUNTY: Newaygo

CITY: Newaygo

CAMPING SITES: 99, all rustic.

SCHEDULE: The campground is open April 1 - December 1.

DIRECTIONS: Approximately 43 miles north of Grand Rapids on US-131, take the Morley exit and go west 7 miles on USFS-5104 (Jefferson Road) to Beech Road. Turn right (north) onto Beech and go a half mile.

FURTHER INFORMATION: Newaygo State Park, 2793 Beech St., Newaygo, MI 49337; (231) 856-4452, summer only.

Duck Lake
STATE PARK

If you're looking for a place to get away from crowds, Duck Lake State Park is for you. The out-of-the-way day-use park is wild, open and undeveloped except where it touches the shore of Duck Lake and a short but striking stretch of Lake Michigan.

The long entrance road cuts south through the heart of the park, which is blanketed by a mixed hardwood/ pine forest, to two parking lots on the north shore of Duck Lake. The east lot faces a sheltered beach, a small bathhouse, and a wooded picnic area (with a shelter) that edges the quiet waters of the small lake. From the west lot a barrier-free sidewalk skirts the edge of Duck Lake, crosses a narrow two-lane road, and continues on to a solitary stretch of Lake Michigan beach that begs you to spread a blanket, unpack a picnic lunch, and soak in the view.

No formal hiking trails mark the park, but the 704 acres give bushwhackers plenty of opportunity to try not to get lost. Hunters successfully go after deer and squirrels, and anglers, who launch from a ramp at the west parking area, pull panfish and northern pike from Duck Lake.

COUNTY: Muskegon

CITY: Whitehall

CAMPING SITES: None

DIRECTIONS: From US-31 about 15 miles north of Muskegon take the Lakewood Club exit and drive west on White Lake Road 4 miles to Zellar Road. Turn left (south) onto Zellar and go 2 miles to Michillinda Road. Turn right (west) onto Michillinda and go 2 miles to the park entrance.

FURTHER INFORMATION: Duck Lake State Park, c/o Muskegon State Park, 3560 Memorial Dr., North Muskegon, MI 49445; (231) 894-8769.

LAKE MICHIGAN

BOARDWALK

Scenic Drive

Todd Rd

Lamos Rd

Michillinda Rd

CHANGING COURTS & TOILETS

DUCK LAKE

CONTACT STATION

Nestrom Rd

Muskegon State Park

You would expect Muskegon State Park — with a half million swimmers, beach-combers, surfers, sailboarders, fishermen, boaters, campers, picnickers and other visitors descending upon it each year — to be crowded.

In most areas it isn't.

A seemingly endless expanse of Lake Michigan sand, a connecting channel to a bay of Muskegon Lake, and the dunes and forest that back all the shoreline soak up the heavy crowds and leave room for more. The many developed facilities are so spread out over 1,357 acres that it's easy to get the feeling you're really visiting several small parks. You can spend a day at any one and have a great time without ever seeing the rest.

Campers who like to fish, or fishermen who like to camp, for instance, haul tackle and boats, if they have them, to the Channel Campground, then go after perch, trout, panfish and salmon in the surrounding waters. The campground's two loops overlook the southern edge of the park where Muskegon Lake flows through a channel to Lake Michigan. Campers can drop fishing lines from two small piers that nudge out into the channel or a walkway that borders the narrow strip of water. (Day fishermen, who park in a convenient, specially designated lot, also use the boardwalk as do non-fishermen, who watch the parade of fishing and pleasure boats that pass through the channel to the

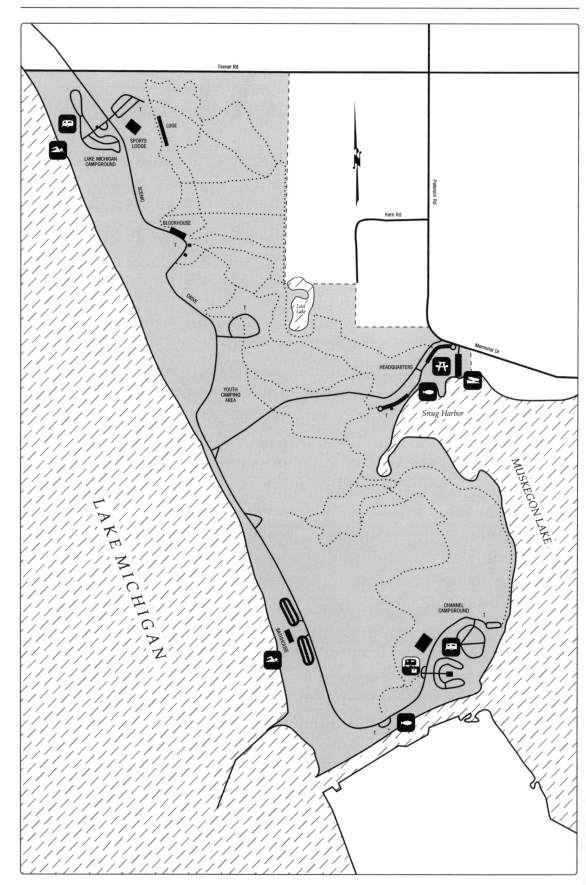

LAKE MICHIGAN

MUSKEGON LAKE

Fenner Rd

Peterson Rd

Kern Rd

Memorial Dr

LAKE MICHIGAN
CAMPGROUND

SPORTS
LODGE

LUGE

SCENIC

BLOCKHOUSE

DRIVE

Lost
Lake

YOUTH
CAMPING
AREA

HEADQUARTERS

Snug Harbor

BATHHOUSE

CHANNEL
CAMPGROUND

Great Lake.)

All 139 sites are completely modern and have paved slips. Lots (105-148), in the east loop, are generally more-private and large. Channel Campground is not fronted by its own swimming area, but the park's huge day-use area, along Lake Michigan, is only a short hike, drive or bike ride away.

For near-immediate access to seemingly endless beach, stay at the north edge of the park at one of 106 completely modern sites that make up the Lake Michigan Camp-ground. The shaded, well-worn lots there spread under a stand of lofty, old hardwoods less than a 100 yards from a wide, open strip of sand that stretches south along Lake Michigan for more than two miles. An added plus: smaller crowds than at the park's other beaches.

All campgrounds are heavily used through-out the summer months and usually fill on weekends, so if the park is your vacation desti-nation, make reservations. If your plans aren't that organized, you can often find a vacant spot if you arrive early in the day, according to park officials. The park is open year round, but the campgrounds' opening and closing dates depend on weather and sand buildup.

Day-trippers, too, can choose from several spots, but the over-whelming favorite is a huge unshaded beach/ picnic area along Lake Michigan at the south end of the park. It's only a few feet from the large bathhouse to superb swimming, but because of the relatively few picnic tables and the large crowds, you may have to eat from a blanket on the sand. For a cozier, less-crowded lunch, but without a beach, try the grassy, tree-sheltered grounds (including the park's two picnic shelters) alongside Muskegon Lake's Snug Harbor.

A fishing pier pokes out into the water there, and day-use boaters can launch from a ramp that borders the picnic area.

No matter where you camp or visit, be sure to take one of the prettiest short drives in the state along the road that follows the park's Lake Michigan coastline. About two-thirds of the way up the route, a trail from a small parking lot leads to a sweeping view of the surrounding countryside and Lake Michigan from a replica rustic log blockhouse.

From the parking lot adjacent to the blockhouse, or for that matter virtual-ly any parking lot or campground, you can access 12 miles of well-marked hiking trails that honeycomb the park's backcountry. And when you can drag your eyes away from the many scenic overlooks on the trail system you'll find an abundance of wildflowers pok-ing from the forest floor in season plus more than 200 species of birds to search for—includ-ing waterfowl, hawks, shorebirds and impres-sive numbers of warblers—which have been documented within the park boundaries.

When snow flies a beautiful lodge — com-plete with fireplace, concession area and restrooms — near the rustic campground area is headquarters for the Winter Sports Complex, which includes one of only three luge runs in the country. On just about any Saturday or Sunday winter afternoon you can literally walk in off the street, take a few beginning luge lessons, then drop through some of the gentler curves of the ice-covered wood chute.

Cross-country skiers can set tracks on five miles of lighted trail, and if you don't own cross-country ski equipment you can rent it at the lodge. Ski-trail maps, available at park headquarters, detail length, direction of travel, and degree of difficulty of the routes.

  Other facilities/attractions

COUNTY: Muskegon

CITY: North Muskegon

CAMPING SITES: 245, all modern, plus a mini-cabin.

DIRECTIONS: From US-31 north of Muskegon exit onto M-120 and go southwest approximately 1.5 miles to Giles Rd. Turn right (west) onto Giles and go 6 miles to Scenic Dr. Turn left (south) onto Scenic and go about a mile to the park.

FURTHER INFORMATION: Muskegon State Park, 3560 Memorial Dr., North Muskegon, MI 49445; (231) 744-3480.

P J *Hoffmaster* Sᴛᴀᴛᴇ Pᴀʀᴋ

The majestic mountains of sand that line the eastern shore of Lake Michigan are the longest stretch of dunes along fresh water anywhere in the world. Some of the finest views of this beautifully unique natural phenomenon come from the nearly three miles of shoreline that edges P. J. Hoffmaster State Park. Towering dunes there stand guard over sandy beach, scenic picnic areas, deep forest, interdunal valleys, miles of hiking trails, and one of Lower Michigan's premier campgrounds.

It's hard not to head right for the beach or the top of one of the dunes. But to better understand and appreciate what you are about to experience, try to first spend some time at the Gillette Visitor Center, near the geographic center of the park. Inside, slide shows in an 82-seat theater, plus dozens of colorful displays and dioramas combine to give you a basic education in the natural forces that created the dunes and the fragile dune ecology.

Nothing, however, can adequately prepare you — especially if it's your first look at dunes — for the feelings that might be stirred by the awesome meeting of crystalline-blue Lake Michigan and the giant ramparts that rise up only yards behind. You can't make even a short visit and leave without a lasting memory of the scene. One of the most striking views comes from a platform less than a quarter mile from the nature center.

It's only a 10-minute walk, but the climb to the sweeping vista of Lake Michigan and surrounding dunes takes at least another 10 minutes up what seems to be an interminable flight of stairs.

You can get other excellent views and more walking from the 10 miles of hiking trails that network the 1,150-acre park. Several routes follow breaks in the high dunes down to remote stretches of beach. Other longer trails climb over dunes, weave through steep-sided interdunal valleys, and cut through the park's

forested backcountry.

Local birdwatchers have spotted a variety of species of waterfowl, shorebirds, and upland birds in the diverse habitat. The park is also a prime area for warblers, and you can often see hawks soaring on the updrafts created by the dunes.

The easiest and shortest route to the shoreline is from the large day-use parking lot. A short walk from there past a concession stand and changing courts ends at a sandy swimming beach that stretches away in either direction for nearly a mile.

A small, open picnic area next to the beach parking lot is the closest in the park to water, but there's little privacy. For more seclusion, plenty of shade, and much less traffic try one of three picnic grounds strung along the road that leads to the visitor center. The first two are nestled in deep woods well away from traffic, and the third, at the end of the road, includes the park's only picnic shelter.

Tucked into a wooded valley on the extreme north edge of the park well away from the picnic areas, visitor center and beach is one of the finest campgrounds in southern Michigan. From the seclusion of any of the 293 spacious, shaded lots that are nestled in a stand of mature red pine or scattered amid towering hardwoods, you'll rarely see or hear any of the day-users who run the park's visitor

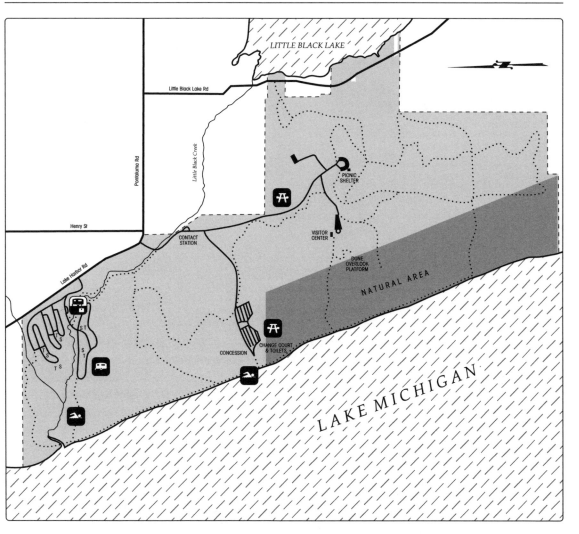

count up to nearly half a million each year. All lots have electrical hookups, and its a short walk from any of the sites to restrooms with flush toilets and showers. An added plus: a quarter-mile walk through the woods leads to a campers-only beach.

The popular campground is heavily used throughout the summer, filling almost every weekend, and you can't always count on finding a vacant lot even in midweek. Weekend use during fall color season can also be heavy.

When snow blankets the dunes, three miles of cross-country ski trails, rated as intermediate, lace the park. Sledding down the face of the dunes and snowshoeing through the backcountry are also popular winter exercises here.

 Other facilities/attractions

COUNTY: Muskegon

CITY: Muskegon

CAMPING SITES: 293, all modern.

SCHEDULE: The park park is open year round. Camping is permitted from April 1 - December 1. Modern restroom facilities are available from April 15 - October 15.

The Gillette Visitor Center and its art gallery, bookstore, and natural-science room, is open year round but is closed on Mondays.

DIRECTIONS: From US-31 about 6 miles south of Muskegon take Pontaluma Road west about 2 miles.

FURTHER INFORMATION: P.J. Hoffmaster State Park, 6585 Lake Harbor Rd., Muskegon, MI 49441; (231) 789-3711.

Grand Haven
State Park

At Grand Haven State Park, what you see is what you get: fine, white sand that stretches for a half-mile along Lake Michigan. Essentially, the park *is* the beach; only a slab of asphalt and a few buildings interrupt the wide, nearly flat expanse.

And, to use upon another adage, the early bird here doesn't get the worm; he or she gets to play in the giant sandbox.

For its size (48 acres) Grand Haven may be the busiest (a million visitors each year) state park in Michigan. Campground demand for prime summer weekends so outstrips available sites that you must make reservations six months in advance to ensure you have a vacation campsite. On those same weekends, if you're planning to just have a picnic or spend a day at the beach, you'd better arrive right after breakfast, not brunch, to get a parking spot.

After you pull into a space in the day-use parking area, it's only a few feet to a large, open, sand-covered picnic area and a modern bathhouse with a concession stand. It's only a few yards farther to the glistening strip of beach and sparkling Lake Michigan water. Picnickers and swimmers all have full views of passing freighters and pleasure boats, windsurfers, a picturesque lighthouse that punctuates the tip of a long pier, and some spectacular sunsets.

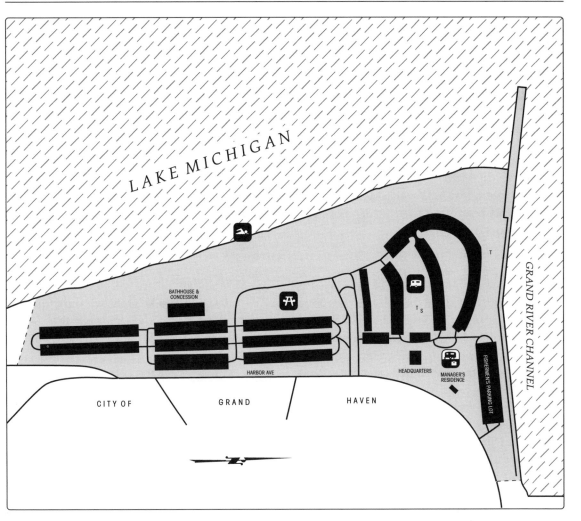

LAKE MICHIGAN

GRAND RIVER CHANNEL

BATHHOUSE &
CONCESSION

HARBOR AVE

HEADQUARTERS

MANAGER'S
RESIDENCE

FISHERMEN'S PARKING LOT

CITY OF   GRAND   HAVEN

North of the day-use area is one of the most-unique campgrounds in the state. The 174 modern sites are nothing more than lines painted on an open asphalt slab completely surrounded by sand, which stretches north to the Grand River and west to Lake Michigan. There is no shade from the broiling sun, no privacy, and no shelter from potentially strong on-shore winds or heavy rain. Setting up motor homes and trailers on the blacktop is a snap, but trying to stake down a tent in the soft sand is like trying to collect fog with a fishnet. Still, this campground is tough to beat if you like beach living. And all sites are reserveable.

Just north of the campground, a pier that juts out into Lake Michigan is curtained by monofilament when fish are biting. Day anglers who use the breakwater, which marks the park's northern boundary, park in their own special lot. Perch, salmon, steelhead, and brown and lake trout are caught from the pier and in the surrounding waters.

If you don't fish and you get tired of eating, breathing, and sweating sand, you can walk or pedal to downtown Grand Haven, only a couple of blocks away.

Other facilities/attractions

COUNTY: Ottawa

CITY: Grand Haven

CAMPING SITES: 174, all modern.

SCHEDULE: The park and campground are open April 1 to October 31.

DIRECTIONS: From downtown Grand Haven at the waterfront, drive south on Harbor Avenue to the park entrance.

FURTHER INFORMATION: Grand Haven State Park, 1001 Harbor Ave., Grand Haven, MI 49417; (616) 798-3711.

Ionia
RECREATION AREA

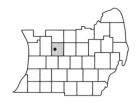

More than three miles of frontage on the Grand River, some of the best bass fishing in the state, great birdwatching, and a 140-acre man-made lake flanked by a large, sandy beach and beautiful picnic areas are reasons more than 260,000 people come to the Ionia Recreation Area each year.

The focal point of most of the day-use activities is small but scenic Sessions Lake. The damming of Sessions Creek created numerous inlets, little bays, and thin peninsulas that jut far out into the water. One that pokes out from the east shore is so narrow that you could blindfold picnickers there, twirl them around several times, and nine out of 10 would still hit water if they tossed a rock. That tree-shaded area is not only the park's most scenic, but also includes a specially designed table, built out to the water's edge next to a fishing pier for people in wheelchairs. You can also cart coolers to tables and shelters at two other areas: among towering hardwoods on the west shore of the lake and near the Grand River on the north edge of the park.

A sprawling swimming beach hugs the north side of Sessions Lake. The open, shadeless area, with excellent views across the water, is the only stretch of shoreline not crowded by trees or marshes.

About a half mile east of the lake, well away from most day-use facilities is the park's 100-site completely modern campground. Just north of it is a 49-site rustic equestrian campground—no electricity, only pit toilets and tethering posts for horses at each lot.

Horsemen ride 17 miles of bridle paths that loop through the southern half of the 4,500-acre park. Hikers, too, use those routes, in addition to the 3.5-mile hiking trail that circles the lake.

Mountain bikers will find nine miles of designated bike paths winding through marsh, meadow and woods near the Grand River, which marks the park's northern boundary.

In the winter the entire park is open to cross-country skiers, and there are three marked ski trails ranging from beginner to expert and ranging in length from a mile to 6 miles.

Snowmobilers are welcome to use the park but must stay off the designated cross-country ski trails and campground.

The park's diverse habitat — from river frontage to lakeshore and open meadows to deep woods — shelters numerous wildflowers and attracts a wide variety of birds. According to the local Audubon Society, 156 different species have been spotted here.

Perhaps the biggest surprise is the fishing in the Grand River, which is rated by the DNR as one of the two or three best bodies of water, lakes included, in the state for bass fishing. The section near the park is especially good, and from Ionia west to Grand Rapids may well be the best smallmouth bass hole in Michigan.

The park's two access points onto the river can only accommodate canoes or cartoppers, but you can launch larger craft from a ramp just off M-66 on the south side of the city of Ionia or in Saranac, to the west.

There is a park launch ramp on the west side of Sessions Lake. A no-wake speed is in effect.

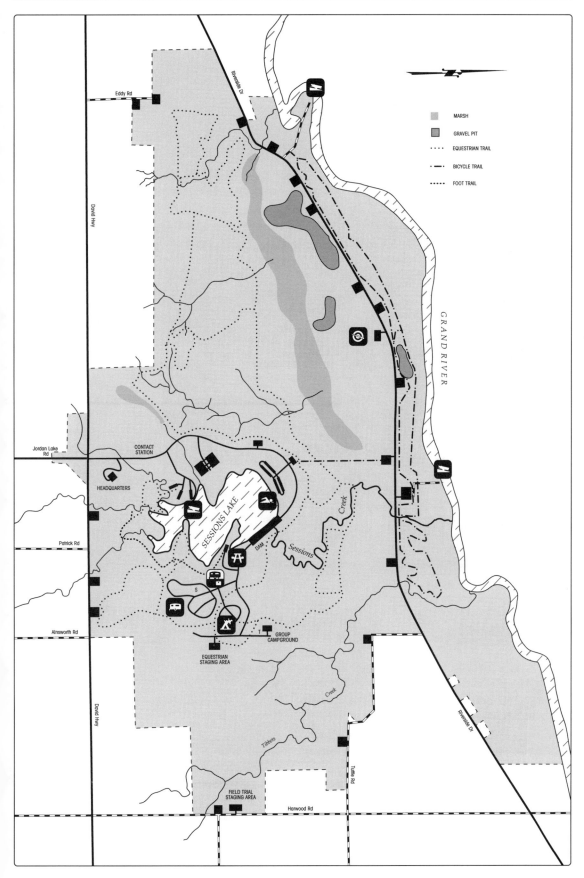

Fishing — including from shore on peninsulas that nearly enclose weed-filled bays — is good for large and smallmouth bass, walleye, catfish and panfish.

 Most of the park is open to hunting. Rabbits and deer are the most-plentiful game, and grouse, waterfowl, pheasants, squirrels, turkey, and woodcock are also successfully taken. During the off-season, sportsmen can hone their shotgun skills at a skeet range, and those with dogs can keep them sharp at a field-trial area.

Other facilities/attractions

COUNTY: Ionia

CITY: Ionia

CAMPING SITES: 149 (100 modern, 49 equestrian) plus an organization/group site.

DIRECTIONS: From exit 64 on I-96 drive 3 miles north to the park.

FURTHER INFORMATION: Ionia Recreation Area, 2880 David Hwy., Ionia, MI 48846; (616) 527-3750.

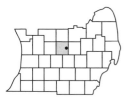

Sleepy Hollow
STATE PARK

The centerpiece of Sleepy Hollow State Park is Lake Ovid, a large, island-dotted lake that was created by damming the Little Maple River.

You can see Lake Ovid from virtually any place in the 2,600-acre park, and most facilities hug its shore. At the north end is a quarter-mile-long swimming beach. The narrow strip of sand separates the water from an immense, treeless lawn that is a perfectly suited to tanners. Facilities there include a modern bathhouse and a few widely scattered grills and picnic tables.

Other large, grass-carpeted picnic areas are scattered around the lake. One on the west shore features a bridge leading to the lake's largest island. All picnic areas provide plenty of room to claim a spot and a view for the day.

Striking views of the lake also come from a couple of lots in the completely modern campground a half mile from the lake on the east side of the park. The line of sight to the water from most of the 181 lots, however, is obstructed, but there is enough variety that you won't have any trouble finding a spot to

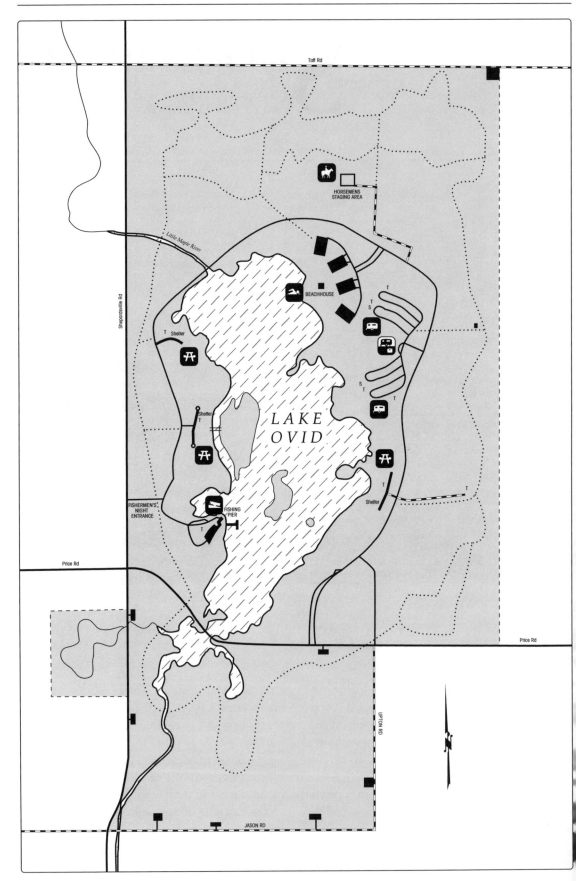

LAKE OVID

your liking.

Many sites are in full sun, old hardwoods shelter others, and a few are almost completely screened by shrubs and low trees. All lots are flat and level, with asphalt slips for easy parking and setup of trailers and RVs. A minimum 100-foot extension cord is required. Reservations are recommended from May 15 to September 30.

Walking is easy on 16 miles of foot trails, which are also open to mountain bikers. The paths cross over open, gently rolling land and occasionally probe into stands of hardwoods that fringe the park's boundaries.

Cross-country skiers use the trails during the winter, and other sections of the park are set aside for snowmobilers where there is four or more inches of snow.

The park has nine miles of bridle trails open to users who trailer their horses in for the day. Mountain bikers are not allowed on bridle trails and likewise horses are not allowed on hiking/biking trails.

Sleepy Hollow is also an excellent birdwatching area. More than 200 species of birds have been recorded in the park, including significant numbers of waterfowl, which use the lake as a spring stopover.

The lake itself is popular with canoeists, who enjoy paddling along the winding shoreline, across small bays and around several islands.

Fishermen can use a pier next to the boat-launching ramp, launch their own boats, or rent one from park's boat concession. Anglers report regular catches of bluegills, bass, northern pike, and channel catfish. Fishing and canoeing is made even more pleasant because Lake Ovid is a no wake lake.

Hunting is allowed, with grouse, deer, rabbits, and squirrels the game most often taken.

 Other facilities/attractions

COUNTY: Clinton

CITY: Laingsburg

CAMPING SITES: 181, all modern

SCHEDULE: The park is open year round from 8 a.m. to 10 p.m. daily. The campground is open April 1-December 1, with water and toilets available May 1-October 1.

On the park's west side, a special night access road for fishermen is open from 10 p.m. to 8 a.m. June 10-Labor Day.

DIRECTIONS: From US-27 approximately 5 miles south of St. Johns, take Price Road east 5.5 miles.

FURTHER INFORMATION: Sleepy Hollow State Park, 7835 Price Rd., Laingsburg, MI 48848; (517) 651-6217.

Holland
State Park

Each year a million and a half visitors take advantage of the fact that the long, broad beach that edges Lake Michigan northwest of Holland is one of the most accessible and beautiful along the Lower Peninsula's west shore. But though this is one of the heaviest-used parks in Michigan, there's always plenty of room on the acres of pillow-soft sand to stroll or spread blankets and towels.

The beach is just a few steps west from the large day-use parking area, which is front-and-centered by a large, modern bathhouse and concession stand. Lining the sand behind the bathhouse are a dozen or so well-used beach volleyball courts. You can picnic at a few tables that are scattered along the edges of the parking lot and around the bathhouse, but you'll feel like you're eating in a Marshall Fields display window. For a little more privacy and, in some spots, even a hint of shade, carry your basket and cooler south from the parking lot to a picnic area that borders Lake Macatawa and the channel that connects it to Lake Michigan. Tables there are also front-row seats for watching the boat traffic on the busy channel.

Across the road from the day-use parking area is one of the park's two widely separated and markedly different modern campgrounds. The newly reconfigured Beach Campground features fewer but much-roomier sites. The 98 (where there used to be 147) sites can accommodate 50-foot rigs and have 30-amp service. Thirty-one sites offer sewer, water, and 50-amp service.

The camping spots are nothing more than lines painted on an asphalt island surrounded by sand, but if you love beach camping and don't mind a lack of privacy, it doesn't get much better than this. You can build sand castles next to your lot, walk just a few dozen steps to a magnificent beach, and bask in the glow of beautiful Lake Michigan sunsets.

The Beach Campground also has a new dump station.

About a half mile inland and separated from the rest of the park by private property is the Lake Macatawa Campground. Here also less is more with 211 larger sites where there used to be 221. All sites also offer 30-amp hookups. The grassy sites — with some privacy, especially those nestled in a stand of red pine — spread in eight loops along the park road, which follows the shore of Lake Macatawa. If you plan to stay at the Lake Macatawa unit, bring your 3- or 10-speed and take it on a pedalers path to the beach and other area bike tours.

During peak summer months, especially on weekends, the only sure way of getting a spot at either unit is by reservation. Even in mid-week if you arrive late in the day without a reservation, you may be turned away.

A new boat launch lies one mile east of Lake Macatawa Campground.

Water skiers skim across Lake Macatawa, and fishermen hook walleyes and perch in its sheltered waters. On the Great Lake, spring runs of lake trout, brown trout and salmon usually provide good action. Pier fishermen, too, pull out salmon and trout in the spring, plus perch throughout the summer, from a breakwater that marks the mouth of Lake Macatawa on the park's southern border.

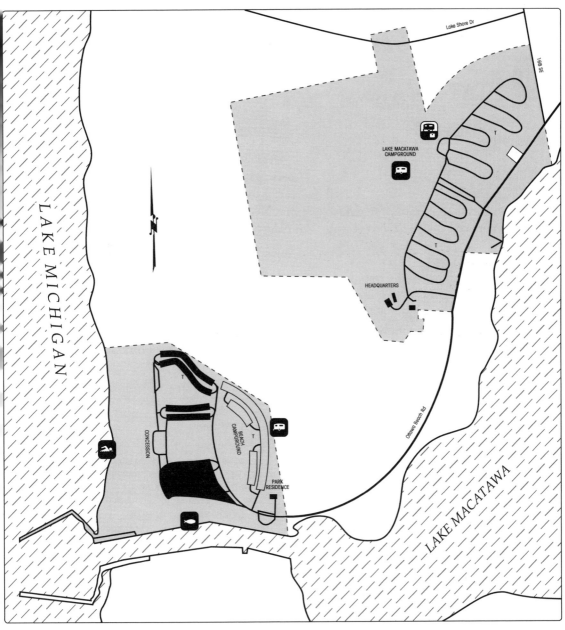

![Other facilities/attractions] Other facilities/attractions

COUNTY: Ottawa

CITY: Holland

CAMPING SITES: 309, all modern.

SCHEDULE: The Beach Campground is open May 25 through the day after Labor Day. The Lake Macatawa campground is open April 1 through October 31.

DIRECTIONS: From downtown Holland drive north on River Avenue across the Macatawa River, then turn left (west) and drive on Ottawa Beach Road about 5 miles.

FURTHER INFORMATION: Holland State Park, 2215 Ottawa Beach Rd., Holland, MI 49424; (616) 399-9390.

S augatuck Dunes
STATE PARK

The DNR calls Saugatuck Dunes a "day-use park." That's false advertising. True, there's no campground, and the park is open only from 8 a.m. to 10 p.m. But there is no way you can take in its 1,100 acres, secluded 2¼ miles of Lake Michigan beach, and 14 miles of marked hiking/cross-country ski trails in just one day.

It's fun to try, but not many people even do that. Saugatuck Dunes is not only one of Michigan's newest (established 1977) state parks, but also one of the Lower Peninsula's least visited. The DNR tallies only 30,000-plus visitors each year, so if you're after exceptional scenic beauty without large crowds, look no further.

The two-plus miles of glistening beach are among the least-used in the state-park system, and for good reason. You don't just drive up, park your car, then drag chairs, coolers, radios and other toys a few yards to the water. The shortest route to the beach here is a l...o...n...g one-mile slog over the wooded dunes from the parking lot. That's quite a hedge against overcrowding.

Adjacent to the 50-car parking area, just inside the park's eastern boundary, picnic tables, grills and a covered shelter are spread under a mixture of evergreens and hardwoods. Vault toilets are located at the both the picnic area and the beach.

The rest of the park is almost totally undeveloped, wild and scenic, and the south end is a designated natural area. Twenty- to 180-foot-high dunes frame the waters of Lake Michigan, and back from them a mixed hardwood/pine forest partially covers the rolling landscape.

Fourteen miles of well-marked trails, all of which begin at the parking lot, network the park and range in length from the two-mile circuit to the beach to a 5.5-mile loop through the southern end of the park. Two paths end at scenic overviews of the lake from the crest of the barrier dunes.

In winter the trails are used by cross-country skiers and range in difficulty from novice to expert.

COUNTY: Allegan

CITY: Saugatuck

CAMPING SITES: None

DIRECTIONS: Take exit 41 (Blue Star Highway) from I-96 and go west less than a half mile to 64th Street. Turn right (north) onto 64th and drive 1.5 miles to 138th Avenue. Turn left (west) onto 138th and go about a mile.

FURTHER INFORMATION: Saugatuck Dunes State Park, c/o Van Buren State Park, 2390 Ruggles Rd., South Haven, MI 49090; (616) 637-2788.

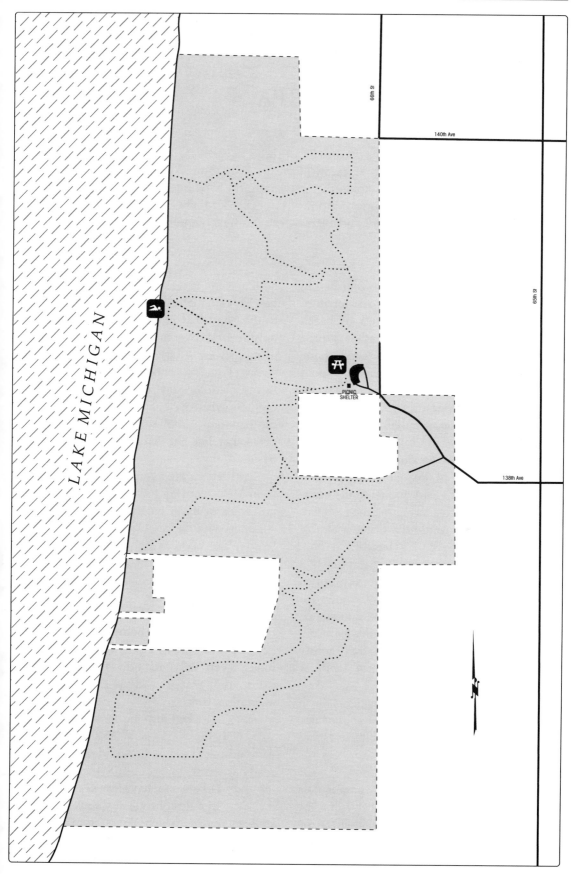

LAKE MICHIGAN

66th St

140th Ave

65th St

138th Ave

PICNIC
SHELTER

Yankee Springs
RECREATION AREA

On hot summer weekends at Yankee Springs Recreation Area, a narrow peninsula that pokes into Gun Lake resembles Times Square on New Years Eve. Before lunch on Saturdays and Sundays, the long, continuous parking lot that centers the strip has filled with the vehicles of swimmers and picnickers who have claimed tables and parcels of beach for the day.

But though it may sometimes seem like it, not *everyone* who crosses into park territory disappears into the massive quilt of beach blankets. For those who'd rather tiptoe through something other than sunbathers, there's plenty to do and plenty of room to do it over the park's 5,000-plus acres, which take in three beautiful campgrounds, miles of hiking trails, and good opportunities to birdwatch, hunt and fish.

There's no doubt, though, that most of the 600,000 people a year who come to the park funnel to the beautiful picnic and beach areas lining the peninsula that juts so far out into the water it almost cuts Gun Lake, the park's largest, in half. Dozens of tables and grills there, plus two large picnic shelters are scattered in open meadows and under shady trees. On the west shore, two bathhouses and concession stands back the day-use area's most popular feature, a long, sandy swimming beach that gently slopes under the water to only knee depth far from shore.

Power boaters and water skiers launch down a ramp on the east shore then, along with those who navigate sailboards and sailboats, put on a continuous show for the land-bound crowd.

Near the peninsula's base, cut off from the busy day-use area by a narrow inlet, is the largest of the park's three camping areas. All 200 large, level lots there have electrical hookups and access to modern restroom facilities. Though mature hardwoods shade the sites to the point that in the center of the area the only ground cover is fallen leaves, there is little or no privacy. A large, sandy stretch of gently sloping Gun Lake shoreline that fronts the area is reserved for day use by campers. Overnighters who tow boats can launch them at a campers-only ramp into the inlet, then tie up to posts that line the banks of the ready-made basin.

Reservations are a must at this campground from Memorial Day to Labor Day. If you have no choice or insist on trying your luck in the summer without reservations, show up late Sunday afternoon or early in the morning during midweek.

In less demand and even farther from the Gun Lake day-use crowds are two small, rustic campgrounds near the park's eastern boundary. Facilities at a 120-site area spread across a bluff that overlooks Deep Lake include a boat-launching ramp and playground equipment but no swimming beach.

Tucked into the southeast corner of the park is a 25-site equestrian campground, used by horse riders as a base for ready access to miles of bridle trails.

Hikers, too, have a web of more than 15 miles of trails to choose from. The diverse routes, which range from ½ to five miles long, cut through an array of wildflowers, pass several interesting geologic features,

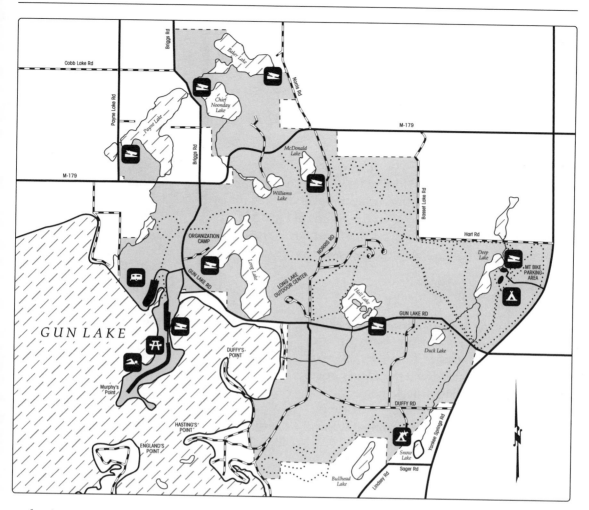

and rise to numerous scenic overlooks. Birdwatching is good, and the area, once the hunting grounds of the Algonquin Indians, is still rich in wildlife.

A 12 mile-long mountain bike trail starts at the Deep Lake campground and takes pedalers from flat, easily biked terrain to some of the park's more-rugged landscape. The trail—with long uphill climbs, deep sand pockets and creek crossings—tests the mettle of even advanced mountain bikers.

In the winter cross-country skiers can follow 10 miles of groomed trails, and snowmobilers can leave tracks over their own large, open area.

All but one (Duck) of the park's nine lakes have boat ramps, which fishermen use to go after panfish, bass, northern pike, walleye and muskies. Gun Lake, is stocked annually with walleyes, but don't fish there on weekends unless you're prepared to be a floating pylon for speed-boaters, sailboaters and water skiers.

Hunters pursue their favorite game both in the park and in the adjoining 15,000-acre Barry State Game Area. Deer are the favored quarry, but rabbits, squirrels and ruffed grouse are also hunted.

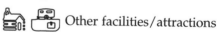 Other facilities/attractions

COUNTY: Barry

CITY: Middleville

CAMPING SITES: 345 (200 modern, 145 rustic), plus 12 rustic cabins at a large outdoor center.

DIRECTIONS: From M-37 where it jogs northwest 2 miles west of Hastings, bear left on Gun Lake Road (M-179) and drive west 14 miles. Or from US-131 take exit 61 and go 8 miles east on M-179.

FURTHER INFORMATION: Yankee Springs Recreation Area, 2104 S. Briggs Rd., Middleville, MI 49333; (616) 795-9081.

Kal-Haven Trail
State Park

At 100 feet wide and 34 miles long, Kal-Haven Trail is one of Michigan's most unusually shaped state parks. The route follows an old, unused stretch of the Penn Central Railroad from South Haven, on the shores of Lake Michigan, to Kalamazoo. The crushed limestone that has replaced the rails and ties is user-friendly to bike, wheelchair and of course foot traffic. In the winter cross-country skiers and snowmobilers share the entire route.

Walking, pedaling, or skiing is easy, with no steep grades or hills. The trail passes through numerous small towns (Alamo, Kendall, Pine Grove, Gobles, Bloomingdale, Berlamont, Grand Junction, La-cota, and Kibbie), crosses picturesque streams on seven old railroad trestles, and passes a variety of scenic vistas.

Camping is not allowed on the trail itself, but state and private campgrounds are located on the South Haven end. Or you can even choose to spend the night at one of several bed-and-breakfasts in towns along the route. You can get a detailed map (see FURTHER INFORMATION) that not only shows the location of public rest areas and staging areas along the way, but also lists grocery stores, restaurants, bike rentals and lodging.

Picnic areas are located at the trailheads at both ends of the park.

You don't need a vehicle permit, but you will need a trail pass, available at both trailheads. Prices are $2 for an individual day pass, $5 for a family day pass, and $10 and $25 respectively for annual passes.

Other facilities/attractions

COUNTY: Van Buren and Kalamazoo

CITY: Trailheads at South Haven and Kalamazoo

CAMPING SITES: None

DIRECTIONS: Kalamazoo trailhead—From US-131 northwest of Kalamazoo, exit onto M-43 and drive west less than a quarter mile to 10th St. Turn right (north) onto 10th and drive approximately 2 miles to the trailhead.

South Haven trailhead—Go one mile north of town on the Blue Star Hwy.

FURTHER INFORMATION: Van Buren State Park, 23960 Ruggles Rd., South Haven, MI 49090; (616) 637-2788.

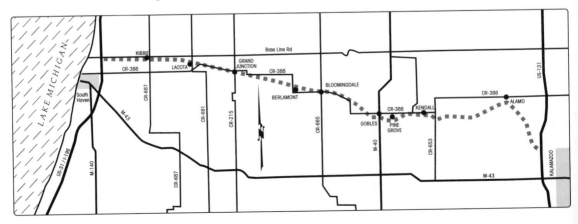

Isle Royale National Park

Van Buren
STATE PARK

Van Buren State Park hides a secret behind the partition of high, wooded sand dunes that lines it's west boundary. A wide sidewalk leads through a single narrow opening, and it's not until you're almost completely through the sand wall that the view opens to reveal the park's main attraction: limitless blue waters of Lake Michigan edged by a broad sweep of fine, black-speckled sand. The dune-backed shore disappears into the horizon on the north and, nearly a half mile to the south, park property ends at the Palisades Nuclear Power Plant.

Just back from the beach, nestled in the narrow gap that cuts through the dunes, are a large bathhouse and a few picnic tables. A little farther inland, more tables, plus grills and a shelter, are spread over an open, grassy meadow that separates the back of the dunes from the large day-use parking lot. (Note: Alcoholic beverages are prohibited in the day-use area.)

Also just a few minutes' walk from the beach, tucked into the park's southeast corner away from the mainstream of traffic, is a fully modern campground. The 220 well-worn sites are arranged in five loops, with a mix of both sunny and shaded lots. And though the lots are large, they are close together, with little or no privacy. Campground use is heavy throughout the summer, usually filling on weekends.

Though there are no marked hiking trails in the 407-acre park, some well-worn routes probe the barrier dunes. Some of the huge, fragile sand mountains, however, are posted with no-trespassing signs to prevent human erosion from adding to the natural wear. You can also stretch your legs along the lengthy shoreline and also wander through the large, rolling, wooded undeveloped parcel in the park's northeast corner.

Cross-country skiers can make their own trails.

Parts of the park are open to hunting in season, with deer and squirrel the game most often taken.

There's no place to launch a boat or fish within park boundaries. If you do want to go after the area's salmon, lake trout and perch, it's only two miles north to public launches, marinas, a pier, and charter boats at South Haven.

Other facilities/attractions

COUNTY: Van Buren

CITY: South Haven

CAMPING SITES: 220, all modern.

DIRECTIONS: Take the Blue Star Highway south out of South Haven for 2 miles to Ruggles Road. Turn right (west) onto Ruggles and go about a mile.

FURTHER INFORMATION: Van Buren State Park, 23960 Ruggles Rd., South Haven, MI 49090; (616) 637-2788.

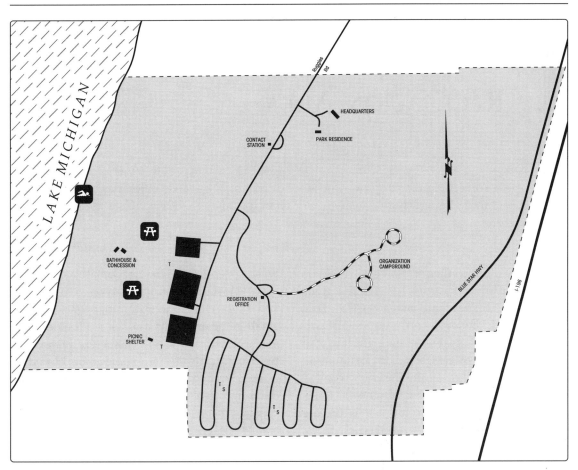

LAKE MICHIGAN

Ruggles Rd

HEADQUARTERS

PARK RESIDENCE

CONTACT
STATION

BATHHOUSE &
CONCESSION

T

REGISTRATION
OFFICE

ORGANIZATION
CAMPGROUND

BLUE STAR HWY

I-196

PICNIC
SHELTER

T

T
S

T
S

Fort Custer
RECREATION AREA

A little something for everyone and a lot of potential outdoor enjoyment for anyone is packed into the sprawling year-round playground named Fort Custer Recreation Area.

When snow flies, cross-country skiers glide over 3.5 miles of marked trails that circle three small lakes — Jackson, Whitford and Lawler — in the southwest corner of the park. If that's not enough, they can also set their own tracks to exhaustion throughout the rest of the heavily wooded park. Snowmobilers, too, can run the gas tanks of their machines empty anywhere on the park's 2,962 acres except the marked ski trails. Many of the winter sportsmen spend the night at one of the park's three rustic, but cozy, frontier rental cabins.

When the snow melts, hikers take the place of skiers on the 22 miles of designated hiking trails. Much of the surrounding land there is part of a wildfowl management area, so you can usually see ducks and geese on the wing and in the water. Hikers also set out on the 16 miles of bridle trails that network the park's remote wooded areas.

The recreation area is also a favorite of cyclists. The extensive system of park roads and four miles of mountain bike trails, coupled with the distance between facilities, not only add up to long, aerobic rides, but also make bicycles a convenient means of getting around the far-flung park. Many bikers also pedal to the small village of Augusta, to the west.

You can bring your own small boat and launch it at ramps on all of the area's lakes and the Kalamazoo River. Or you can rent one at the Eagle Lake day-use area and go after bluegills, bass and pike. A no-wake speed limit is in effect on all lakes here.

Most of the park is also open to hunters, who take the full range of Michigan small game and deer in season. Hunters need to check with park officials before planning a hunt because there are some areas closed to hunters and hunting is restricted to specific dates in different areas of the park.

The recreation area's only swimming beach edges the north shore of the largest body of water in the park, Eagle Lake. The long, wide stretch of sand and beachhouse is backed by a large, open picnic area that overlooks the water from a low bluff. Extensive plantings of young trees promise shade in the future, but for the next few years the only available protection from the sun will be under two picnic shelters.

A smaller, more-scenic, and much-more-private picnic area hugs the west shore of the two-lakes-in-one, Whitford and Lawler. You can plop your cooler on a table right at the water's edge or under shade trees in full view of the lily pads, rushes, and marshy edges of the inlets that ring the shoreline. The trails that circle the lakes are only a step away, and shore-fishing near the picnic area looks promising.

North of Jackson Lake, 219 sites divided between two loops make up the park campground. Mature trees, which hover over most sites, plus dense shrubs and wide spacing create excellent privacy, and all lots have paved slips. Campers on both loops have access to modern restrooms and electrical hookups. The campground is only moderately

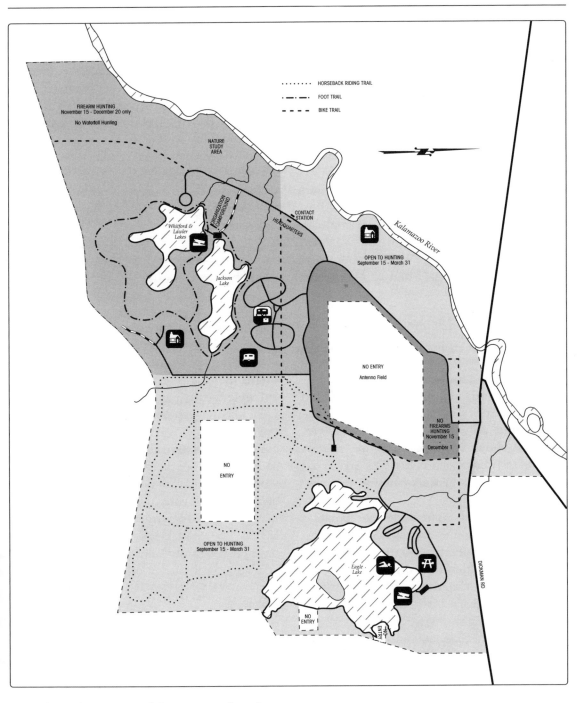

HORSEBACK RIDING TRAIL
FOOT TRAIL
BIKE TRAIL

FIREARM HUNTING
November 15 - December 20 only
No Waterfall Hunting

NATURE
STUDY
AREA

ORGANIZATION CAMPGROUND

CONTACT
STATION

HEADQUARTERS

Whitford &
Lawler
Lakes

Jackson
Lake

Kalamazoo River

OPEN TO HUNTING
September 15 - March 31

NO ENTRY
Antenna Field

NO
FIREARMS
HUNTING
November 15
-
December 1

NO

ENTRY

OPEN TO HUNTING
September 15 - March 31

Eagle
Lake

NO
ENTRY

NO
ENTRY

DICKMAN RD

used throughout most of the summer, but does usually fill to capacity every weekend in July and August.

The park has three frontier cabins for rent: two on the east side of Whitford Lake that sleep 16, plus a smaller and more recently built family cabin on the banks of the Kalamazoo River that sleeps six. The cabins are heavily booked year round, so make reservations well in advance.

 Other facilities & attractions

COUNTY: Kalamazoo

CITY: Battle Creek

CAMPING SITES: 219, all modern, plus two mini cabins and three rustic cabins.

DIRECTIONS: Drive approximately 10 miles west of Battle Creek on M-96.

FURTHER INFORMATION: Fort Custer Recreation Area, 5163 W. Fort Custer Dr., Augusta, MI 49012; (616) 731-4200.

Grand Mere
STATE PARK

Many visitors come to Grand Mere State Park because it is an extremely secluded spot of uncommon beauty, a rare retreat from the modern world. The dunes, forests, Lake Michigan shoreline and string of small interdunal lakes are part of the reason that Grand Mere is one of only a dozen Michigan areas listed among the country's National Natural Landmarks. If you're a backwoods pro, dedicated birdwatcher, or experienced naturalist, you'll revel in the isolation and nearly total undeveloped beauty.

The vegetation that grows in the Grand Mere area is an almost classic example of plant evolution and succession — from aquatic to terrestrial, from bare sand to climax forest — that began shortly after glaciers retreated from the state some 10,000 years ago. Because the area is unusually protected, representatives from just about every phase of the process remain, and biologists, naturalists and other scientists comb the park looking for the often-rare species.

Grand Mere has also earned a reputation as one of the finest birdwatching areas in the state. The list of some 250 species that have been spotted include such rare Michigan visitors as Yellow-throated Warblers, Dickcissels, Mockingbirds, Bell's Vireo, Summer Tanager, and Worm-eating Warblers. The spring migration season is an especially good time to carry binoculars and bird books here. Throughout the warm-weather months, ducks, loons, cormorants and shorebirds find refuge throughout the interdunal lakes, and you can usually spot a wide variety of thrushes, warblers and songbirds in the bordering cover and surrounding woods. Spring and fall are both good for observing flights of migrating hawks.

From the park's picnic area a trail heads west from the picnic shelter along the marshy shoreline of South Lake. Because the first half-mile of the route is paved and is lined with dense vegetation on the South Lake side and wooded dunes on the other, it is one of the finest wheelchair-accessible birding spots in the state. At a couple of points along this section of trail, worn paths cut off to the right and lead to a mile of pristine Lake Michigan shoreline. Where the main trail pavement gives way to sand the route then curves to the south, climbs a high bluff on the south side of South Lake, and winds through wooded dunes lying between the smaller lake and Lake Michigan.

Fishermen with craft less than 14 feet long can put in at an unimproved sandy launch site on Middle Lake and go after a variety of panfish. The lake is shallow and weedy and so electric motors only are advised.

Hunting is allowed in some areas of the park, but special regulations are in effect. Contact the park for details.

Other facilities/attractions

COUNTY: Berrien

CITY: Stevensville

CAMPING SITES: None

DIRECTIONS: Take exit 22 (Stevensville) from I-94 and go west about 400 feet on Grand Mere Road to Thornton Road. Turn left (south) onto Thornton and go about a half mile to the park entrance, on the right.

FURTHER INFORMATION: Grand Mere State Park, 12032 Red Arrow Hwy., Sawyer, MI 49125; (616) 426-4013.

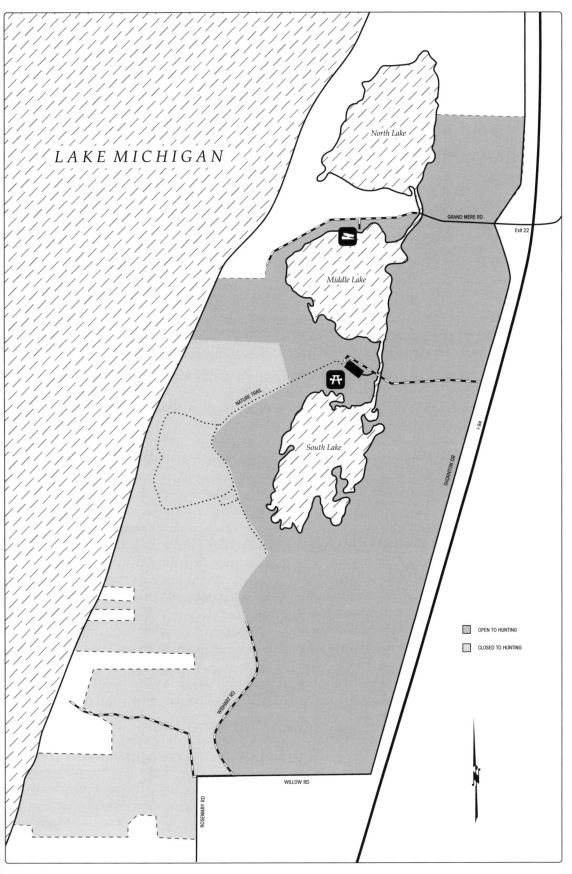

LAKE MICHIGAN

North Lake

GRAND MERE RD

Exit 22

Middle Lake

NATURE TRAIL

South Lake

THORNTON DR

I-94

OPEN TO HUNTING

CLOSED TO HUNTING

WISHART RD

WILLOW RD

ROSEMARY RD

W arren Dunes
STATE PARK

We should somehow require every out-of-state tourist who comes into Michigan from the southwest corner to stop at Warren Dunes State Park, less than 10 miles north of the state line. What a stunning introduction to our state, to a coastline that is repeated for hundreds of miles to the Straits of Mackinac, to a coastline that is only one of four. Even if you're a longtime resident who has seen what wind, water, and sand has created elsewhere along our 3,121 miles of Great Lakes frontage, you will be unprepared for your first-time visit here.

The views from the entrance road leading to the beach are so outstanding that the DNR has had to post signs advising the drivers who chauffeur in 1.3 million visitors each year that stopping is not allowed. Huge dunes tower over the asphalt on the right, while from their base to the left, the wide expanse of sand falls sharply away to deep-blue Lake Michigan waters that blend into the horizon. It's hard to keep your foot off the brake.

When you do stop, it's at one of the largest, most beautiful beaches in the state. Fine, soft sand drops none too gently to the water from two large beachhouses set on high, sandy ridges. Each of the change facilities fronts its own immense parking lot, and directly behind the asphalt are mountains of sand that cut off the area from the rest of the park. The strenuous climb to any of the peaks ends with excellent views of the expanse of water and sand that swallows up the buildings, acres of blacktop, and thousands of visitors. To the north a virtual wilderness of sand arches past the park boundary to the horizon.

Shouldering the coast and rolling inland to blanket much of the rest of the 1,523-acre park are the Great Warren Dunes. You can get a taste of the tree-spiked dunes from eight miles of marked hiking trails (six miles of cross-country ski trails in the win-

ter), or you can feast on them away from the crowds by heading into hundreds of open, undeveloped acres. A good way to explore the dunes plus learn a little of their natural history is to walk the one-mile Warren Dunes Nature Trail. A self-guiding brochure with numbered paragraphs that match numbered posts along that route is available at the trailhead located on the park road leading to the park's fully modern campground.

That overnight area is located well away from the hustle, bustle and heavy traffic of the beach area. One hundred eighty large sites are arranged in two loops in such a pattern that, usually, no two lots end up back to back, which makes for good privacy. Many sites are heavily wooded, some are grass covered, and a few are well worn—good evidence that reservations are a must throughout the summer to ensure a spot. For the most privacy and shade, try for heavily wooded lots 1-99, which make up the south loop. A long hiking trail through the dunes to the beach also begins at that loop. Or if you don't feel like walking, it's only a five-minute drive.

Northwest of the modern campground, 24 rustic campsites are widely scattered along the looping gravel road that used to encompass an organizational campground, which has been relocated to Floral Lane, at the park's north end.

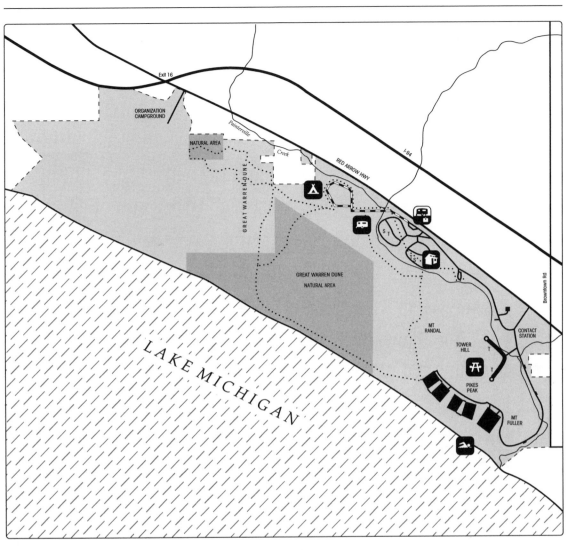

Several picnic tables are scattered along the road to the beach. But for the most beauty and seclusion take a short road that branches north, only a few hundred feet past the contact station, to its end at what is left of the park's largest picnic area, on the lee side of a giant dune. Nearly one entire wing of the picnic area has been buried under the shifting mountain of sand. At the remaining wing, trees shelter tables, grills, playground equipment and modern restroom buildings from the sun, but not from the wall of sand that is slowly creeping ever closer.

Some areas of the park are open to hunters. Contact the address or phone number below for details.

  Other facilities/attractions

COUNTY: Berrien

CITY: Bridgman

CAMPING SITES: 204 (180 modern and 24 rustic) plus three mini-cabins and two rental tipis.

SCHEDULE: The park and campground are open all year, but the restroom buildings are closed from October 15 to April 15.

DIRECTIONS: From I-94 12 miles south of St. Joseph, take exit 16 and drive 2 miles south on Red Arrow Highway.

FURTHER INFORMATION: Warren Dunes State Park, 12032 Red Arrow Hwy., Sawyer, MI 49125; (616) 426-4013.

Warren Woods
State Park

Tucked away in the extreme southwest corner of Michigan are 300 acres of forest so sublimely beautiful that they have not only been set aside as a state park, but are also designated as a National Natural Landmark. The forest includes the last known stand — with outstanding individual specimens — of virgin beeches and maples left in southern Michigan. Axes or saws have never touched this tract; even centuries' worth of deadfalls lie where they have fallen.

The unique area is the legacy of E.K. Warren, a local businessman who in the 1870s, when most people saw nothing but dollar signs in Michigan's great forests, had the unusual foresight to purchase the virgin hardwood stand with the sole intent of saving it for posterity.

If Warren could visit the park today he would be happy to see that it has remained as one of the least developed in the state. Pit toilets, a small parking lot, and a one-table picnic area are about the only concessions to visitors.

It doesn't matter, because the reason for a visit is to walk through the majestic broad-leafed hardwoods accented by the needles of occasional huge red pines. You can do so on two miles of well-trodden paths, with access from Warren Woods Road. (You used to also be able to access the trails from the main entrance on Elm Valley Road, but high water wiped out the footbridge crossing the Galien River.) Not surprisingly, fall — when the trees, trails, and air are filled with bright yellow splashed with orange and red — is an especially good time to visit.

Warren Woods is also one the state's premier birding sites. During spring migrations the woods attract numerous warblers, many of them uncommon to Michigan and usually only seen much farther south. Cerulean, Hooded and Kentucky warblers, along with Acadian Flycatchers and Louisiana Water-thrushes, are regularly spotted all summer. The woods are also an ideal location for seeing woodpeckers, including the crow-size Pileated Woodpecker.

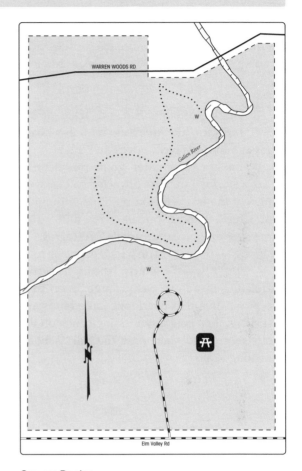

COUNTY: Berrien

CITY: Three Oaks

CAMPING SITES: None

DIRECTIONS: From I-94 take exit 6 (Union Pier) and go east on Elm Valley Road about 2.8 miles. To reach the Warren Woods entrance, continue east another 0.75 miles to Three Oaks Road. Turn left (north) onto Three Oaks and drive a mile to Warren Woods Road. Turn left (west) onto Warren and drive 0.75 miles to a parking area on the south (left) side of the road.

FURTHER INFORMATION: c/o Warren Dunes State Park, 12032 Red Arrow Hwy., Sawyer, MI 49125; (616) 426-4013.

L*ake Hudson* RECREATION AREA

Lake Hudson Recreation Area — established in 1979 amid the open, rolling plains of southern Michigan only seven miles north of Ohio — remains almost totally undeveloped, so most of its 90,000-plus annual visitors are hunters and fishermen.

Anglers after panfish and tackle-jarring muskies like to duck into the lake's many semiprivate bays, coves and inlets.

Hunters come after good numbers of waterfowl that are attracted to the open waters of the lake, created by the damming of Bear Creek. Others pursue deer and small game over the recreation area's 2,700 acres.

The park's entrance road winds through wide, undulating meadows past a large, open treeless picnic area that overlooks Lake Hudson's east shore, then past a swimming beach on the south shore, and then past the park's boat-launching ramp.

The road ends at the park's semimodern campground. All 50 sites are grassy and open, and all campers get views of the lake. Facilities include electric hookups, a hand water pump, and pit toilets.

COUNTY: Lenawee

CITY: Hudson

CAMPING SITES: 50 semimodern.

DIRECTIONS: From M-34 11 miles west of Adrian, turn south onto M-156 and go one mile.

FURTHER INFORMATION: Lake Hudson Recreation Area, c/o W.J. Hayes State Park, 1220 Wampler's Lake Rd., Onsted, MI 49625; (517) 445-2265.

Coldwater STATE PARK

Coldwater State Park, located in Branch County, exists as a park in name only. There are no developed facilities nor any way to access the 400-plus acres. Currently, more than 80 per cent of the property is being farmed under a use permit, and there are no plans to develop the area or open it to the public in the near future.

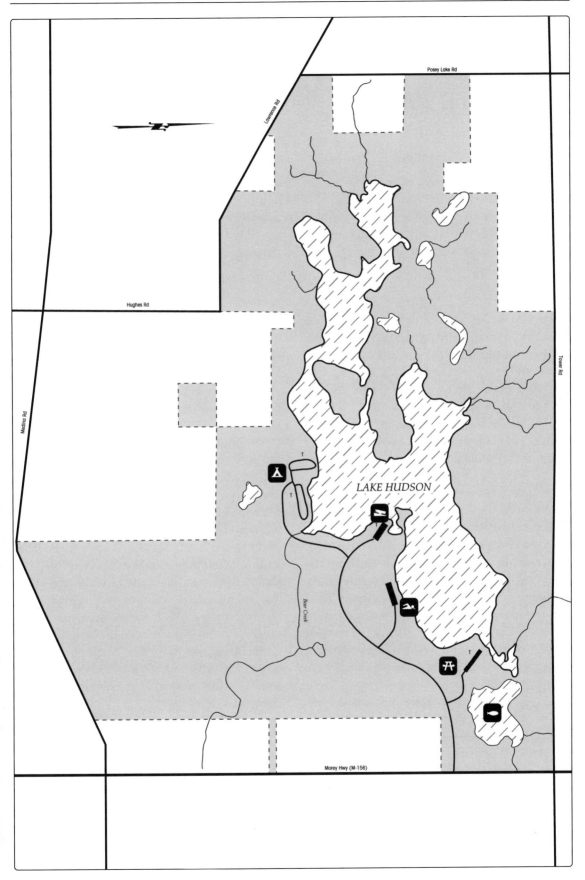

LAKE HUDSON

Posey Lake Rd

Lawrence Rd

Hughes Rd

Medina Rd

Tower Rd

Blair Creek

Morey Hwy (M-156)

S terling STATE PARK

It's no wonder why so many of Sterling State Park's nearly one million annual visitors are fishermen and birdwatchers. Almost half of its 1,000 acres is water — Lake Erie and, back from it, large lagoons separated by narrow causeways and dikes. One causeway that leads from the mainland, in fact, is the only thin thread that prevents most of the park's land mass from being an island surrounded by two creeks, several lagoons and the Great Lake.

Sterling is Michigan's only state park on Lake Erie, a water body considered a little over 20 years ago to be nothing short of a 10,000-square-mile stagnant, polluted pool. The lake was near death after years of taking in raw sewage and industrial poisons. But stringent anti-pollution laws and a ban on commercial fishing resulted in a remarkable rebirth of water quality and sport fishing.

Today, at the right time, in the right place on western Lake Erie, you can't bait a hook fast enough to please hungry walleyes, the lake's number-one gamefish. Anglers also pull yellow perch, white bass, crappie, bullhead, black bass and pike from the lake. Park rangers say that the lakeside walkway, long popular with casual strollers is turning into an early spring walleye shorefishing hot spot. The lagoons are also popular with shore fishermen, and the two lagoons marking the back of the picnic area come equipped with their own parking area.

Boat fishermen have quick and easy access to Lake Erie from a multiramp launch facility (with an immense parking lot for cars and trailers) onto a large, protected basin off the Sandy Creek Outlet.

The park's extensive shoreline and sheltered lagoons also make for very good birdwatching. You can spot herons, egrets, gulls, terns and an occasional osprey, often without even leaving your car. Birders also use 2.6 miles of trails that wander through the park, with the best chances for sightings coming from a path that completely circles the park's largest lagoon and the observation tower located on its southern edge. All trails are open in the winter for cross-country skiing.

Sterling State Park also makes a good base for exploring surrounding areas that make up one of Michigan's prime birdwatching zones. The park sits about dead center in a complex network of lagoons and marshes that line the western shore of Lake Erie south to Toledo and north to the mouth of the Detroit River. That strip attracts huge numbers of waterfowl and shorebirds, including some rarely found in the rest of the state. You can set up camp at Sterling, then make the easy drive to several excellent spots — such as Pointe Mouillee State Game Area and Lake Erie Metropark, to the north, and the Erie Marsh Preserve, to the south — that will always reward you with numerous sightings.

Birders, along with fishermen and other overnighters, pitch tents or set up trailers at a large, completely modern 288-site campground that overlooks the boat basin and launch ramps. Though they lack privacy and shade, the level lots on the grassy meadow are excellent front-row seats to all the boating activity. Campground use is heavy throughout the summer, but park officials report that you

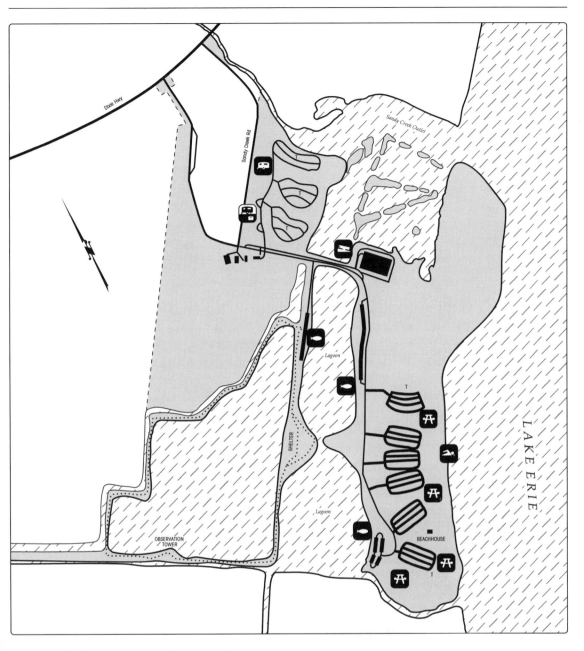

can usually find a site in midweek and even on most weekends.

From the campground, the park entrance road crosses a narrow causeway to a sprawling picnic area that almost seems to float in Lake Erie. The grass-covered, tree-clad grounds rise to a low crest — with commanding views of the lagoons and the vast waters of the Great Lake — that runs down the center of the odd-shaped peninsula. A sandy swimming beach stretches along the Lake Erie side, and a bathhouse with change courts stands between two large parking lots at the south end.

Note: The park is scheduled to be closed during 2002 for construction and renovation.

Other facilities/attractions

COUNTY: Monroe

CITY: Monroe

CAMPING SITES: 288, all modern.

DIRECTIONS: From I-75 near Monroe, take exit 15 and go northeast on Dixie Highway about a mile.

FURTHER INFORMATION: Sterling State Park, 2800 State Park Rd., Route 5, Monroe, MI 48161; (734) 289-2715.

Walter J. Hayes

STATE PARK

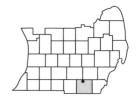

With 654 acres of rolling, wooded hills and open meadows, all nearly framed by the shores of two lakes, Walter J. Hayes State Park would be a nice vacation destination in itself. But there's more. Located in the heart of an area that has drawn vacationers for decades, the park makes a fine base for exploring the attractions in the beautiful section of the state known as the Irish Hills.

Highway M-124 neatly bisects the park into a day-use area on the west side and large campground on the east. Several small, quiet picnic areas strung along the entrance road to the day-use area are great places to spread a blanket and drowse away a few hours under the shade of a tree.

If you prefer sun, crowds and people watching, plus the convenience of having only a short walk until you're up to your knees in water, try the sprawling, open picnic

grounds that nearly surround the park's beach at Wampler's Lake. The large swimming area — with its long, wide, stretch of sand and gently sloping lake bottom — is heavily used.

You can rent a boat or canoe at a concession area adjacent to the bathhouse or launch your own at a ramp at the north end of the beach. From near the ramp, boaters have access not only to Wampler's Lake but also — via a narrow channel, navigable by most pleasure boats — to Round Lake on the park's northeastern edge.

Hayes' large 185-site campground sits on low, wooded hills overlooking Round Lake. The fully modern campground is heavily used throughout the summer months and fills up almost every weekend.

Nearly half the park's acreage is undeveloped, and the various habitats host a wide variety of flora and fauna. The marsh, wetlands and woods provide shelter and food to many bird species, so bring binoculars and bird books.

Fishermen pull bass, panfish, and a few pike and muskies from both Round and Wampler's lakes.

Snowmobilers and cross-country skiers are allowed in the park, but no trails are marked for them.

Within a short drive of the park there are enough attractions to keep you and your family busy for several days. Water slides, fun-parks, a wild-west town, a "mystery spot," and

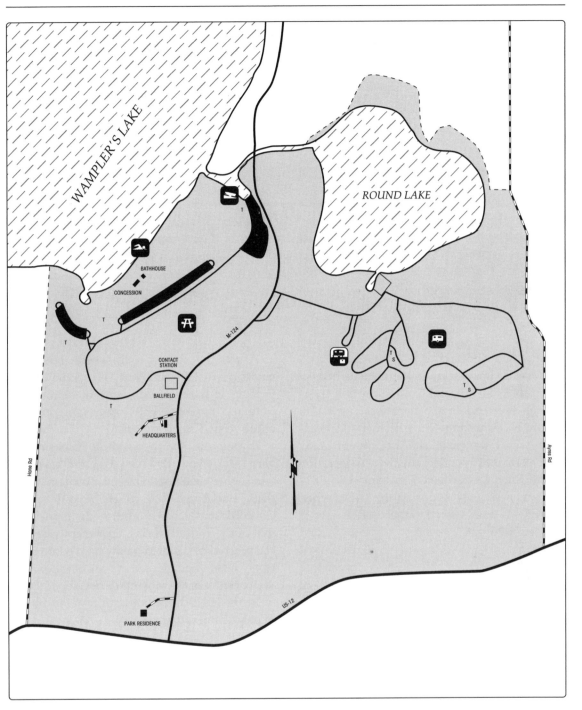

a prehistoric-forest park line US-12 from Hayes' entrance. Michigan International Speedway and Cambridge State Historic Park are only a few miles west, and Hidden Lake Gardens, one of the most unique outdoor botanical showcases in the state, is a few miles south, near Tipton.

  Other facilities/attractions

COUNTY: Lenawee

CITY: Onsted

CAMPING SITES: 185, fully modern plus a mini-cabin.

DIRECTIONS: From the intersection of US-12 and M-50, go 4 miles east on US-12.

FURTHER INFORMATION: Walter J. Hayes State Park, 1220 Wampler's Lake Road, Onsted, MI 49265; (517) 467-7401.

Cambridge Historic
State Park

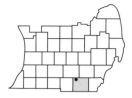

In the 1830s a trip by wagon or stagecoach through south central Michigan over the road that connected Detroit and Chicago was hell on wheels. The spine-crunching route, called the Chicago Military Road, was "constructed" basically by cutting trees low enough to the ground for wagons to clear the tops of the stumps. It snaked around as many obstacles — hills, bogs, streams and swamps — as possible and rarely ran straight for long. Lowlands that couldn't be avoided were made passable by lashing logs crossways over the soft ground, but wagons still commonly became stuck up to their axles in mud while traveling those sections of "corduroy" road.

After hours or days of such travel, the good food, tap room, blazing fire and rustic beds at the Walker Tavern, built on a low hill overlooking the road in the northwest corner of Lenawee County, must have seemed like heaven to weary travelers. The inn, one of many built along the 250-mile route, was in operation before Michigan achieved statehood in 1837 and was at its busiest during the 1840s, when passengers from several stagecoaches a week stepped into the two-story, clapboard-sided structure.

Walker Tavern still stands on its original spot, at the junction of today's US-12 and M-50. Although empty mugs no longer clunk onto the small wood cage bar and no aroma of fine food wafts from the dining room, it isn't hard to imagine what the inn must have felt like to road-weary travelers 150 years ago.

Start at the visitors center, where a tour guide, an exhibit gallery, and an audio-visual program gives you a glimpse into the history of taverns and stagecoach travel when Michigan was young.

From the visitors center, it's a short walk to the large, white saltbox-style tavern. Inside, two first-floor rooms have been restored to reflect a "busy/in-use" 1840s' tavern. In the tap room a scattering of empty straight-back chairs, trunks, and a cage bar overlook US-12.

Across the narrow hall, several Hitchcock chairs, a side table and stove fill a sitting room. Exhibits in the restored first-floor rooms illustrate the tavern's daily operations, but the entire second story is closed.

Behind the tavern stands a reconstructed barn, complete with a New England basement and cobblestone floor. The cellar contains a carriage, buckboard and sleigh. A scale model Concord stagecoach (unfinished), representative of those used during the tavern's heyday 150 years ago, is stored on the barn's first floor.

A small picnic area in back of the visitors center is the only other developed facility in this field museum administered by the Michigan Bureau of History.

County: Lenawee

City: Cambridge Junction

Camping Sites: None

Schedule: Open daily 10 a.m.-5 p.m. from May through October.

Directions: The park entrance is on M-50 a quarter mile north of the intersection of US-12.

Further Information: Cambridge State Historic Park, 1220 Wampler's Lake Rd., Onsted, MI 49265; (517) 467-7401.

Waterloo
RECREATION AREA

With 16 fishing lakes, a swimming beach, picturesque picnic grounds, four diverse campgrounds, miles of hiking and bridle trails, the Gerald E. Eddy Discovery Center, and most of its land open to hunting, it's sometimes hard deciding what you want to do at Waterloo Recreation Area.

And once you do choose, it's not always easy to find your way. The huge area — at 20,000 acres, the Lower Peninsula's largest state park — sprawls across two counties in a crazy quilt-patchwork of state land intermingled with private property. You have to pay careful attention to roadside park signs and the park map to negotiate your way along the twisting, picturesque dirt roads to the many fine facilities and activities hidden among the rolling, wooded hills. But no matter what your outdoor interests, you will be rewarded for your efforts.

Amateur naturalists, for instance, will have a literal field day here and should start with a visit to the Gerald E. Eddy Discovery Center. The center introduces visitors of all ages to the fascinating world of natural history through an array of hands-on exhibits, displays, programs, and even trails that explore wetlands, mature forests, and other Michigan habitats.

From the Center, beautiful, serene nature trails wander over rolling hills and through deep woods, swamps and open fields. Rated the most interesting (and fragile) are one route through a magnificent stand of mature beech and another that crosses over a floating bog. From two of the park's campgrounds, Sugarloaf and Big Portage Lake, short nature trails loop into the surrounding scenery. If you like wildflowers, you can often wade through a near-riot of color here.

If you want more of a challenge than the nature trails or other short loops and paths

throughout the park, you can test yourself on part or all of the longest hiking trail in southern Michigan. The 39-mile-long route winds through both Waterloo and Pinckney recreation areas, and by connecting to the trail networks in both you have access to a tremendous variety of week-long trips. The main trail — which runs from Big Portage Lake Campground, on the west side of the Waterloo Recreation Area, to Silver Lake, on the east side of the Pinckney Recreation Area — passes through some of the most beautiful countryside in southern Michigan, including 13 lakes, pine plantations, open meadows, hardwood forests and wetlands. Maps available at both recreation areas show trail details, including locations of numerous campgrounds along the route.

Three of those camping areas are in the Waterloo Recreation Area, but hikers have to share them with other overnighters. Least-used is Green Lake Campground, just off M-52 on the park's east side, probably because its 25 sites, though well-shaded by a stand of pines and hardwoods, are rustic, with no electricity or modern restrooms.

Campers who like seclusion but prefer modern facilities gravitate to Sugarloaf Campground, located at the end of a winding, seldom-traveled dirt road near the center of the sprawling park. Surrounded by dense woods, marshes and the shore of Sugarloaf Lake, the open, level, grassy campground almost looks like a putting green set down in the wild. Its

170 sites, only about a third of which have any shade, are far from the day-use facilities, but campers do have their own beach, and there is playground equipment for children. Park personnel report that this campground is heavily used on summer weekends, but say you can usually find a spot in midweek.

A second modern campground covers a low bluff a hundred yards back from the brush-covered edge of Big Portage Lake, on the park's west side. Pluses at this 136-site area include modern restrooms, electrical hookups, and glimpses of the lake from shaded, grass-covered lots. Uneven terrain, which breaks the camping sites into different elevations, adds to the beautiful setting. The lots are quite close together, however, and privacy is limited. Also, the unevenness makes it difficult to set up large trailers and motor homes on at least half the sites. Like the Sugarloaf unit, this campground also fills up almost every summer weekend.

The park does have a fourth campground, a 50-site rustic area for equestrians with a day-use staging area. From there, riders have easy access to more than 12 miles of bridle trails that loop through the southern edge of the park. This campground receives its heaviest use, sometimes filling, on weekends in early spring and late summer.

Only a few hundred feet from the Big Portage Lake Campground is Waterloo's major day-use area. A swimming beach there stretches for almost 150 yards down the lakeshore. There's plenty of space on the wide ribbon of sand, plus an immense open lawn that extends back 200 yards from it, for hundreds of sun worshippers to rotisserie themselves. A large bathhouse and camp store perch on a slight rise at the back of the meadow like a southern mansion overlooking its huge front lawn.

Picnickers, too, have room to spread out on the rolling grounds and can set up at a table and grill overlooking the lake or in a quiet corner well back from the water in the shade of huge, old hardwoods.

The Portage Lake day-use/camping area and the Discovery Center are among the few sections in the park closed to hunting. Sportsmen who carry guns or bows can pursue game over much of the rest of the park's acreage. Deer, rabbits, ducks and geese are plentiful, and there are enough grouse and pheasants to make hunting them worthwhile. Wild turkeys were released in the park during the mid-1980s, and their numbers may increase enough in the near future to support hunting.

Birdwatching is good in the diverse habitat. And for a memorable sighting of Sandhill Cranes, visit the Haehnle Audubon Sanctuary, a roosting area for the huge birds that abuts one of the park's western parcels.

Anglers can go after the panfish, bass and pike that inhabit the park's lakes, many of which have public fishing-access sites and boat ramps.

In the winter, cross-country skiers can glide over the rolling terrain on 15 miles of trails, and snowmobilers can set tracks in many other areas of the park.

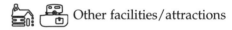 Other facilities/attractions

---

COUNTIES: Jackson and Washtenaw

CITY: Chelsea

CAMPING SITES: 383 (308 modern, 75 rustic) plus two 20-person frontier rental cabins available year round and another 8-person cabin available during the winter only.

DIRECTIONS: From I-94 west of Chelsea take any of exits 147, 150, 153, 156 or 157.

FURTHER INFORMATION: Waterloo Recreation Area, 16345 McClure Rd., Chelsea, MI 48118; (734) 475-8307.

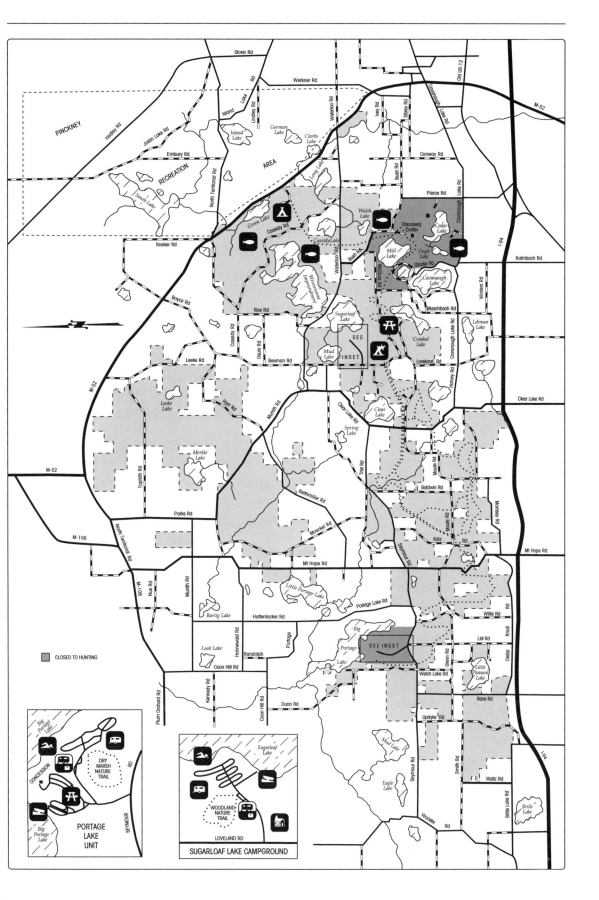

Pinckney
RECREATION AREA

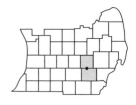

The Pinckney Recreation Area's near-11,000 acres are jam-packed with a variety of facilities and opportunities to enjoy the out-of-doors for a day, weekend or week.

Canoeists, for instance, can put in at Bruin Lake, then glide eastward across an interconnected chain of a half-dozen quiet, undeveloped lakes, plus make short portages to others, all in the heart of the recreation area. Some paddlers simply ferry a picnic lunch to a deserted shore, then return. Others use a modern campground at Bruin Lake as a base for extended day trips.

Hikers can explore the area on more than 60 miles of trails. One, the 17-mile-long Potawatomi Trail, circles the entire park. That well-marked route travels through completely wild, scenic country abundant in small lakes, creeks and streams, and wildlife. The triple-stacked loops of the Losee Lake Trail connect wetlands east of Losee Lake to the day-use area at Silver Lake. If you're after even more of a challenge you can start at Silver Lake, on the east side of the park and, after 35 miles of walking on the longest trail in southern Michigan, finish at Big Portage Lake, on the west side of the Waterloo Recreation Area. If you'd prefer just a casual stroll, you'll like a pair of easy 3-mile-long trails that swing through the backcountry from the Silver Lake beach parking lot.

Walkers can also use several miles of bridle trails that loop through the northeast section of park land. Park officials strongly advise calling ahead for trail conditions, especially when they may be wet and muddy.

The Waterloo-Pinckney and Losee Lake Trails are reserved for foot traffic only, but most of the other trails within the park, including the Potawatomi Trail, are open to mountain bikers.

Located well away from roads and day-use areas on top of a low, wooded plateau and extending well back from the west side of Bruin Lake are 220 sites that make up the park's modern campground. A small campers' beach, playground equipment, and a boat-launching ramp line the shore in front of the lots. This campground is heavily used, and you will need reservations on weekends. Or, if you don't mind doing without flush toilets, showers and electricity, you can use the park's rustic campground at Crooked Lake.

Day-use visitors have their choice of two swimming beaches. On the east side of the area, a grassy meadow wraps around a beach on Silver Lake. In the center of the park, on the east tip of Half Moon Lake is a larger swimming area with more facilities. A picnic grounds, with pleasing views of the water, flanks that sandy beach on both ends. On the grass just back from the beach are tables, grills, a picnic shelter, a beachhouse and a concession stand, and a boat-launching ramp marks the west end of the area.

Boat-launching ramps provide access to seven other lakes scattered within park property. Fishing, especially for bluegills and pike, is reportedly good on all of them, and canoeists and boaters will find great bass action on the chain of lakes.

Hundreds of the park's acres are open to hunting, with deer and rabbits the most-sought-after game.

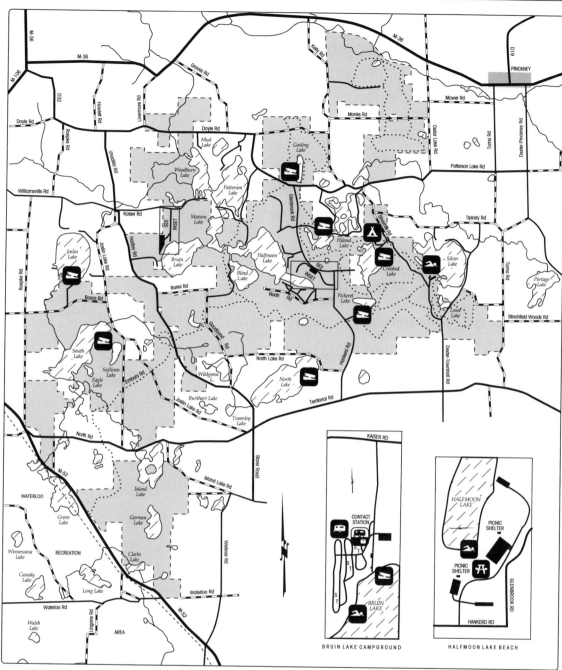

BRUIN LAKE CAMPGROUND

HALFMOON LAKE BEACH

 Much of the winter activity is centered around Silver Lake. From the parking lot in back of the swimming beach there, two skiers-only trails — one two miles long, the other four — strike out into the park's low, rolling, wooded hills and valleys. Snowmobilers aren't forgotten; more than 5,700 acres of park property are set aside for their use when snow depth is four or more inches.

Other facilities/attractions

COUNTIES: Washtenaw and Livingston

CITY: Pinckney

CAMPING SITES: 255 (220 modern, 35 rustic).

DIRECTIONS: From US-23 6 miles north of Ann Arbor, take exit 49 and drive west on North Territorial Road approximately 7 miles.

FURTHER INFORMATION: Pinckney Recreation Area, 8555 Silver Hill, Route 1, Pinckney, MI 48169 (734) 426-4913.

Lakelands Trail
State Park

One of the state's newest (opened spring 1993) linear parks, Lakelands Trail State Park joins three other state rails-to-trails parks that have converted old railroad grades into fine hiking/biking trails.

Hikers, bikers, and equestrians all share this level, gravel-covered, 13-mile-long route that runs generally east/west through rolling, rural farmland and forested areas between the small villages of Pinckney and Stockbridge.

A spring walk is especially rewarding because of the spectacular displays of wildflowers through which the trail passes.

Cross-country skiers frequent the trail in the winter.

Plans call for the trail to be blacktopped on the north half so that hikers, bikers and those in wheelchairs can be separated from horseback riders, who will use the south side. Plans also call for the trail to eventually stretch for 38 miles through Livingston, Ingham and Jackson counties.

COUNTY: Livingston

CITY: Pinckney

CAMPING SITES: None

DIRECTIONS: From M-36 in downtown Pinckney, turn north onto D-19 and drive a quarter mile to the trailhead. The west trailhead is located on M-52 in Stockbridge.

FURTHER INFORMATION: Pinckney Recreation Area, 8555 Silver Hill, Rte. 1, Pinckney, MI 48169; (734) 426-4913.

Hoffmaster State Park

Brighton
Recreation Area

More than a quarter of a million people visit the Brighton Recreation Area each year and for good reasons: fine facilities, lots of room, and plenty of choices year round for outdoor fun.

Picnickers and swimmers, for instance, have two attractive options. At the park's original day-use area, on the northeast shore of Bishop Lake, tables and grills are widely scattered over a spacious, hardwood-canopied picnic grounds that gently slopes to the water. Almost all sites have nice views of the lake and the narrow strip of sand that makes up the swimming area. Chilson Pond has a much larger swimming area and a broader expanse of sand. Open, grassy picnic grounds flank both ends of the beach and extend well back from the water. Facilities at both day-use areas include a bathhouse and changing court. The Chilson Pond area additionally features four picnic shelters with water and electricity. Each shelter will accommodate up to 120 people , and volleyball and horseshoe courts are immediately adjacent. The shelters are available for rent by contacting the park office.

Hikers, too, have choices. A pair of well-established trails — 2-mile-long Kahchin and 5-mile-long Penosha — depart from the Bishop Lake Beach parking lot and then circle through the heart of the 4,913-acre park over old, rolling farmland and through deep woods full of deer, fox, raccoon, pheasant and other wildlife.

Mountain bikers have their own trail system, off Bishop Lake Road east of Bishop Lake.

If you want to rough it, you can choose from two primitive campgrounds. A total of 50 large, relatively private, shaded, rustic lots are divided among areas on both Murray and Little Appleton lakes. Park officials say that you can usually get a site, even on summer weekends, at these moderately used campgrounds.

Seven rustic cabins, which can accommodate 8-20 people, are located in isolated areas of the park and can be reserved by contacting the park office.

If you prefer modern facilities, including electrical hookups and restrooms with flush toilets and showers, head for 140 sites spread along the north shore, near the narrow "waist," of hour-glass-shaped Bishop Lake. This campground is the park's most heavily used and usually fills on weekends. Lots 1-58 border the edge of a low bluff overlooking the east section of the lake. All of those sites are roomy, grass covered and level, and about half provide some shade. Lots 59-140 are spread over a sunny, open meadow near the shore of the lake's west half. The sites there are dead-level and spacious enough to pull even the largest RVs into and out of with ease.

Equestrians can ride over 18 miles of bridle trails, as well as tether their mounts at a 25-site horsemen-only campground, adjacent to a riding stable off Bishop Lake Road on the west side of the park. If you'd like to ride but don't have your own mount, you can rent a horse at the livery stable.

Fishermen can drop hooks into any of the park's 10 quiet lakes and go after bluegills, sunfish, bass, pike and perch. Appleton Lake is stocked with rainbow trout. Three lakes have fishing access sites, and

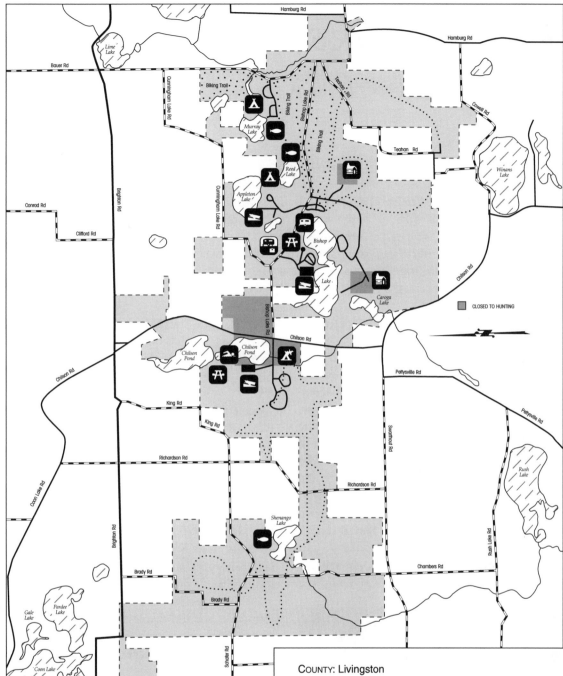

three others have boat-launching ramps.

Much of the park is open to hunters, who take squirrels, rabbits, deer, fox, geese, ducks, pheasants, partridge, woodcock and raccoon.

During the cold months, cross-country skiers and snowmobilers make heavy use of the park.

COUNTY: Livingston

CITY: Brighton

CAMPING SITES: 225 sites (75 rustic, 150 modern), plus seven rustic cabins.

DIRECTIONS: From I-96 approximately 0.5 miles west of US-23, take exit 147 (Spencer Road) and go west through Brighton. Continue west approximately 6 miles out of town to Chilson Road. Turn left (south) onto Chilson and go 1.5 miles to Bishop Lake Road. Turn left (east) onto Bishop Lake Road and go one mile into the park.

FURTHER INFORMATION: Brighton Recreation Area, 6360 Chilson Rd., Route 3, Howell, MI 48843; (810) 229-6566.

Island Lake
Recreation Area

The name of this 4,000-acre park gives no hint as to what the high point is for most visitors. True, two lakes (including one named Island Lake) guard the park's eastern and western boundaries. But most first-time visitors are surprised to find that the beautiful, gently flowing Huron River is the area's main attraction. The 7.5-mile section of the stream that makes lazy loops through deep woods, small marshes and open meadows in the heart of the park was designated "Country Scenic" in 1977 under the Natural Rivers Act. After pulling up a picnic table or spreading a blanket along its banks, it's hard not to be hypnotized by the gentle sweep of current as it quietly, effortlessly makes its way to Lake Erie.

The 40- to 60-foot-wide river and the park are ready-made for canoeists, even novice paddlers. Near the center of the area and accessible only by canoe is one of the state-park system's few canoe campgrounds. Facilities at the two sites include vault toilets, picnic tables and fire circles. (Contact park headquarters before planning an outing.) Also nestled along the river's edge are two small picnic areas — reachable by car or canoe — which include two of the park's four picnic shelters. Rental canoes are available at a livery on Kent Lake. If you bring your own, you can put in at either Kent Lake or an access not quite halfway along the

river's course through the park.

The Huron River may be Island Lake Recreation Area's most spectacular feature, but an arm of Kent Lake that pokes into the east end of the park is the most heavily used. Visitors gravitate to a sandy beach and bathhouse near the bay's west end and a picnic area, the park's largest, that stretches along its southern shore. Picnickers there have plenty of space to spread out over the attractive, sprawling, partly shaded grounds, which cover a hill overlooking the lake. The park's other two picnic shelters are located in this area.

At the opposite (west) end of the park, two attractive, shaded picnic areas face each other across the narrow southern end of Island Lake. The park's southern section features a sandy swimming hole, with a modern toilet building, located on 8-acre Spring Mill Pond. Because of its small size and location in the middle of a large, unshaded open meadow, this spring-fed pond probably warms faster in early summer than any of the other swimming waters.

In the middle of the park is one of the most unique picnic grounds in the state. The sunny, open Meadow Picnic Area is the site of the first and only balloonport in a Michigan state park, and you can down your hot dogs, hamburgers

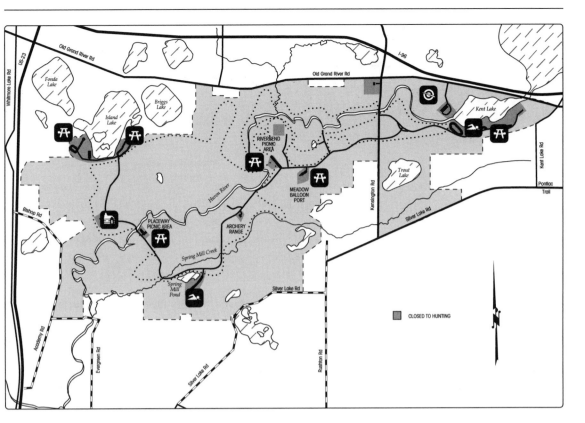

and potato salad while watching launches of colorful hot-air balloons.

You can hike, cross-country ski or mountain bike over all or part of a 14-mile trail that borders the river, crosses hills that overlook the river valley, and passes through deep woods, marshes and open fields. The wide diversity of cover and habitat promises good birdwatching and abundant wildflowers. A few hardy hikers, skiers or bikers tackle the entire 14-mile loop. But since the trail links all facilities, most explore it in sections from several places in the park. Also, a paved 4.5-mile biking/hiking trail cuts through the heart of the park, connecting Kent Lake to the Riverbend Picnic Area.

If you want to overnight here, you're only option if you're not a canoe camper are two secluded frontier cabins nestled in the woods not far from the river on the western edge of the park.

Fishermen will find action good for crappies, perch, bluegills and bass on Kent Lake; Spring Mill Pond is stocked with trout in the spring; and panfish, bass and an occasional pike are pulled from both Island Lake and the Huron River. There's no boat ramp in the park, but you can launch at Kent Lake in Kensington Metro Park, just across I-96 from the state park.

Most of Island Lake Recreation Area's acreage is open to hunters during the fall and winter. Pheasants are released in the park, and other small game, as well as deer, are also taken. Hunters can sharpen their skill at the park's modern handicap-accessible shooting, skeet, and trap ranges.

Snowmobiling is permitted in the winter.

COUNTY: Livingston

CITY: Brighton

CAMPING SITES: Two canoe-camping only, and two frontier rental cabins.

DIRECTIONS: From I-96 2.5 miles east of US-23, take exit 151 onto Kensington Lake Road and drive 0.75 miles south.

FURTHER INFORMATION: Island Lake Recreation Area, 12950 E. Grand River Ave., Brighton, MI 48116; (810) 229-7067.

M aybury
STATE PARK

Old McDonald would feel right at home in Maybury State Park; it's the only state park in Michigan that features a working farm. The Maybury Farm is a unique chance to experience a way of life that is fast disappearing from Michigan and the nation. It may, in fact, be the *only* opportunity many Michigan children will have to learn what an actual farm looks, sounds and, yes, smells like.

Youngsters who do visit will return with a long list to fill in the "On this farm he had some ..." of the Old McDonald jingle. A large barn and several pens hold draft horses, pigs, sheep, chickens, dairy goats, ducks, geese, beef cattle, dairy cows and rabbits. You can observe them close-up all year, but spring is the most rewarding when calves, colts, kids, chicks, lambs, piglets and other newly born and hatched creatures fill the stalls and pens. In fields adjacent to the barn are vegetable gardens, an herb garden, and selected plantings of

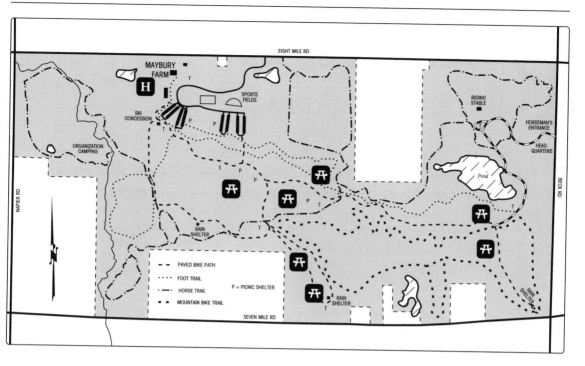

field crops that are worked by non-motorized machines and equipment only.

Within sight and sound of the Detroit metropolitan area, Maybury is also a convenient place for urban dwellers to get an introduction to Michigan's natural environment. The park's 945 acres of rolling hills, alternately covered with dense stands of mixed hardwoods and open meadows, shelter a variety of wildflowers and wildlife. A good way to see it all is along four miles of paved bicycle paths and an estimated six miles of hiking trails, which begin at two large parking areas at the end of the entrance road and wind throughout the park. The park also boasts a 4-mile-long, challenging mountain-bike trail.

Small, secluded picnic sites, isolated tables, and rain shelters are scattered along all bike and hiking paths, and most require a healthy walk or pedal from the nearest parking area. There is no large, central picnic grounds, but one small area and pavilion is conveniently located about 100 yards south of the easternmost parking lot. Four picnic shelters are available; reservations are recommended.

Ten miles of bridle trails also roam into the far corners of the park from the horse-men's area, on the east side off Beck Road. Rental horses are available there, at a stable located near the staging area.

In the winter both beginning and experienced cross-country skiers can glide over an extensive 17K network of one-way trails, more than half of which are rated as difficult. The concession area near the west parking lots rents skis, poles and shoes; sells refreshments; and usually has a blazing fire in their large fireplace. Complete novices can arrange for lessons before testing their mettle on the marked trails.

COUNTY: Wayne

CITY: Northville

CAMPING SITES: None

SCHEDULE: Living Farm—Summer Hours, 10 a.m.-6 p.m. daily; Winter Hours, 10 a.m.-5 p.m. daily.

Cross-country ski rentals—Monday through Friday, 12 noon-6 p.m.; Saturday and Sunday, 9 a.m.-6 p.m.

DIRECTIONS: Go 6 miles west of I-275 on Eight Mile Road. Or go 3.8 miles south of I-96 on Beck Road to Eight Mile Road, then one mile west on Eight Mile Road.

FURTHER INFORMATION: Maybury State Park, 20145 Beck Rd., Northville, MI 48167; (248) 349-8390.

Proud Lake
Recreation Area

In a setting of splendid natural beauty only minutes from metropolitan Detroit, the Proud Lake Recreation Area has catered to the widely varying interests of millions of outdoor lovers since its establishment in 1944. Within a valley framed by gently rising hills, the park's 4,000 acres straddle both the scenic Huron River and a chain of lakes created by the damming of it. Marshes, meadows, bogs, pine plantations and large expanses of natural forest add variety to a landscape dominated by the river.

That wide diversity of habitat makes the area ideal for wildflower hunters, birdwatchers and walkers, who can take anything from a casual stroll to a challenging hike on the park's 2l-mile-long trail system. Many of the paths wind east from a parking lot next to park headquarters through a large nature-study area. That tract, south of the river between the campground and Wixom Road, covers nearly a quarter of the park's acreage and is closed to hunting. Longer routes extend from the nature-study area into the farthest corners of the park, and five miles of the trail system are open in the winter to cross-country skiers.

Just across the river from the west end of the nature study area is the Huron River Fishing Site. A foot bridge crosses from a parking lot on Wixom Road south of the river to the pleasant area that hugs the river's edge on the opposite bank.

Just a quarter of a mile north, at the end of a long entrance road west off Wixom Road, is Powers Picnic Area, sheltered by a stand of impressive oaks, perches on a grass-covered hill with panoramic views of the river and valley.

Hugging the bottom of the hill below that picnic area is Powers Beach. This day-use swimming area — actually a medium-size pond at the head of a bayou connected to the river — could more appropriately be called a swimming pond. It does, however, have a bathhouse, and sunbathers like the wide, grassy strip that flanks the swimming area.

Almost directly across the river from Powers Beach and reached by car from Garden Road is the park's canoe-rental concession. If you bring your own you can put in nearby at the Huron River Fishing Site. The river in this west section of the recreation area is an ideal setting for paddlers. Old channels, bayous, and islands mark the flow as the river continuously loops back on itself.

Horsemen and mountain bikers will also like the western park area. Riders can saddle up in a staging area at the end of Childs Lake Road, then travel eight miles of bridle paths that roam over park property south of the river, west of Wixom Road. The same trails are also open to mountain bikers.

At the opposite end of the recreation area, a completely modern campground stretches along the crest of a hill on the south side of Proud Lake. The 130 lots line up in four long rows well up the hill away from the lake, so the entire shoreline — including a campers-only beach and boat-launching ramp — are accessible to all overnighters. Most sites are small and lack shade and privacy, but because of the area's long, narrow layout, there is little feeling of being cramped. Best shade and views of the lake come from sites at the extreme western edge. The heavily used campground is almost always full on summer week-

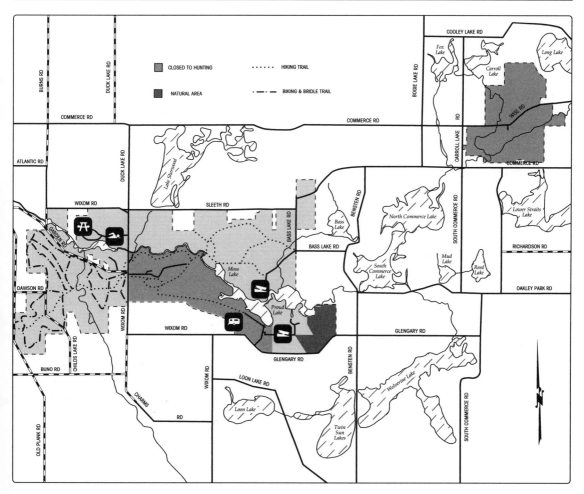

ends, but during the week you can usually find an open site.

 The Huron River and its chain of lakes yield panfish and some bass and pike, and fly-rod aficionados come after the 16-inch rainbow and brown trout that are released into the river each spring. From April 1 through the last Saturday in April a 2-mile stretch of the Huron River, within the park, features catch and release fishing for trout. Regular fishing rules apply during the rest of the year. A public boat-launching ramp is located on the north shore of Proud Lake off Bass Lake Road.

More than half of the recreation area is open to hunters, who take rabbits, squirrels, deer and an occasional pheasant.

During the winter, snowmobilers use 10 miles of trails.

 Other facilities/attractions

COUNTY: Oakland

CITY: Milford

CAMPING SITES: 130, all modern, plus two mini-cabins.

DIRECTIONS: From I-96 approximately 12 miles east of US-23, take exit 159 (Wixom Road) and go north about 6 miles to park headquarters. The campground is on Glengary Road about a mile east of Wixom Road.

FURTHER INFORMATION: Proud Lake Recreation Area, 3500 Wixom Rd., Milford, MI 48382; (248) 685-2433.

Highland
Recreation Area

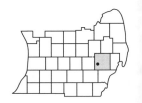

What's attractive about the Highland Recreation area is what's not there. For its size, nearly 6,000 acres, it is the least developed of the many state parks that arc around the northwest Detroit area. There are no large facilities, and thus no large crowds, in this vast chunk of land that sprawls across western Oakland County. The campground, picnic areas and swimming beach are not only small, but also are located on the fringes of the park, leaving a large, undeveloped, wide-open central portion to roam on foot, horseback, mountain bike, snowmobile or cross-country skis.

A couple of other features set Highland apart from most other state parks. The first is Haven Hill Natural Area, a 550-acre parcel in the northeast corner of the park, on which grows every forest type found in southern Michigan. Wildflower enthusiasts, too, will not be disappointed, and birdwatchers can look for more than 100 species that are attracted to this unique area, a National Natural Landmark. Nature trails from the Goose Meadow Picnic Area follow the shoreline of Haven Hill Lake and penetrate to the heart of the nature area north of the lake.

Second is a 30-site, hitching-post-equipped equestrian campground on the east side of the park. The camping area is primitive — no showers, flush toilets or electricity — but is conveniently close to the miles of bridle trails that range through the heart of the park, climbing to several panoramic vistas from some of the highest elevations in the region. Those without horses can walk the bridle trails or rent a mount at a livery stable on the main park road.

Mountain bikers who like a challenge can depart from a trailhead on Livingston Road and set out on 15 miles of very technical trails. Novices have 2 miles of easier trails to pedal.

Cross-country skiers, too, can glide over three marked trails

totaling 12 miles, and several areas of the park are open to snowmobilers. Snowmobiles are only allowed when snow depth reaches a minimum four inches, however, and each machine must have a motor vehicle permit.

Skiers and snowmobilers are among the many visitors who overnight at the park's lone rustic cabin, which sits in splendid isolation near Bass Lake just off Pettibone Lake Road.

Also just off Pettibone Lake Road north of the cabin is one of the park's most attractive picnic grounds—a quiet, peaceful area surrounded by woods. Two newer picnic areas on the west side are accessible from Livingston Road. One overlooks a large field trial area, and the other snuggles up to a small lake.

Three more picnic areas are strung out from the park entrance along the twisting main road. Facilities at Goose Meadow, in a large, open field beside Haven Hill Lake, include a pavilion, a ballfield, and immediate access to the Haven Hill Natural Area. At another area farther south, grills and tables perch on a high hill, with scenic views, over the north shore of Teeple Lake.

From the end of the park's main road, a short walk leads to the last picnic grounds, which consists of a few tables that hug the shore near the park's only swimming

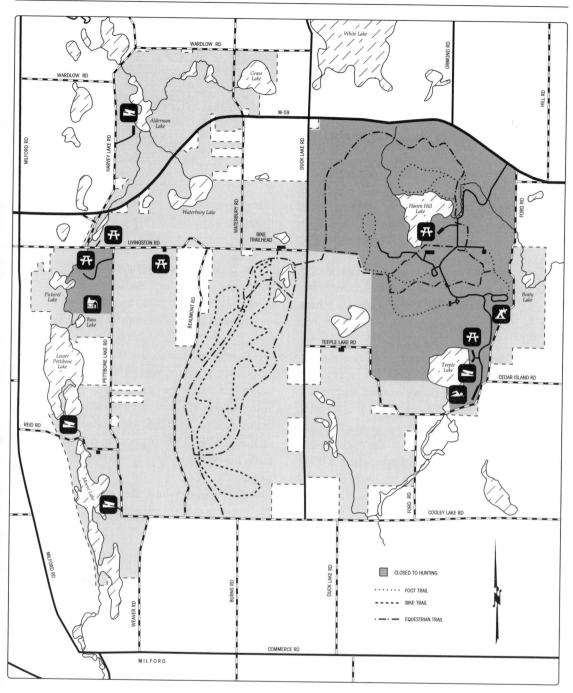

beach, on the southeastern shore of Teeple Lake. Nestled behind the small beach are a changing room, a pavilion and grills.

Fishing is good for pike and bass in the park's 10 lakes, four of which have boat-launching ramps.

More than half of the park property is open to hunting, and deer, rabbit and pheasant are all successfully taken.

Oh yes, and to all the other special features

at Highland, add one more: three dog field trials that are open all year.

COUNTY: Oakland

CITY: White Lake and Highland townships.

CAMPING SITES: 30, all rustic, plus a rustic cabin.

DIRECTIONS: Go 15 miles west of Pontiac on M-59.

FURTHER INFORMATION: Highland Recreation Area, 5200 E. Highland Rd., White Lake, MI 48383; (248) 889-3750.

Dodge Brothers No.4
State Park

The main attraction at Dodge #4 State Park is Cass Lake, and it's easy to see why. The park spreads across the tip of a peninsula that nudges out into the lake, so water defines it's boundaries on three sides.

The mile-long, scalloped shoreline is beautifully distinctive, with narrow beach-hugging islands, odd-shaped little promontories, three foot bridges, backwater bayous, and an old channel.

The narrow channel, in fact, creates a small peninsula within the larger one. At the tip of that thin finger of land and nearly cut off from the rest of the park is a narrow, sandy 150-yard-long swimming beach. After crossing a foot bridge to get to the picturesque area, you have the option of spreading a blanket on sand in the full sun or, back from the beach, on a thick carpet of grass in the heavy shade of stately trees. Nearby is a concession stand and bathhouse. On the shore just west of the beach you can rent a sailboard.

You can also bring your own craft and join the steady stream of fishing boats, speedboats, sailboats and runabouts that are put in and pulled out of Gerundegut Bay at the park's ramp.

Anglers who dare to brave the busy waters of Cass Lake, Oakland County's largest, will discover some of the best fishing in southeastern Michigan, particularly for smallmouth bass. Fishing for largemouth bass and northern pike is also good, especially in the less-heavily used waters of Gerundegut Bay. Panfish, channel catfish and lake trout are also taken from the 1,280-acre lake.

Any of Dodge 4's 139 acres that aren't paved, sand-covered, or reserved for boat launching are set aside for picnickers, who have their choice of three attractive, distinctly different areas. One, on top of a hill near the center of the park, radiates out from a circular parking lot into the deep shade and seclusion of a stand of mature pines. The other two are near water. Across the channel from the swimming beach, picnic tables and small trees dot a grassy meadow that spreads from a parking area to the shore of both the channel and the lake. Many of the tables are right at the water's edge, with full view of all the activity on Cass Lake. On the opposite, west, side of the park, tables are widely spaced in full sun along Gerundegut Bay. And, in spite of the availability of a large pavilion, this area appears to be the most quiet and least used of any in the park.

Other facilities/attractions

COUNTY: Oakland

CITY: Pontiac

CAMPING SITES: None

DIRECTIONS: From the intersection of M-59 (W. Huron) and M-24 (Telegraph Rd.) in Pontiac, go west on M-59 approximately 1.5 miles to Cass Road. Turn left (south) onto Cass and go about one mile to Cass-Elizabeth Road. Turn right (west) onto Cass-Elizabeth and go one mile to Parkway Drive. Turn left (south) onto Parkway and go 0.75 mile.

FURTHER INFORMATION: Dodge Brothers No. 4 State Park, 4250 Parkway Dr., Waterford, MI 48328; (248) 666-1020.

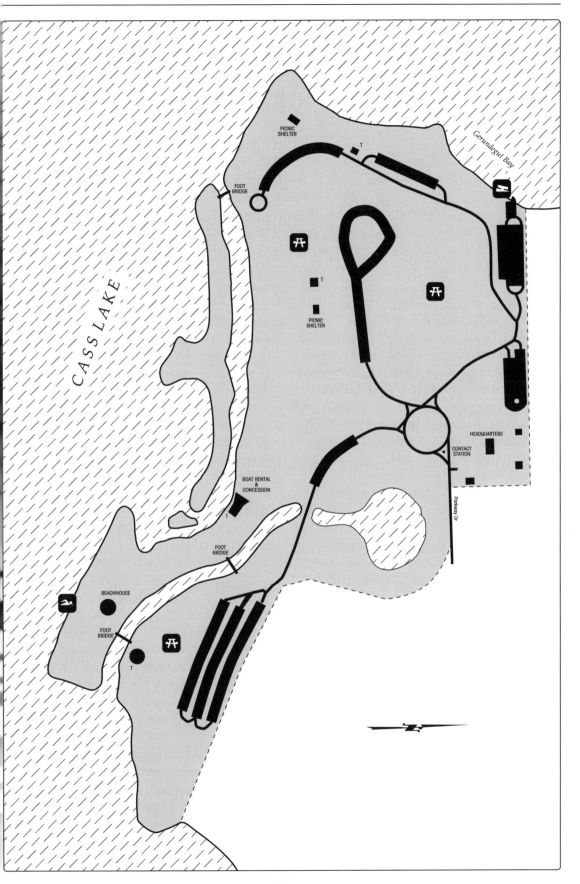

CASS LAKE

Gerundegut Bay

PICNIC SHELTER

FOOT BRIDGE

PICNIC SHELTER

BOAT RENTAL & CONCESSION

FOOT BRIDGE

HEADQUARTERS

CONTACT STATION

Parkway Dr

BEACHHOUSE

FOOT BRIDGE

Pontiac Lake
Recreation Area

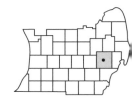

For out-state residents, the Pontiac Lake Recreation Area is an inexpensive base from which to take advantage of the Detroit Zoo, Pontiac Silverdome, Meadow Brook, Joe Louis Arena, Greenfield Village, The Palace, Cobo Hall, Pine Knob, Greek Town, and other Detroit-area attractions and facilities. The big city's dwellers, on the other hand, can enjoy open spaces and a true sense of the out-of-doors only minutes from the end of their driveways.

The park's wide diversity of habitat and ecosystems makes for such good wildlife observation that local colleges use the area for biology field trips and bird study. An excellent cross section of Michigan wildflowers also pokes up from the area's woods, fields and hills. Morel mushroomers forage through the park in the spring, and modern-day hunter-gatherers pick a wide variety of fruits and berries throughout the summer.

The best way to explore is on foot or horseback along 17 miles of bridle trails (horses can be rented at the park's livery stable) that cut through the heart of the park, border the Huron River and rise to several scenic overlooks. The main trail-access is at the horsemen's staging area, livery stable and campground on Maceday Road.

A mile west of the rustic equestrian campground is a lightly used modern campground. One hundred seventy-six sites are divided between two widely separated wings that spread over rolling, partially wood-ed hills in the heart of the park. Neither crowded nor hemmed in by busy roads or day-use facilities, the lots are — with some exceptions — large, well shaded and fairly private. Generally, those in the west loops (sites 1-95) are the most-shaded and private. Every site in the campground has a paved slip and is served by modern restrooms with flush toilets and showers. Park officials recommend reser-

vations for weekends during the peak summer months.

Campers can reach the large day-use area by either walking 1.8 miles on the park's sole hikers-only trail or driving five miles on gravel and paved roads. A swimming beach there stretches nearly 400 yards along a section of Pontiac Lake's north-east shore, and just back from the water are a large bathhouse and snack bar. Wrapping around the entire beach area and extending several hundred yards inland is an immense grass-covered, tree-shaded picnic grounds dotted with tables, grills, a ballfield, swings, slides, volleyball courts and horseshoe pits.

At the extreme southeast end of the day-use area, pleasure boaters, water skiers and fishermen all use a boat-launching ramp to get onto the popular lake. Panfish, catfish, walleye, and pike are regularly pulled from the water, and in the recent past the park has been the site of bass-fishing tournaments. A wheelchair-accessible fishing dock welcomes handicapped fisher-men.

Much of the area is open to hunt-ing, and squirrels, pheasant, grouse, woodcock, rabbit and deer are all taken in season. Experienced hunters can also sharpen at a modern shotgun, rifle, pistol and archery range, across Gale Road from the day-use area.

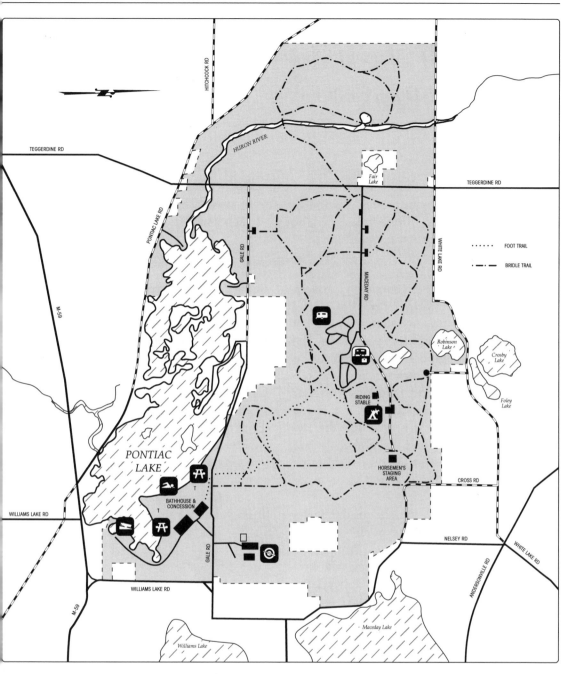

An 11-mile mountain bike trail here is ranked among the top 100 in the country.

No groomed cross-country ski trails crease the park's snow during the winter, but skiers are welcome to break their own paths through the property. Snowmobilers may do the same in a large portion of the park.

Other facilities/attractions

COUNTY: Oakland

CITY: Pontiac

CAMPING SITES: 176 modern.

SCHEDULE: The park is open all year, but the campground is closed from October 26 to April 30. The shooting range is open 10 a.m. to 6 p.m. Wednesday-Sunday in the fall and Thursday-Sunday the rest of the year

DIRECTIONS: From Pontiac, drive approximately 8 miles west on M-59 to Williams Lake Road. Turn right (north) onto Williams Lake and drive one mile to Gale Road. Turn left (west) onto Gale and go a few hundred yards.

FURTHER INFORMATION: Pontiac Lake Recreation Area, 7800 Gale Rd., Waterford, MI 48327; (248) 666-1020.

Seven Lakes State Park

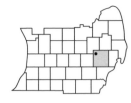

Seven Lakes State Park is a pleasing 1,378-acre blend of water, woods, and large, open meadows that accommodates a wide variety of uses. The area does not, however, include seven lakes. At one time it did, but the seven small lakes were flooded to create one large one — Big Seven Lake.

An added plus: a completely modern campground, which opened in spring 1992. The 71 grassy, sunny sites with asphalt pads line the north side of tiny Sand Lake. The lake and the campground are tucked into a bowl shaped depression surrounded by wooded hills on three sides and a working gravel or sand pit on the east end of the lake. In fact, the campground and lake are probably the by-product of excavating sand and gravel. A wide camper's-only beach stretches the entire length of the campground, only a few steps away from any site.

On the west shore of Big Seven Lake, the park's 800-foot-long day-use swimming beach fronts a large picnic area. Warm water, a gently sloping lake bottom, and wide expanse of sand draws large summer crowds to the sun-drenched area. A large concession stand with restrooms and changing courts stands just back from the beach. Around the shore on the north side of the large lake, a less-crowded, slightly shadier picnic grounds overlooks the water from a hill. Facilities there include two large pavilions.

A third picnic grounds, which overlooks Dickinson Lake from a wooded bluff, is more shaded and considerably less crowded than the two at Big Seven Lake. Still, the small, quiet area seems to be the third choice of most visitors, probably because it's the farthest from the swimming beach. A no-alcohol ban is in effect at all beach and picnic areas from April 1 through Labor Day.

Fishermen walk the shores of all the park's lakes and toss lures for walleye, trout, panfish and bass, including some good-size largemouths in Big Seven Lake. Others rent boats or canoes from a concession, open Memorial Day to Labor Day, on Big Seven Lake. Or you can bring your own craft and launch it from ramps at Big Seven Lake and Dickinson Lake. A no-wake speed limit is in effect.

The park's diverse habitat and small lakes undisturbed by boat motors make for very good birdwatching. A wide range of species find cover in the large meadows bordered by wooded groves, shrubs and thickets; the open waters in spring attract numerous migrating waterfowl; and special efforts to attract bluebirds have been very successful. The same conditions that create good birdwatching opportunities are equally good for

COUNTY: Oakland

CITY: Fenton

CAMPING SITES: 71, all modern.

DIRECTIONS: From I-75 approximately 20 miles north of Pontiac take Grange Hall Road (exit 101) and go west about 5 miles to Fish Lake Road. Turn right (north) onto Fish Lake and drive one mile.

Or from US-23 take exit 79 and go east on Silver Lake Road into Fenton. At the stoplight in the downtown area, jog right (north) onto Fenton Road, cross the railroad tracks, then turn east onto Grange Hall Road and follow it approximately 3 miles to Fish Lake Road. Turn left (north) onto Fish Lake and go one mile.

FURTHER INFORMATION: Seven Lakes State Park, 2220 Tinsman Rd., Fenton, MI 48430; (810) 634-7271.

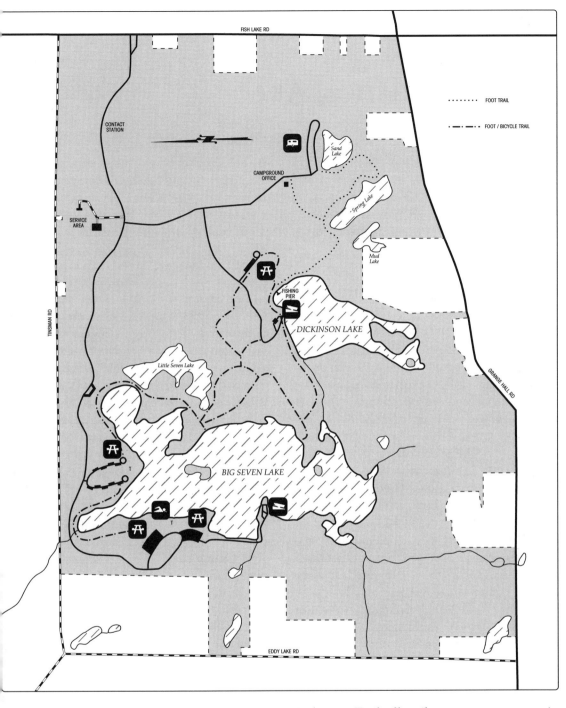

wildflower hunters.

You can roam just about anywhere in the park, but if you're more comfortable with established routes you can confine your wanderings to the more than six miles of well-marked trails that run between Big Seven Lake, Dickinson Lake and Sand lake. Except for the 0.7 mile Nature Trail, which circles south of Sand Lake, and the even-shorter Dickinson Trail, all trails are open to mountain bikes.

In the winter, through-the-ice anglers go after pike, and snowmobilers and cross-country skiers set tracks over the large, open park.

Much of the acreage is also open to hunters in season. Rabbits, deer and pheasants are the game most often taken.

Holly
RECREATION AREA

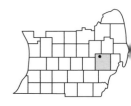

Crowded swimming beaches and picnic areas are likely to be your first impression of the Holly Recreation Area, especially if you come on a weekend. You'll turn onto the entrance road, roll over the crest of the hill that hides Heron Beach from view, and see the area covered beach blanket to beach blanket with young people who come to troll for dates, show off tan lines, and soak up sun and anything else they can carry past the sharp-eyed park attendants.

Don't turn around and go home. As so often happens, first impressions can be misleading. There's actually plenty of both space and quiet corners in this sprawling 7,800-acre recreation area. And, except for the flood of visitors at Heron Beach, Holly Recreation Area's hilly, wooded landscape, wet with more than 20 lakes, seems to soak up visitors like a dry sponge.

The park's centerpiece is a large day-use area that surrounds three connected lakes — Heron, Valley, and Wildwood. The first turnoff from the day-use entrance road leads to Heron Lake and its largely treeless, sun-baked picnic area and large, usually jam-packed beach. Just back from the sand is a large bathhouse, a concession stand, and canoe and boat rentals.

Past the Heron Beach turnoff the road winds between Heron and Valley lakes, then sweeps to its end at the park's only other swimming area, a small, quiet, shaded beach on the south shore of Wildwood Lake. Both sides of the road along the route are marked by secluded, grass-covered, tree-shaded picnic areas. Each either overlooks one of the three lakes from atop a hill or is nestled into one of the wooded, serpentine shorelines. You can also take easy walks around both Valley and Wildwood lakes. Alcohol is not allowed in the day use area from April 1 through Labor Day.

 Also common along the drive is the sight of anglers slouched in folding chairs — tackle boxes, coolers and portable radios within arm's reach. The shore-fishermen eye floating bobbers on all three lakes, and a parking lot near the isthmus that separates Heron and Wildwood lakes is reserved especially for them. Both Heron and Valley lakes do have boat-launching ramps (as do other area lakes — more in a moment). Only electric motors are allowed on Heron Lake. Gas motors are permissible on Wildwood and Valley lakes but at no-wake speed.

Across McGinnis Road from the day-use area is the undiscovered gem of the entire recreation area, a 161-site campground perched on hills north of McGinnis Lake. The large lots are arranged around four loops off the access road, and most are heavily shaded and screened from other sites by thick stands of trees. Paved slips, which alternate off each side of each loop, make for easy setup of trailers and motor homes. Facilities at the campground include flush toilets, showers, a dump station and electric hookups (except for lots 147-161). On weekends during the summer and fall months, the campground usually fills.

Many visitors use the campground as a base for making use of the park's other half dozen parcels, which horseshoe around the day-use/campground areas. Holly Recreation Area's lakes, many with fishing-access and boat-launching sites, yield good catches of sunfish, walleyes, muskies, bass, bluegill, perch,

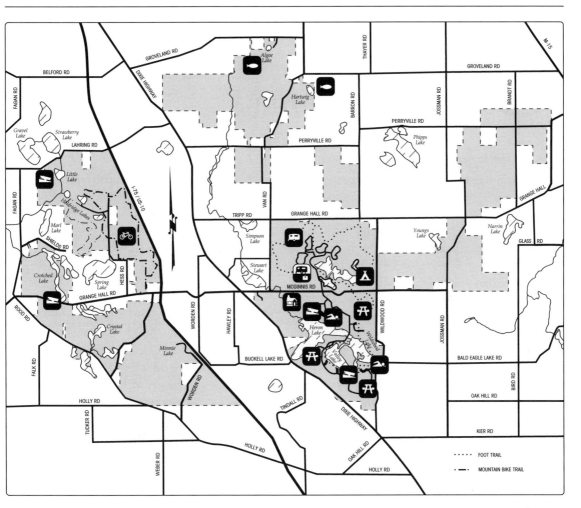

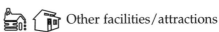

bullheads and crappies.

Much of the park land is also open to hunters, who take deer, rabbits, grouse, squirrels and turkey.

Mushroom hunters, too, as well as wild-flower enthusiasts and other amateur naturalists will not be disappointed by a search through the park's wide range of habitat. Birdwatchers have spotted 190 different species, including such rare visitors as American Avocets, osprey and Caspian Terns.

Ten miles of hiking and cross-coun-try ski trails probe some of the park's remotest corners.

In the winter, snowmobiles are permit-ted on 1,000-plus acres of the park lying on the west side of I-75.

A new, extensive labyrinth of mountain bike trails on a large parcel of park land off Hess Road crosses some of the region's highest and most-scenic hills. The trails range

in length from an easy 0.75-mile pedal great for kids, to a slightly more challenging 2.25-mile pleasant route, to a gut-busting 18-mile, 3-hour-plus slog that includes log jumps, off-camber climbs, and miles of single track.

For detailed descriptions and routes of all trails in the park, inquire at the headquarters building, just west of Dixie Highway on Grange Hall Road.

Other facilities/attractions

COUNTY: Oakland

CITY: Holly

CAMPING SITES: 160 (all but 16 completely modern), includ-ing a mini-cabin and a frontier cabin.

DIRECTIONS: From I-75 north of Pontiac take exit 101 (Grange Hall Road) and go east about 2.5 miles.

FURTHER INFORMATION: Holly Recreation Area, 8100 Grange Hall Rd., Holly, MI 48442; (248) 634-8811.

Ortonville

RECREATION AREA

The 5,400-acre Ortonville Recreation Area spills across the extreme southwest corner of Lapeer County like a giant Rorshach ink-blot test. If, while studying the abstract-looking map of the area, you envision fishing, hunting, swimming, trap shooting, horseback riding, hiking, mountain biking, and a myriad of other outdoor activities, you're not only sane but also in the perfect frame of mind to enjoy this great outdoor playground.

The park's 25 site rustic campground — vault toilets and a hand pump for water — lays along the north shore of Algoe Lake. The park also has a rustic cabin nestled in the woods near the trailheads of the Bloomer #3 unit. The single-room structure with triple-high bunks sleeps 20. It is only accessible by foot, has no electricity, and requires a two-night minimum stay.

Nineteen lakes are nestled into the park's rolling, wooded terrain. Three — Big Fish, Davison, and Algoe — have boat-launching ramps. Big Fish Lake, the area's largest, is popular with water skiers and power boaters, most of whom come from cottages and homes on the lake's east shore.

The park's other lakes, though smaller, are generally quieter and less congested and make angling for the area's bass, bluegills and trout the solitary, contemplative sport it was intended to be. Trying the same on the weekend on Big Fish Lake would be as enjoyable as dropping a fish hook in the middle of a drag strip.

But drag strips can be fun to watch, and a large picnic/swimming area that rims the lake's west shore makes an excellent grandstand for all the activity on the water. The grassy spectator area/picnic grounds extend to a low sea wall fronting the lake and marking the transition from grass to sand. At the base of the wall, six to eight feet of beach provides an ideal area for those who enjoy playing in the sand. Facilities include two rental pavilions, a playground, and horseshoe and volleyball courts, with occasional shade provided by several scattered groups of tall, old trees.

Hikers and mountain bikers share a 2.75-mile loop at the Bloomer #3 area off State Park Road, and cross-country skiers can access a 1.5-mile loop from the same trailhead in the winter.

Also open to hikers are seven miles of bridle trails, which lead from a staging area and equestrian campground on Fox Lake Road into some of the park's most remote sections. The paths border several small lakes and pass over some of the area's highest hills, with striking views of the surrounding countryside.

Hunters have plenty of room to move over the nearly 4,500 acres not set aside for picnicking, hiking or camping. Park officials say that deer and rabbit are the game most often taken, and success is fair for both.

During limited dates and times, shooters can sharpen their skills at the park's rifle/trap range on Sawmill Lake Road. Call (248) 627-3828 for a current schedule.

COUNTIES: Lapeer and Oakland

CITY: Ortonville

CAMPING SITES: 25 rustic sites and a rental cabin.

DIRECTIONS: From Ortonville, go west on Oakwood Road about one mile to Hadley Road. Turn right (north) onto Hadley, which cuts through the park and provides access to most points of interest.

FURTHER INFORMATION: Ortonville Recreation Area, 5779 Hadley Rd., Route 2, Ortonville, MI 48462; (248) 627-3828.

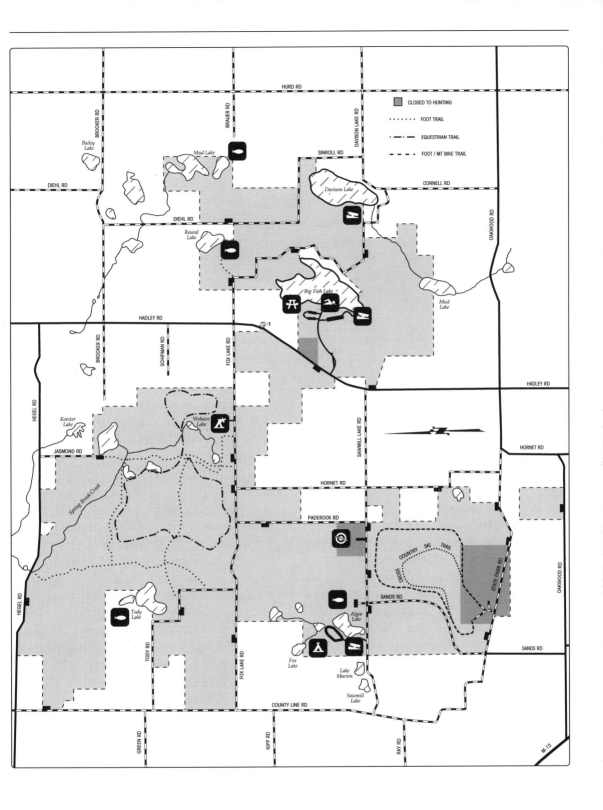

M etamora-Hadley
RECREATION AREA

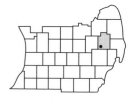

Only minutes from urban sprawl, yet tucked into an out-of-the-way corner of Lapeer County far from major expressways or even busy secondary roads, the Metamora-Hadley Recreation Area offers a welcome respite from everyday metropolitan life. This quiet, heavily wooded park, with rolling hills that overlook Lake Minnewanna, might even make you feel like you're several hundred miles farther north.

The park's facilities circle Lake Minnewanna, a twisting, narrow body of water created by the damming of a small creek that flows through the center of the property. Stretching along nearly the entire west shore is a 198-site campground, divided into roughly equal northern and southern sections. The south loops overlook the water from a low bluff blanketed by a mature stand of hardwoods. Panoramic views of the lake come from about a quarter of the sites that are perched right at the edge of the bluff. All lots are roomy, deeply shaded and fairly private.

The lots that make up the north half of the campground are smaller, less private, and sparsely covered with small hardwoods and evergreens. On the plus side, you can fish, sunbathe, or relax on the lawn-like shore just a few yards from your tent or trailer on a quarter of the lots that are immediately adjacent to the lake. The campground usually has vacancies on Sunday through Thursday nights, but unless you have made a reservation, you'll have trouble getting a spot on weekends during the peak summer months. A camp store is located at the entrance to the campground.

Swimming is not allowed in the campground area, but it's just a short walk to the day-use area on the east shore. There, a long, sandy swimming beach, with a bathhouse and concession stand, fronts a grass-covered, almost-treeless picnic area.

Plenty of tables and grills are scattered throughout the large, open grounds, with many close enough to the beach for you to keep a wary eye on children in the water. If you want a little more privacy and a lot more shade, take your basket and cooler to an area nestled in heavy woods on a bluff that overlooks the water about halfway down the lake's east side.

You can get onto the lake, too, with a canoe, rowboat or pedal boat, all available to rent at the day-use area's concession stand. There is a boat-launching ramp next to the dam on the lake's north end. A no-wake speed limit is in effect.

Two fishing piers jut into the water, one at each of the camping areas. Shorefishing is an equally popular way here to go after the lake's bluegill, crappie, bass, and northern pike.

In the fall, hunters take grouse, rabbit, squirrel, deer, raccoon, pheasant and geese.

Wildflower enthusiasts (picking not allowed), mushroom hunters and birdwatchers will also usually be rewarded, although the area is not a prime location for those pursuits.

The six miles of hiking trails that circle the lake, climb gentle hills, and pass through deep woods on the outer edges of the 723-acre park are, nevertheless, quiet, secluded leg stretchers.

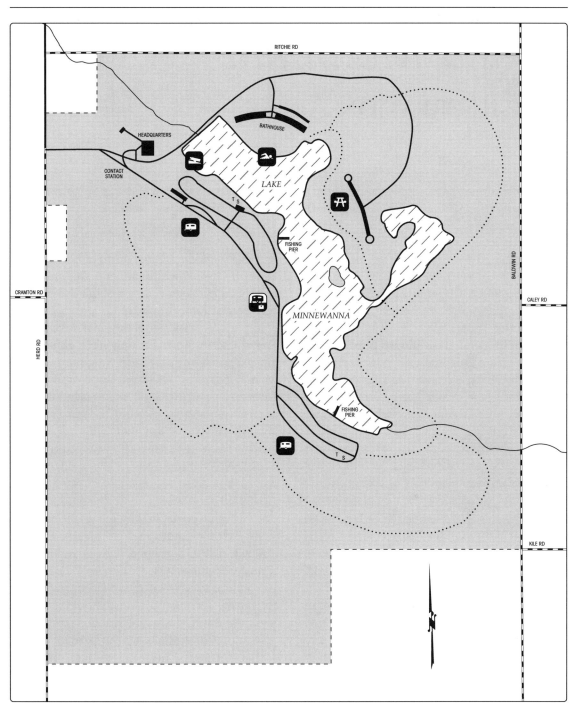

  The park is open for cold-weather camping, ice fishing, cross-country skiing and snowmobiling.

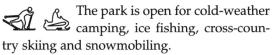 Other facilities/attractions

COUNTY: Lapeer

CITY: Hadley

CAMPING SITES: 212, all modern, plus two mini-cabins.

SCHEDULE: The park and campground are open all year, but water is turned off from the end of October until April.

DIRECTIONS: From M-24 approximately 7 miles south of Lapeer or 10 miles north of Oxford turn west onto Pratt Road and drive 2 miles to Herd Road. Turn left (south) onto Hurd and go about a half mile.

FURTHER INFORMATION: Metamora-Hadley Recreation Area, 3871 Hurd Rd., Metamora, MI 48455; (810) 797-4439.

Bald Mountain
RECREATION AREA

The swimming beach in the Bald Mountain Recreation Area is *the* best in southeast Michigan for small children, according to a prominent Detroit-area magazine.

The wide, sandy shore, gently sloping lake bottom, and shallow waters that reach far out into Lower Trout Lake add up to peace of mind for parents and a near-perfect water play place for small fry. Back from the sand, a bathhouse fronts a large grass-covered picnic area. An added plus for parents: the long entrance road to the swimming/picnic area crests some of the highest elevations, with sweeping views, in northeast Oakland County.

If you want or need to escape the noise and activity of the swimming beach, you have several options. Away from that south-shore area, several quiet, picnic areas with shelters ring the rest of Lower Trout Lake, the park's largest. Or you can drift through the lake's colonies of lily pads and past its forested edges in a canoe or paddle boat, available to rent at the beach concession area.

If you really want to roam, step or pedal onto the 15.1 miles of hiking/mountain biking trails that crisscross two of the three large tracts that make up the 4,637-acre recreation area. Trail maps, available at park headquarters, detail both a 7.1-mile system that explores an area north of Lower Trout Lake off Greenshield Road, and an 8-mile network that connects a dozen small lakes in the park's northernmost parcel.

Several of the small lakes in the northern unit have either fishing access sites or boat-launching ramps. A no-wake speed is in effect on Upper and Lower Trout lakes, and just about all lakes in the recreation area yield bass, bluegills and crappies. Fly fishermen can test their skill against the brown trout that inhabit Trout and Paint creeks, which flow through the southern section of the park.

Bald Mountain's wide diversity of habitat and cover makes for such excellent birdwatching that the Oakland County Chapter of the Audubon Society holds their annual Christmas bird count here. Wildflowers also abound, and if weather conditions cooperate, mushrooms pop up throughout the area.

At Bald Mountain, hunters and other firearms enthusiasts can practice at one of the country's most up-to-date shooting ranges, complete with skeet, trap, rifle, pistol and archery areas. The complex, located on the west side of Kern Road north of Greenshield Road, also includes a classroom, lounge, and sales area where guns can be rented. A ranger is always on duty.

Hunting is allowed in several areas of the park. Deer and rabbits are the most plentiful game, but a few pheasants and ruffed grouse are also taken.

In the winter eight miles of trails are groomed for cross-country

---

COUNTY: Oakland

CITY: Lake Orion

CAMPING SITES: Two frontier rental cabins.

SCHEDULE: The shooting range schedule varies according to the season. Call (248) 814-9193 for exact hours.

DIRECTIONS: Drive 3 miles south of Lake Orion on M-24 and watch for park signage.

FURTHER INFORMATION: Bald Mountain Recreation Area, 1330 E. Greenshield Rd., Lake Orion, MI 48360; (248) 693-6767.

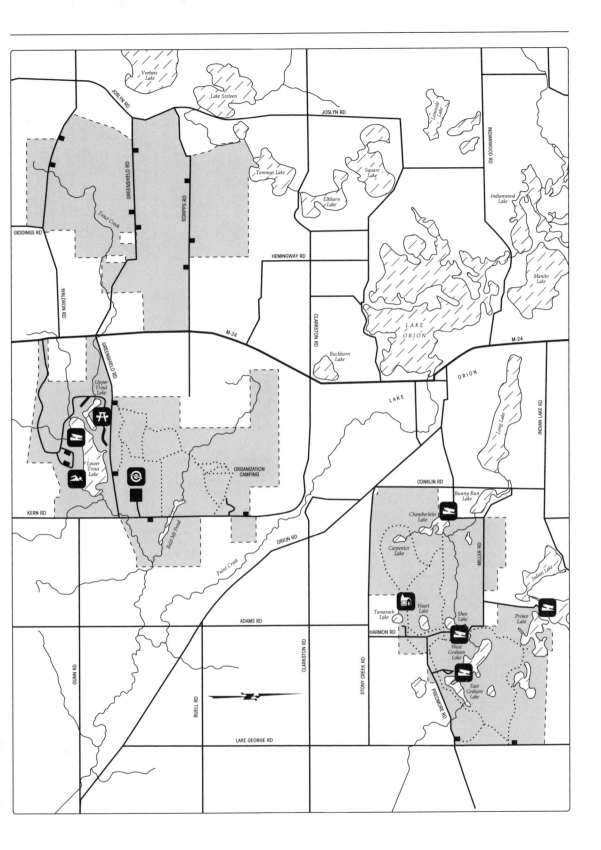

skiers. Snowmobilers can motor over seven miles of marked trails and an additional 2,500 acres set aside for their use.

 Other facilities/attractions

Wetzel
State Park

Although it hasn't been worked in years, if not decades, this 844-acre tract of former farmland still shows the imprint of cultivation in its open fields and near absence of trees.

There are no facilities except for a scattering of small parking sites on roads bordering the park. The area is used mainly by hunters and cross-country skiers, although hiking and snowmobiling are also available.

Also, the Radio Control Club of Detroit has obtained a use permit to establish both a 25-car parking lot north of 27 Mile Road and a 400-foot by 400-foot take-off and landing field for the flying of model airplanes. For the foreseeable future, that area will most likely be the center of most activity in the park.

COUNTY: Macomb

CITY: New Haven

CAMPING SITES: None

DIRECTIONS: From New Haven, drive approximately 2 miles west on 26-Mile Road to where it ends in a parking lot.

FURTHER INFORMATION: Algonac State Park, 8732 River Rd., Marine City, MI 48039.

Algonac STATE PARK

Since its establishment in 1937, Algonac State Park has been providing one of the best seats in the state for watching the world go by. The park stretches for a half mile along the banks of the St. Clair River, one of the world's busiest shipping lanes. Huge Great Lakes and ocean-going vessels, many with international markings, continuously ply the narrow waters, and freighter-watching is one of the park's chief attractions. Almost as many *Geez, look at that*'s are directed at the flotilla of large pleasure boats that also makes its way up and down the waterway connecting lakes Huron and St. Clair.

Each year a quarter of a million visitors spread blankets or set up lawn chairs on picnic and campground areas across M-29 from the river, then sit mesmerized for hours by the passing show. Campers at a dozen-plus sites that immediately border the highway experience the astonishing sensation of watching 1,000-foot-long ore carriers and other ships pass what appears to be less than a boat length from their tents or trailers. And from the narrow strip of bank on the river side of the highway the huge slow-moving vessels seem to block out almost everything else.

But don't tell avid fishermen that freighter-watching is the main attraction. They're liable to give you a long lecture on just how good fishing is in the river and, a few miles downstream, Lake St. Clair. Following spring breakup of river ice comes smelt dipping and good catches of king and coho salmon. In spring, summer and fall walleyes are abundant throughout both the

113

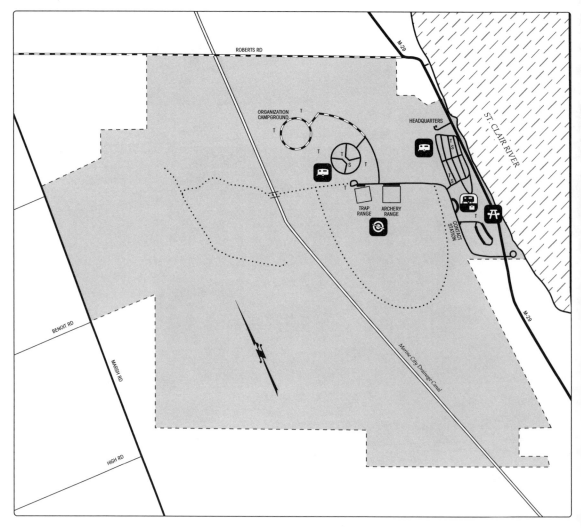

river and lake. Anglers also hook white bass, channel catfish, sturgeon and muskies, and the village of Algonac, a couple of miles south of the park, is known as the "pickerel capital of the world."

There is a small boat ramp near the park's scenic turnout, but better-equipped public-launch facilities are available downstream in Algonac or north of the park at Marine City. Judging from the number of anglers who toss lures from the riverbank, fishing from shore is as popular as from boats.

Much of the 1,311-acre park, which stretches well back from the river and is covered by a sometimes-dense mixed-hard-wood forest, is also open to hunting. Rabbits and squirrels are plentiful, some deer are taken, and a few lucky hunters get a shot at a pheasant.

In the off-season, sportsmen can test their aim at the park's trap and archery ranges.

Other interesting, but more-subtle, attractions are also available if you can tear your attention away from the show on the river. Hidden amid the park's lush landscape, for instance, is a special treasure: four patches of original Michigan prairie, the last remnants of the great grasslands that once spread across much of southern Michigan. The four plots total roughly 62 acres and, according to the Michigan Natural Areas Council, support nearly 300 types of grasses and plants, including many rare and threatened species.

The park is also home to a wide variety of birds, mushrooms and wildflowers. Three hiking trails, totaling about six miles, penetrate the park's interior and lead to three of the four prairie areas.

 Algonac State Park is also open in the winter to cross-country skiers and snowmobilers.

Campers have a choice of 296 sites divided between two separate campgrounds. The most desirable lots are the 220 in the Riverfront Campground, which borders M-29 and the St. Clair River. The very best for freighter watching are the lots closest to the river. There is a trade-off for the great view, however. Campers at those sites have to put up with being a few feet from a fairly busy state highway. The rest of the lots in the Riverfront Campground spread back in several rows from the highway. All sites are small and offer little privacy, but most are shaded and over half have gravel pads for easier parking. There are several drive-through sites for those who can't back onto a lot.

The newest and prettiest campsites are located in the Wagon Wheel Campground, several hundred yards inland from the river. This heavily shaded area offers flush toilets, showers, electricity and blacktop roads and pads, and it's just a few minutes' walk to fishing or freighter watching.

Both camping areas are heavily used throughout the summer, so make a reservation to ensure a site for a weekend visit.

Day visitors have plenty of room to enjoy a cookout and the scenery from a sprawling grass-covered, partially shaded picnic area that also borders the west side of the highway, just south of the modern campground.

Other attractions/facilities

COUNTY: St. Clair

CITY: Algonac

CAMPING SITES: 296, all modern.

SCHEDULE: The park and campgrounds are open all year.

DIRECTIONS: Go 3 miles north of Algonac on M-29.

FURTHER INFORMATION: Algonac State Park, 8732 River Rd., Marine City, MI 48039. (810) 765-5605.

Lakeport
STATE PARK

For day-users and campers alike, the focal point at Lakeport State Park is a mile and a half of beautiful Lake Huron shoreline. The park lies just three miles north of where the lake empties into the St. Clair River, and from the park's low bluffs come distant views of freighter traffic heading in and out of that gateway to the upper Great Lakes. Most visitors, however, don't come here to look at freighters but rather to build sand castles, sunbathe, swim, picnic, and laze away the day on a golden ribbon of sand that is easily accessible from nearly anywhere in the park.

The small village of Lakeport splits the park into two unequal sections. Abutting the village's southern border is a day-use area (Franklin Delano Roosevelt Unit), and to get to its half mile of Lake Huron frontage you have to cross over busy M-25 on a pedestrian bridge. It's a long way to lug a heavy cooler but worth the effort. Panoramic views of the lake come from a picnic area that lines the low bluff, and several

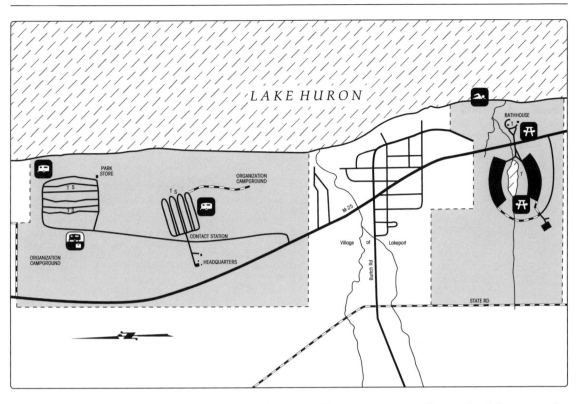

tables are nestled near the base right at the sand's edge. There's plenty of room for sunbathers and swimmers to spread out blankets and towels on the beach and even more room on the grassy bluffs overlooking the lake. The lake bottom shelves steeply here and the water gets deep fast, so keep a close eye on youngsters who take dips. Centrally located on the beach side of the highway is a large bathhouse and restrooms. Children's playground equipment is spread throughout the grounds.

If you don't want to mount a caravan to get your baskets, bags, and coolers across the highway, you can use a spacious picnic area, including a pavilion, adjacent to the large parking lot.

North of the village, 284 sites that make up the park's completely modern campground are divided into two areas. Farthest from the highway and closest to a mile of beach reserved for campers only are lots 1-228. The sites that make up that wing, the park's original campground, are shaded but crowded, with little or no privacy. Best views come from even-numbered lots 16-46, which are closest to the water. The park store is located at the shore edge of this section.

About a quarter mile south of that area, the park's newest camping sites, 301-356, are arranged in four loops near the contact station. Though somewhat less shaded than those in the older unit, these lots are much roomier and have paved slips for easy parking and setup of RVs. The beach is less than a 100-yard walk past a play area and through a dense stand of trees.

Both units fill to near capacity June through Labor Day, so make reservations if you're coming during that period to ensure a site. Many overnighters use Lakeport's campgrounds as a base for excursions into Canada over the Bluewater Bridge, just 10 miles south.

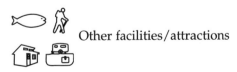

Other facilities/attractions

COUNTY: St. Clair

CITY: Lakeport

CAMPING SITES: 284, all modern, and two mini-cabins.

DIRECTIONS: Go 10 miles north of Port Huron on M-25.

FURTHER INFORMATION: Lakeport State Park, 7605 Lakeshore Rd., Lakeport, MI 48059; (810) 327-6224.

S anilac
Historic Site

In an area remarkable only for its quiet small towns, prosperous large farms, and tabletop-flat landscape lies one of Michigan's most haunting and intriguing mysteries. Poking a couple of feet out of the ground on the banks of the Cass River in Sanilac County is a 20- by 40-foot sandstone outcropping etched with strange markings.

H Scientists have known *what* the figures are ever since a forest fire cleared the land and exposed the rock 100 years ago. They're the best known petroglyphs — that is, prehistoric Indian carvings — in the state. Ancient artists — using stones, bones and antlers — laboriously gouged, scraped and chiseled animals, hunting scenes, animal tracks, human figures and abstract designs into the soft rock.

What nobody knows for sure is when and why. Man has roamed the Cass River basin off and on for more than 10,000 years, according to archaeological evidence. But traditional meth-

ods, such as carbon dating or links to other artifacts found in the area, have so far not conclusively determined the carvings' age. Most researchers theorize that they were done during what is called the Late Woodland Period, which makes them anywhere from 400 to 1,500 years old.

Why were the 100 or so figures carved? Speculation ranges from the recording of dreams, visions or significant events to their being done during hunting rituals or religious ceremonies.

You don't have to know the answers to get caught up in the spell of this very special place. Little known and far from major tourist routes through the Thumb, the Sanilac Petroglyphs receive few visitors. So usually in quiet solitude you can sit on one of the log benches and contemplate what the region's ancient inhabitants were preserving for posterity.

But please don't walk on the rock. The soft sandstone and fragile figures wear easily, albeit imperceptibly. (A large, octagonal roof constructed over the rock partially protects it from the corrosive effects of wind and weather.)

Other faint petroglyphs mark smaller outcroppings scattered along the 240-acre park's two miles of trails, but they're almost impossible to spot. No matter. The walk alone, through some of the most beautiful country in the Thumb, is worth it. The south fork of the north branch of the Cass River winds along the southern edge of the park. Large, majestic hardwoods form cathedral-like arches across the narrow stream, which is bordered in several places by sandstone outcroppings. Away from the river, the trails pass through open meadows, dense thickets, and stands of second growth forest.

Sanilac Petroglyphs State Park's only amenities are pit toilets; there isn't even a picnic table.

The park is open May 28 through Labor Day, 11:30 a.m.-4:30 p.m. Wednesday through Saturday. The park is closed Mondays and Tuesdays.

COUNTY: Sanilac

CITY: New Greenleaf

CAMPING SITES: None

DIRECTIONS: From the junction of M-53 and M-81 drive 4 miles north on M-53 to Bay City-Forestville Road. Turn right (east) onto Bay City-Forestville and drive 4 miles to Germania Road. Turn right (south) onto Germania and go about a half mile to the park entrance. A wide foot trail leads from the parking lot about a quarter mile west to the petroglyph enclosure.

FURTHER INFORMATION: Michigan Historical Center, 717 W. Allegan St., Lansing, MI 48918; (517) 373-3559.

Port Crescent
State Park

When you first see Port Crescent State Park's three miles of unsurpassed Saginaw Bay shoreline, blanketed with low dunes and a white sand so fine it was used for smelting, you'll immediately realize that you are at one of the premier parks in southeast Michigan. By the time you leave — after experiencing its exceptionally fine, beautiful facilities — you'll probably have decided that this 565-acre park is one of the most outstanding in the entire Lower Peninsula.

No matter where you stay in Port Crescent's completely modern campground, you will be drawn to a beach covered in a sand so soft that even with shoes on you often sink to your ankles. Only a few of the 137 sites are immediately on the beach, however, and a few more line an old channel of the Old Pinnebog River, which marks the campground's western edge.

The next-best spots are the 23 scenic lots directly across the narrow campground street from the lake. Many of those sites and the few on the shore are covered with such fine, soft sand that they are partially paved so cars, campers and motor homes can park without getting stuck.

The remaining lots are back from shore, most on a grassy shelf. Almost all of those sites are just a short walk from the campers' beach, and from many you can catch glimpses of the lake through the trees that provide both shade and privacy. Every evening, campers from all lots form a parade to the beach to watch the sun go down over a distant point of land.

The campground (the site of the former village of Port Crescent, which gave up the ghost in the 1930s and left only the stump of a smoke stack to mark its passing) is heavily used from June 15 to Labor Day, and the only sure way to get a spot then is to reserve one.

Almost two miles west of the campground on M-25, an entrance road leads to a day-use area with panoramic views of Saginaw Bay, miles of beach, and acres of low dunes that wet their toes along the shoreline before reaching back into the interior. Scattered between the twisting Pinnebog River and lakeshore throughout the large area are secluded, private picnic tables and grills. And from a change house and large, covered picnic shelter at the swimming beach, boardwalks lead to two of the best picnic spots on the east side of the Lower Peninsula — large decks perched on the lip of dunes overlooking Saginaw Bay. Stretching east, the expanse of low dunes nearly disappears over the horizon. No marked trails cross the area, but it's a great place to casually wander over the unique landscape past wildflowers and dune grasses.

More than 2.5 miles of beautiful hiking and cross-country trails do loop through a large, undeveloped parcel between the picnic area and campground. The Pinnebog River and Saginaw Bay all but surround the area, and the paths pass through quiet, secluded woods, over low sand ridges and dunes, along the beach, and to several scenic spots that overlook the lake and river.

The entire park offers excellent birding, with the trail bordering the old river channel a prime area for warbler watching in late April and early May. Campers can reach the trails from a spot on their beach where shifting sands have blocked the river's original

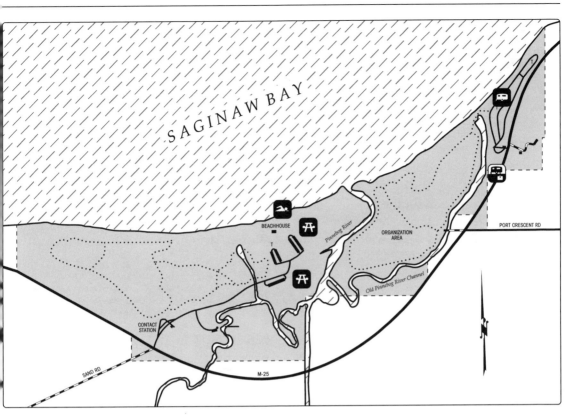

mouth. Day visitors have to cross over the Old Pinnebog River Channel on a footbridge directly across M-25 from the end of Port Crescent Road.

Canoeists can spend an entire day exploring the Pinnebog, a river that seems to tie itself in knots as it searches for an outlet to Saginaw Bay.

The nearly four miles of river that slowly moves through the park also attracts fishermen, who take trout, walleye, salmon and perch from both the river and the channel. There's plenty of shore space for anglers to spread out, and a launch site limited to car-top boats and canoes is located on the river just inside the day-use area. Campers can fish the old channel from three fishing docks built out over the water on the campground's west edge. The village of Port Austin, about five miles east of the park, has a modern harbor and state boat-launching facility, and pier fishing is also permitted there.

Sections of the park are open to hunters, who take deer with both bows and firearms, plus small game in season.

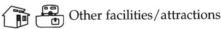 Other facilities/attractions

---

COUNTY: Huron

CITY: Port Austin

CAMPING SITES: 137, all modern and a mini-cabin.

DIRECTIONS: Go 5 miles west of Port Austin on M-25.

FURTHER INFORMATION: Port Crescent State Park, 1775 Port Austin Rd., Port Austin, MI 48467; (989) 738-8663.

Albert E. Sleeper
State Park

Practically from the day it first opened in 1924, Albert E. Sleeper State Park has attracted vacationers from southeast Michigan who want the feel of being in the northern parts of the state without the long drive. Vast and largely undeveloped, the park's heavily forested 723 acres extend well back from a half-mile strip of beautiful, sandy Saginaw Bay beach in a series of undulating sand ridges and ancient shorelines. The pine-scented setting is ideal for hiking, cross-country skiing, nature enjoyment, hunting of small game and white-tails, and other outdoor pastimes.

Highway M-25 slices off the day-use area from the rest of the park. Its half-mile of white-sand beach, plus the gently sloping bottom and warm waters of Saginaw Bay are magnets to hundreds of swimmers, waders, beachcombers and sun-

bathers. Back from the shore, widely scattered picnic tables and grills are tucked into a stand of mature trees between low, wooded dunes and the highway. Although the dunes cut off views of the lake, picnickers have extraordinary privacy and will only have to share their space with troops of busy chipmunks. Other facilities at the day-use area include a large beach house, concession stand, and a picnic shelter.

Directly across M-25 from the beach is Sleeper's grass-covered, heavily shaded campground. All 223 sites have electrical outlets and access to modern restrooms with flush toilets and showers. Campers get to the beach without dodging highway traffic by using a pedestrian overpass. The campground is busy and fills up nearly every summer weekend, and park personnel strongly encourage reservations.

Schools, church groups and other organizations can rent the wilderness cabins, large kitchen and dining hall, and nature center that comprise a large outdoor center, located in the heart of the park. (For information and reservations contact the National Wildlife Education Foundation, 810-583-4863.)

Except for that center, park property in back of the campground is wild and undeveloped. Most of the acreage is unscarred by any path, to the joy of "bushwhackers" who like to

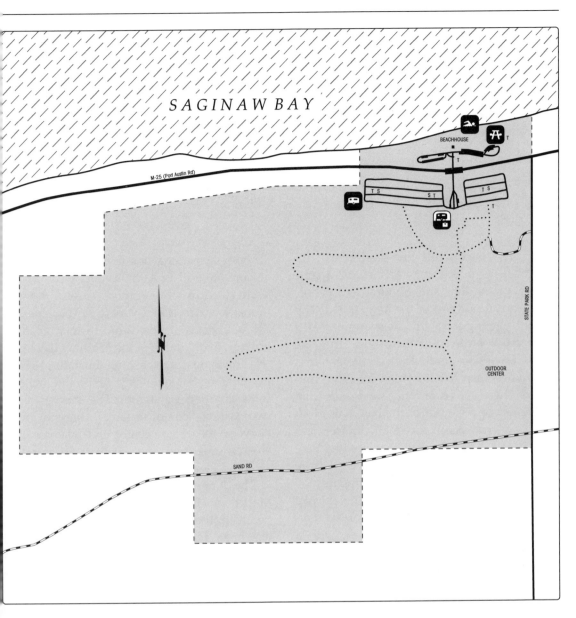

SAGINAW BAY

BEACHHOUSE

STATE PARK RD

OUTDOOR
CENTER

M-25 (Port Austin Rd)

SAND RD

plunge into the area.

 For conventional hikers, four and a half miles of hiking and nature trails also probe the area. Along one, the Ridges Nature Trail, you can use a self-guiding brochure to not only identify the fascinating array of native trees, shrubs and wildflowers along the route, but also learn how Indians used the plants in everyday life. Other trails follow ancient Saginaw Bay shorelines and skirt wetlands. The wide variety of ecosystems here — lakeshore, dunes and woodlands — attracts many birds.

 Cross-country skiers use the trails in the winter, and large sections of the park are also open to snowmobilers (though there are no designated trails) when snow depth reaches four inches.

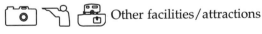 Other facilities/attractions

COUNTY: Huron

CITY: Caseville

CAMPING SITES: 223, all modern and a mini-cabin.

DIRECTIONS: Go 5 miles east of Caseville on M-25.

FURTHER INFORMATION: Albert Sleeper State Park, Caseville, MI 48725; (989) 856-4411.

B*ay City*
STATE RECREATION AREA

One adjective fits just about all of the facilities — beach, picnic grounds, and one of the state's finest nature-study areas — at Bay City State Recreation Area: *E x p a n s i v e.*

The park's soft fine-sand beach, for instance, stretches for nearly a mile along Saginaw Bay, and hundreds of people can stake out portions of the long, broad strip without creating a crowd. The swimming area also extends farther out then most. The lake bottom slopes so gradually that the water is barely knee deep 100-150 feet from shore, and waders there move around sand bars that nudge into or poke out of the bay. This obviously is a great beach for small children and their watchful parents. Facilities, located well back from the water's edge, include a large bathhouse, a nature center, and restrooms.

Behind the beach and paralleling the bay for almost the entire length of the day-use area is an immense picnic area, with a choice of either views of the water from open, sunny meadows, or shade and seclusion amidst towering hardwoods. Playground equipment is scattered along the picnic grounds/beach line, and five picnic pavilions are available.

Across State Park Drive from the picnic area and beach is the park's completely modern campground. A dense woods screens the area from the road and the rest of the park, and the high leafy canopy shades the 193 large, well-worn lots. Nearly a quarter of the sites, those which back up to heavy woods, also have a fair amount of privacy. The beach is only a few-hundred-yard walk from the campground. Reservations are recommended at this busy park.

Bay City State Recreation Area is one of the finest areas in the Lower Peninsula for both recreational and dedicated birdwatchers and naturalists. At the Saginaw Bay Visitor Center, north of the picnic area, you can immerse yourself in a variety of displays and exhibits that tell the natural history, geology, ecology, and wildlife of the Saginaw Bay area.

Then you can experience the natural splendors of Saginaw Bay first-hand on two trails that begin at center. The shorter of the two, which circles a small lagoon lying between the visitor center and Saginaw Bay, crosses over two boardwalks and leads to splendid views of the bay.

The longer trail heads north into Tobico Marsh, which because of its "exceptional value in illustrating the nation's natural heritage," has been registered as a National Natural Landmark. The first mile of trail is paved and cuts through deep woods and marshes before edging the eastern side of the vast wetlands. There are two observation decks along the trail, and a paved branch trail leads to a tall observation tower on the west side of the marsh. The pavement ends at the tower, but a well-worn extension circles farther north along the west side of the marsh, cuts through an impressive stand of hardwoods and leads to a boardwalk that reaches out into the marsh and another tall observation tower.

Tobico Marsh is not only one of the finest birdwatching areas in the state, but also is nationally famous for its wetland bird life. More than 200 different species of birds have been spotted in the marsh, and rare Michigan species such as the Ruddy Duck and Yellow-headed Blackbird nest there. Birds aren't the

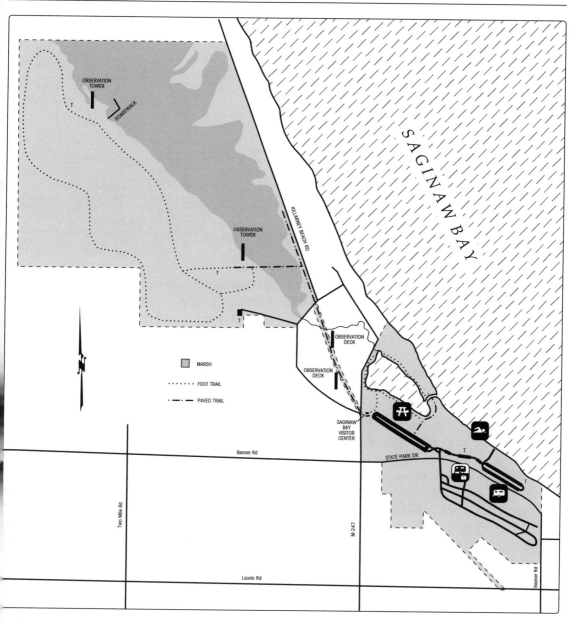

Within the map:

SAGINAW BAY

OBSERVATION TOWER

BOARDWALK

OBSERVATION TOWER

OBSERVATION DECK

OBSERVATION DECK

SAGINAW BAY VISITOR CENTER

KILLARNEY BEACH RD

MARSH

· · · · · FOOT TRAIL

— · — · PAVED TRAIL

Beaver Rd

STATE PARK DR

Two Mile Rd

M-247

Lauria Rd

Beaver Rd

only wildlife that call the area home. Deer, beaver, mink, fox, rabbit, turkeys, coyote and muskrat are among the many other animals that inhabit the area, and rare wildflowers also grow throughout the site.

Hunting is allowed in some areas, with waterfowl, game birds and deer being the prime targets.

Anglers catch perch from a dock built on the shore of a lagoon in the park, and both perch and walleyes are pulled from the open waters of Saginaw Bay.

  Other facilities/attractions

COUNTY: Bay

CITY: Bay City

CAMPING SITES: 193, all modern, plus two mini-cabins.

SCHEDULE: The park is open year round from 8 a.m. to 10 p.m. daily. The Saginaw Bay Visitor Center is open Tuesday through Sunday, noon to 5 p.m.

DIRECTIONS: From I-75 north of Bay City, exit onto Beaver Road (168), and drive east approximately 5 miles.

FURTHER INFORMATION: Bay City State Recreation Area, 3582 State Park Dr., Bay City, MI 48706, (989) 684-3020.

Wilson
STATE PARK

Granted, Wilson State Park, with only 36 acres, is small. And yes, Old US-27 crowds the campground. And no, there aren't any hiking trails or even any undeveloped areas to speak of in the park.

So why do more than 90,000 visitors come here each year, year in and year out?

A look at a state map supplies part of the answer. Wilson is the first "up-north" state park that campers from southeast Michigan can reach in an easy drive. Geographically you could argue the point, but at least psychologically the ambiance of the place says "up north" to a lot of tired city dwellers — so many, in fact, that the campground is filled to capacity on weekends and holidays from mid-June to mid-August. About the only time you'll find a vacancy in the summer is on a weekday.

Another reason for the park's popularity with campers is that they have the whole place almost to themselves—the beach and the picnic area are only lightly used by day visitors. Shaded tables, grills and a large playground are scattered over a gentle rise that overlooks Budd Lake, and the sandy swimming beach edges a small point that juts out into the water. At the base of the little peninsula is a combination bathhouse/picnic shelter.

Wrapping around the day-use area from behind while hugging the highway down the narrow strip of park land is a 160-site modern campground. A stand of mature hardwoods shades most lots, but there's not much privacy and most spots are worn bare of grass. You get nice views of the lake and fair privacy at lots 1-8, 10, 12, 14-16, 25, 27 and 28, which are relatively distant from the road. Farthest from the highway and closest to the lake are odd numbered lots 121-133.

If you don't own a tent or RV (or even if you do) and want to try a nearly unique camping experience, stay in Wilson State Park's tipi which is permanently and visibly set up just off the highway near the entrance. The large blinding-white canvas-and-pole accommodation rents for $23 a night and comes equipped with cots. An electric light and a cooler are available at an additional charge of $3 per night. (Call 1-800-44PARKS for reservations.)

The park also has a mini-cabin that you can rent for $32 a night.

Budd Lake was one of the first in the state to be stocked with northern muskies, and in more-recent years tiger muskies have also been released. Fishermen who launch at private marinas, also pull in good catches of bass and some panfish.

Other facilities/attractions

COUNTY: Clare

CITY: Harrison

CAMPING SITES: 160, all modern, plus one rental tipi and one mini-cabin.

SCHEDULE: The park is open year round; the campground is open April 15-December 1.

DIRECTIONS: Go a half mile north of Harrison on Old US-27

FURTHER INFORMATION: Wilson State Park, 910 N. First St, Harrison, MI 48625; (989) 539-3021.

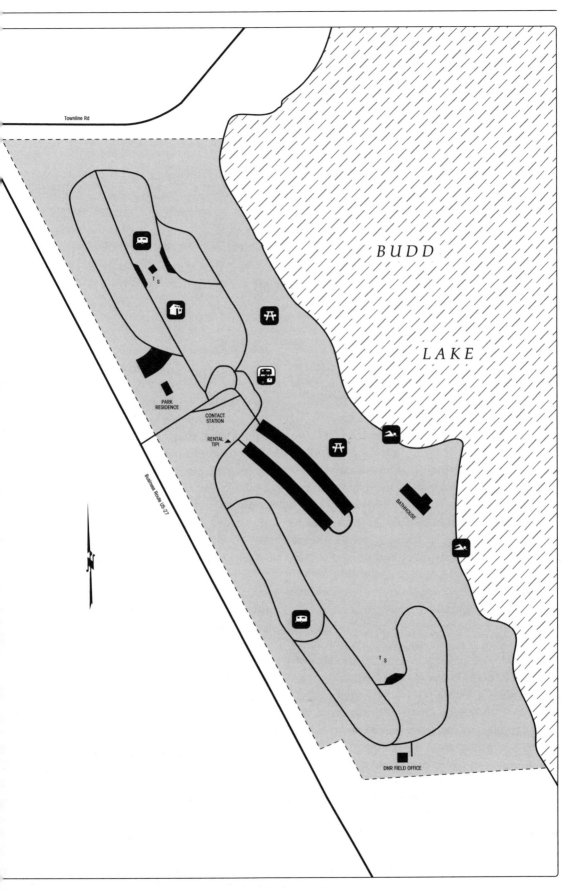

Townline Rd

BUDD

LAKE

PARK
RESIDENCE

CONTACT
STATION

RENTAL
TIPI

Business Route US-27

BATHHOUSE

DNR FIELD OFFICE

Rifle River
RECREATION AREA

One of the best ways to enjoy the scenic Rifle River Recreation Area is on a bicycle. Several miles of paved and good dirt cycling roads cross one-lane bridges, pass forest-fringed lakes, and climb high hills to broad vistas of tangled stands of cedar cut by narrow, fast-moving streams, including the Rifle River. Some of the best views come from Ridge Road, a one-way dirt route that passes over the park's highest elevations. Campers who bring bikes even pedal to nearby villages on the lightly traveled surrounding highways.

If pedal power to you means pressing the accelerator, you can frame many of the same beautiful scenes through the window of a slow-moving car. Or to get an even more intimate perspective than that from a bike seat, you can walk 14 miles of hiking trails that skirt several lakeshores, follow almost countless picturesque streams, and probe the 4,449-acre park's most remote corners.

Many of the area's 100,000-plus annual visitors carry fly rods and creels and for good reason: the Rifle River and its upper tributaries, particularly Gamble and Houghton creeks, have earned reputations for yielding good catches of brown, rainbow and brook trout. Here at the beginnings of its journey to Saginaw Bay, the shallow Rifle widens to 50 feet in many stretches to accommodate several fishing methods, but waders should watch out for occasional 5-foot-plus holes. Some steelhead and Chinook salmon are caught on the upper reaches of the river, and pike, bass and panfish are pulled from the park's 10 lakes and ponds, many of which have public access sites.

Some trout fishermen like to stay at Birch Cabin, one of five frontier cabins for rent in the park. Birch is close to the river, and the other four sit on the shores of the park's lakes. All are located in beautiful, secluded surroundings far from campgrounds and day-use areas. And all are rustic, with vault toilets, hand water pumps, and only the barest necessities for furnishings. (Contact park officials for reservation information and a list of what to bring to set up housekeeping.)

Other trout fishermen favor two rustic campgrounds that border the Rifle River. Spruce Campground, farthest of the park's overnight areas from the entrance, envelopes campers in deep shade and seclusion on widely spaced lots. Upriver, equally close to the water is Ranch Campground. Overnighters who stay at a third rustic area, at Devoe Lake, have easy access to a lightly used beach and a boat ramp. The shaded, private, well-spaced lots there are nestled in a dense stand of trees on the south shore of the lake.

The only modern sites in the park are 75 that make up Grousehaven Lake Campground, near the park entrance. A small campers' beach edges the lake, and good views of the water come from most of the lots, which are large and grassy, but with little shade or privacy. If you have a large RV, try to avoid lots 40-80, because many in that group are uneven. The campground receives heavy use throughout the summer and fills to capacity on most weekends.

Up the Grousehaven Lake shoreline is a boat launching ramp and, even farther east, the

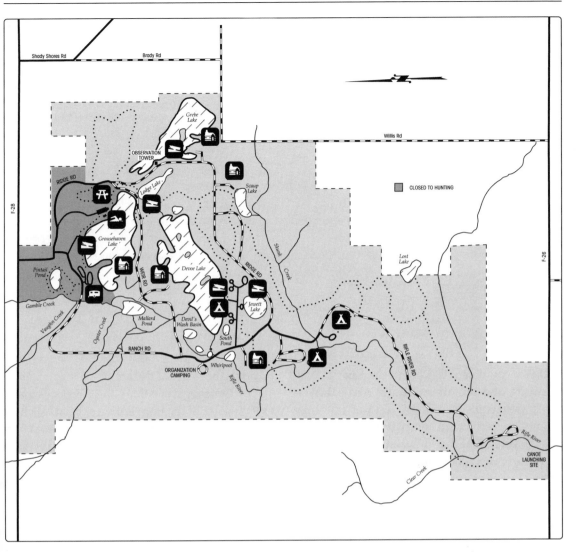

park's day-use area, where a small picnic area, including a shelter, has been cut out of the woods that borders the lake. There's plenty of room to spread out blankets on the grass, which runs almost down to the water's edge, but swimming conditions are only fair.

Land in the Rifle River Recreation Area originally belonged to H.M. Jewett, an early auto-industry tycoon, who used it as a private hunting preserve. The park still lives up to that heritage. Deer are the most plentiful game, but hunters also go after ruffed grouse, woodcock, waterfowl, rabbits, raccoon and wild turkeys on the 90 percent of the park's acreage that is open in season.

Cross-country skiers, ice fishermen and snowmobilers all use the park in the winter.

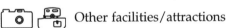 Other facilities/attractions

COUNTY: Ogemaw

CITY: Lupton

CAMPING SITES: 174 (75 modern, 99 rustic) plus five frontier cabins.

DIRECTIONS: Go 4.7 miles east of Rose City on Co. Rd. F-28.

FURTHER INFORMATION: Rifle River Recreation Area, P.O. Box 98, Lupton, MI 48635; (989) 473-2258.

Tawas Point
STATE PARK

You can come to Tawas Point State Park every year and never see the same place twice. Its 183 acres cover the sharp tip (barb included) of the fishhook-shaped peninsula that pokes out into Lake Huron to form Tawas Bay. Annual winter storms pummel the exposed point to create small islands where there were none, carve out chunks of shoreline, and otherwise rearrange the landscape. In addition to those stunning effects of wind and wave power, serious and recreational naturalists can also study a near-perfect model of interdunal wetlands, examine nature's patient attempts to colonize bare sand with plants, and binocular their way through one of the best birdwatching areas in the Midwest.

If you could care less about the finer points of nature and are after nothing more than a day's, weekend's or week's worth of sunning, swimming, picnicking and playing in the sand, this "Cape Cod of the Midwest," as the peninsula has been called, will also fit the bill perfectly.

Acres of glistening, white sand — sprinkled with patches of dune grass and backed by low dunes — make up the park's expansive day-use beach along the Lake Huron side of the peninsula. Ringing the parking area well back from the beach are picnic tables and grills scattered among small groupings of pines and hardwoods. Other facilities include a picnic shelter and a bathhouse with modern restrooms.

Opposite the day-use area on the shore of Tawas Bay is the most photographed feature in the park — a classic, more than 100-year-old lighthouse.

South of the lighthouse and day-use area, the peninsula quickly tapers around marshes, interdunal ponds and shrubs to its point. Footpaths loop through that area, and in places skirt the water's edge so closely that they are often partially obliterated by the winter storms. A dirt access road to a foghorn at the tip also cuts a broad, level swath through the heart of the area.

On foggy evenings the deep, resonant voice of the horn adds a special touch to an already-pleasant modern campground, on the sheltered bay side of the peninsula just inside the park's northern boundary. From June through Labor Day, unless you plan to arrive early in the week, it's best to reserve a spot. On weekends, when all 195 sites consistently fill, it's a must. All sites are large, level, and grass covered, but lack privacy. The sparse tree covering, however, makes it easy for even the biggest trailers and RVs to pull in and out. A campers' beach on the bay—with warmer water and fewer people than the day-use beach on Lake Huron—is just a short walk from most lots.

Campers who tow boats can beach them next to the campground but, since the park doesn't have a launch ramp, have to put in at a commercial marina a few hundred feet from the park entrance or at a DNR ramp across the bay in East Tawas. The Tawas Bay area is fast gaining a reputation for consistent good catches of smelt, perch, coho and Chinook salmon, walleye, and lake and brown trout.

Birding is good throughout the park in spring and fall, but especially in May,

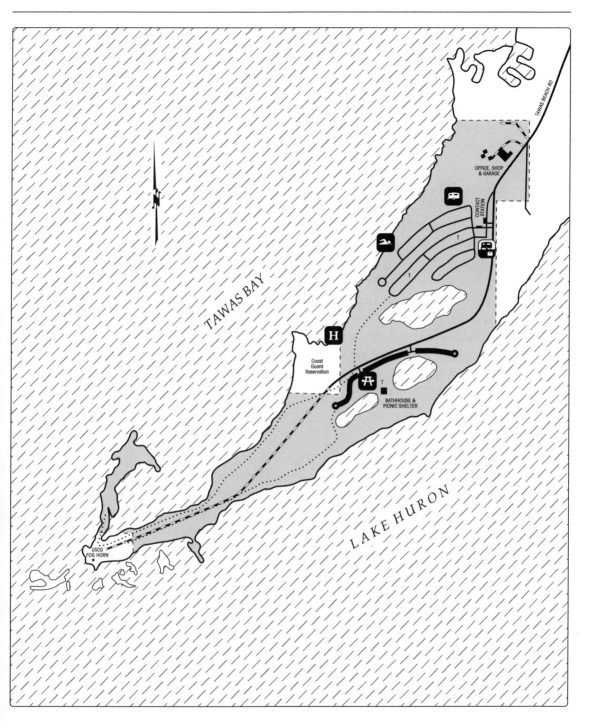

when the tip of the peninsula is alive with migrating birds and birdwatchers. A checklist of different birds spotted within the park numbers 205, including 31 species of warblers and 17 species of waterfowl.

  Other facilities/attractions

COUNTY: Iosco

CITY: East Tawas

CAMPING SITES: 195, all modern, plus two mini-cabins.

SCHEDULE: The park is open year round, but modern restroom facilities and electrical hookups are only available from mid-April to mid-October.

DIRECTIONS: From US-23 just northeast of East Tawas drive east on Tawas Beach Road about 2.5 miles.

FURTHER INFORMATION: Tawas Point State Park, 686 Tawas Beach Rd., East Tawas, MI 48730; (989) 362-5041.

Harrisville
State Park

Except for a wide swatch of sand that meets Lake Huron, trees blanket nearly all of Harrisville State's 107 acres. Fragrance of cedar permeates the air, and a scattering of maple, birch, ash and balsam add visual accents. Add to that an exceptionally fine campground, picnic area and swimming beach, and it's easy to see why this park draws 150,000-plus visitors year after year.

At Harrisville you have to look hard for a sunny camping site and even harder for an undesirable one. All 195 large, flat, grass-covered lots, with electrical hookups and access to modern restrooms, are snuggled among the trees. Most are well shaded, and the trees and shrubs create natural privacy screens around many. Even with all the vegetation, 32-foot trailers fit comfortably on most lots. About 25 of the most desirable campsites, with blacktop pads, border the shore. Park officials suggest that you make reservations during the

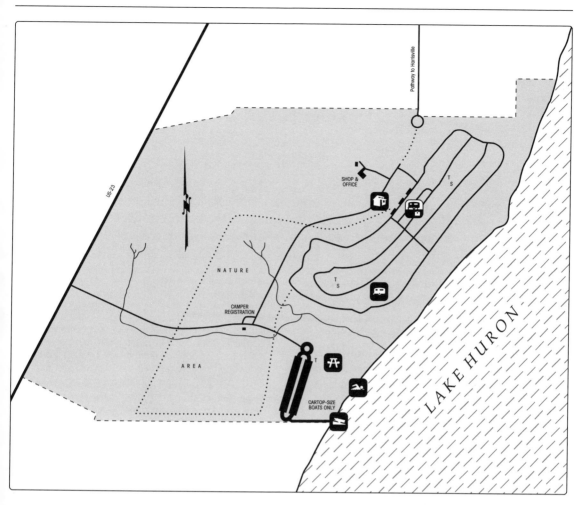

summer months.

Tucked into the park's southeast corner is the day-use swimming and picnic area. Tables and grills there are spread under towering trees, in open meadows, and along the sandy beach. A large pavilion sits a few yards in front of the center of the parking area, and playground equipment is scattered throughout the grounds.

If you want to work chair-webbing marks out of your backside you can hike the Cedar Run Nature Trail, which loops through deep woods in back of both the campground and day-use area. You can walk the quiet path in 45 minutes without breaking a sweat, and if you look closely along the way you'll see wildflowers, which range with the season from ladyslippers and black-eyed susans to marsh marigolds and trillium. If you seek civilization and stores instead of wildflowers, another trail, about a mile long, heads north from the campground to the little town of Harrisville.

Anglers with car-top-size boats can put in at a small site at the end of a blacktop road off the day-use parking area. If you have a large craft, you can launch in the village of Harrisville, less than a mile north. Brown trout, salmon and some prodigious lake trout are pulled from the waters off the village and the park.

 Other facilities/attractions

COUNTY: Alcona

CITY: Harrisville

CAMPING SITES: 195, all modern, plus two mini-cabins.

SCHEDULE: The park is open year round and the campground is open April 1-November 1, but the modern restrooms are closed from October 28 to May 9.

DIRECTIONS: Go one mile south of Harrisville on US-23.

FURTHER INFORMATION: Harrisville State Park, 248 State Park Rd., P.O. Box 326, Harrisville, MI 48740; (989) 724-5126.

# Negwegon
State Park

At Negwegon State park, a negative is turned into a positive. The same lack of facilities that keep most vacationers away from this beautiful 1,775-acre chunk of northern Michigan real estate make it all the more appealing to those who gladly forego creature comforts in order to enjoy an unspoiled natural attraction free of crowds.

"Facilities" here amount to a gravel access road, a parking lot, pit toilets, a water spigot, and bulletin board with a map of the park's trails. And park personnel caution that Sand Hill Trail, the route to the park, is only a two-track whose sand, during dry summer months, "becomes so sugary that most two-wheel vehicles are apt to get stuck."

But for adventurous outdoor lovers, nature has provided a serene and beautiful retreat. The park boasts some of the most beautiful stretches of beach on the sunrise side of the state. The waters of Lake Huron have sculpted the park's 6.5 miles of shoreline into a chain of softly curving bays and coves. A wide, sandy beach marches back from the water's edge, and the broad band of sand is framed by a palisade of green. Behind the tree-lined beach, a forest of birch and cedar blankets the park.

You're welcome to swim and picnic anywhere along the shore. Ten miles of hiking trails, currently under development, cut through the forest and border the beach. Hunting is also permitted within the park, with a variety of small game and deer being taken.

COUNTIES: Alcona and Alpena

CITY: Harrisville

CAMPING SITES: None

DIRECTIONS: From Harrisville drive 12 miles north on US-23 to Black River Rd. Turn right (east) and go about 1.5 miles to Sand Hill Trail (unmarked). Turn left (north) and drive approximately 2.5 miles to a gravel road. Turn right (east) and go 1.25 miles to the parking lot.

FURTHER INFORMATION: Harrisville State Park, 248 State Park Rd., Harrisville, MI 48740; (989) 739-9730.

Tawas Point State Park

Clear Lake State Park

Park officials can be too modest. When I asked a ranger at Clear Lake if there were any unusual, special or scenic attractions in his park, he replied, "Just a beautiful, clean, spring-fed lake." He almost sounded apologetic that he didn't have anything else to brag about.

No apology is necessary. Framed by a forest of dense hardwoods and evergreens, the clear, blue waters of the small, nearly tear-drop-shaped lake; its sandy, gently sloping bottom; and the fine facilities that half circle it are more than enough reason to visit. Another drawing card at this quiet little park is that it sits smack dab in the middle of elk country. You can often see and hear elk in the surrounding area, and there are plenty of country roads to drive in hopes of catching a glimpse of the majestic creatures.

A parcel of private property separates the lightly used (only about 60,000 visitors annually) 289-acre park into a day-use area, on the southwest shore, and a campground, at the tip of the teardrop on the north.

Overnighters can almost always find an empty spot among the 200 campsites, which are divided into two large double-looped wings separated by a playground. The flat, partially grass-covered lots range from open and sunny to deeply shaded, and all are large enough to comfortably accommodate even the biggest RV. All sites have electrical hookups, and all campers have access to completely modern restrooms with flush toilets and hot showers.

It's also an easy walk from any campsite to a large, sandy campers-only beach, where parents with young children will appreciate the shallow, gently sloping lake bottom that reaches far out from shore. At the east end of the beach is a boat launch that camping fishermen

use to go after the lake's splake and small-mouth bass.

Day anglers launch from a ramp on the opposite shore at the west edge of the day-use area. Scattered south from that access along the park's extensive, grassy, tree-shaded shoreline are picnic tables and grills, set up only a few feet from the shimmering lake. A changing court and picnic shelter at the center of the grounds overlooks a fine swimming beach.

A trail on the west side of the lake joins the two sections of the park and is part of a much larger trail system whose loops go around the north and south shores of Clear Lake, rejoin southeast of the park, then continue over rolling terrain to the Jackson Lake State Forest Campground. Points of interest along the way include a gravel pit rich in fossils plus the ghost of the lumbering-era town of Valentine. The round trip to Jackson Lake — either around the south shore of Clear Lake from the day-use area (red and yellow markers) or around the north shore from the campground (blue and yellow markers) — is about six miles round trip. A shortened four-mile round trip to where the loops rejoin also makes for a pleasant outing with many scenic views. (A detailed map of the trail system is available at park headquarters.)

If that's not enough hiking, part of the Clear Lake system helps make up of one of the longest hiking trails in northern Michigan. The High Country Pathway, which cuts through

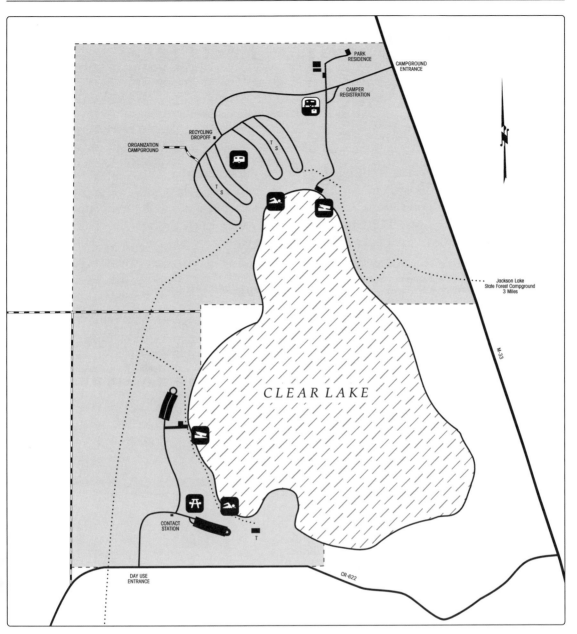

the park (blue markers) on its tour of the Pigeon River State Forest, crosses some of the state's most wild and beautiful country in a nearly circular, 70-mile loop. Clear Lake's campground is one of eight on the trail, but because it's the only one with modern facilities, it makes the best base camp for tackling the long and difficult trek. You can get a detailed map of the High Country Trail from almost any DNR field office.

In the winter a 4.5-mile cross country ski trail runs from the park north to Canada Creek.

Other facilities/attractions

COUNTY: Montmorency

CITY: Atlanta

CAMPING SITES: 200, all modern, and one mini-cabin.

DIRECTIONS: Go approximately 10 miles north of Atlanta on M-33. The campground entrance branches off M-33 at the north end of the lake. To get to the day-use area, go about a mile south on M-33 to CR-622. Turn right (west) onto CR-622 and go about 0.75 mile.

FURTHER INFORMATION: Clear Lake State Park, 20500 M-33 North, Atlanta, MI 49709; (989) 785-4388.

T*hompson's Harbor*
State Park

In the future, 5,247-acre Thompson's Harbor State Park may prove to be one of the jewels of the state park system. Even in its present undeveloped state, it's considered to be more than a diamond in the rough. As early as 1958, a survey by the National Park Service and the Michigan Department of Conservation rated this area as one of the 221 sites along the state's Great Lakes shoreline most worthy of preservation.

The focal point of the park is 7.5 miles of absolutely gorgeous, untouched Lake Huron shoreline accented by low limestone points that break up the waterfront into a series of picturesque bays and harbors.

A narrow, sandy beach lines a designated natural area and a small cove to the west. Elsewhere, a cobble shoreline gives way to a series of low dunes covered by grasses and shrubs. Farther inland a mixed coniferous /hardwood second-growth forest blankets the park.

In the summer of 1992, an access road and parking lot were constructed, and a three-loop hiking trail system totaling more than six miles was blazed. (The trails have had limited maintenance since, but a vault toilet was installed at the trailhead.) The trail's three separate loops (1.4, 2.4 and 2.6 miles in length) all eventually reach the shoreline, but the shortest route to Lake Huron is via Loop 1, which brushes the shore after about a third of a mile. To reach the trailhead, turn onto the park's entrance road from US-23, then take the first right. (If you stay on the entrance road and don't take the turnoff to the trail head, you will eventually come to a parking area only a short walk from the beach.) All park roads are undeveloped, and so it's a good idea to call ahead for driving conditions.

The park is open to hunting.

COUNTY: Presque Isle

CITY: Rogers City

CAMPING SITES: None

DIRECTIONS: Go 12 miles south of Rogers City or 24 miles north of Alpena on US-23.

FURTHER INFORMATION: Hoeft State Park, US-23 North, Rogers City, MI 49779; (989) 734-2543.

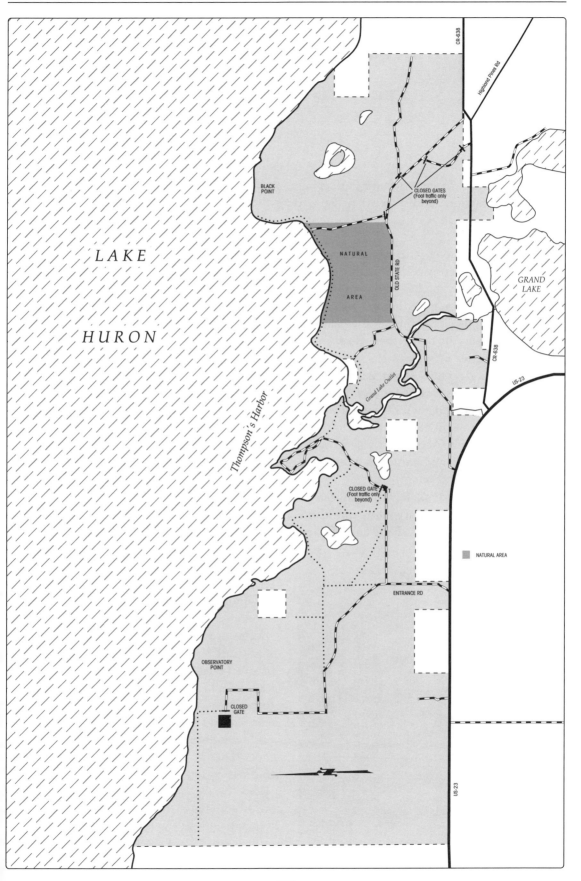

LAKE

HURON

Thompson's Harbor

BLACK
POINT

NATURAL
AREA

OLD STATE RD

CLOSED GATES
(Foot traffic only
beyond)

GRAND
LAKE

Grand Lake Outlet

CR-638

US-23

Highland Pines Rd

CR-638

CLOSED GATE
(Foot traffic only
beyond)

NATURAL AREA

ENTRANCE RD

OBSERVATORY
POINT

CLOSED
GATE

US-23

PH *Hoeft*
STATE PARK

Many rate P. H. Hoeft State Park as the most beautiful state park along Michigan's Lake Huron shore, and it's easy to see why.

A near-mile-long strip of pristine, soft, white sand gently rises from the water's edge and gradually builds into low, rolling dunes. Like ramparts guarding the park from the Great Lake, they march inland for at least 50 yards, where the land then rises more sharply in a series of shelves stacked with a mixed hardwood/conifer forest. Add to this a top-notch picnic area, as beautiful a campground as you can find anywhere in Michigan, and the clincher — an attendance record that ranks the park as one of the least visited in the Lower Peninsula — and you come very close to an outdoor-lover's Shangri-La.

The 144-site completely modern campground — set amidst mature pines and hardwoods, with plenty of shade and privacy — is only moderately used, except on summer

weekends. All lots are level and unusually large, most are well worn, and more than half are arranged in single rows not backed up to other lots, which creates even greater privacy. The *creme de la creme* are lots 1-33, which are only a few steps from the beach and water.

At the day-use picnic area you can dine in a degree of privacy you usually won't find at other parks. Tables and grills, some within view of the water, are nestled in small clearings cut out of the forest. Facilities include an array of playground equipment and a large picnic shelter, and it's just a short walk to one of the finest beaches in any Michigan state park, with great swimming, hours of beachcombing, and enough sand and room to build Windsor Castle.

From the picnic area south to the park boundary, almost half the shoreline and park property behind it is totally undeveloped dunes and woods that abounds in wildlife and vegetation. Some 40 species of wildflowers, including orchids and irises rare to Michigan and North America, bloom here. More than four miles of trails, most of which begin at the day-use area, loop through the wild parcel along the beach, over and around the low dunes, and across the highway into the backcountry. The trails, though not groomed, are open in the winter to cross-country skiers.

Bikers can't use those trails, but they do have their own designated path, which begins at the back of the campground, crosses US 23, and heads south toward Rogers City through dense, quiet woods.

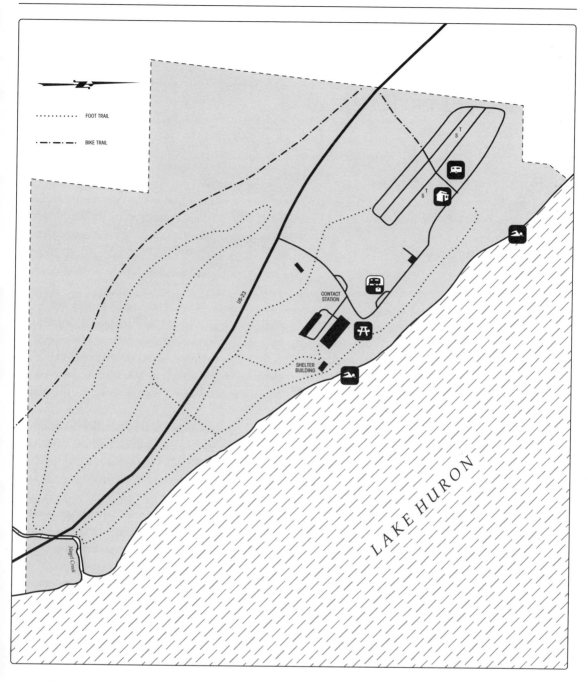

Hunters, too, are allowed on about half the park property. Deer, squirrels, and snowshoe hares are the most-sought-after game, and some partridge and woodcock are also taken.

Recent plantings in the Rogers City area have stirred the interest of anglers who go after lake trout, steelhead, and Chinook and coho salmon. There's no boat access at the park, but you can put in at a ramp in Rogers City, four miles south.

  Other facilities/attractions

COUNTY: Presque Isle

CITY: Rogers City

CAMPING SITES: 144, all modern, four rent-a-tents and one mini-cabin.

DIRECTIONS: Go 5 miles north of Rogers City on US-23.

FURTHER INFORMATION: P.H. Hoeft State Park, US-23 North, Rogers City, MI 49779; (989) 734-2543.

O naway
STATE PARK

Established in 1921, Onaway State Park has aged and mellowed like a fine wine. Yet few people come to taste. With only 44,000 visitors annually, Onaway is one of the most ignored parks in the Lower Peninsula. Probably the lack of a glorious swimming beach and the absence of nearby tourist attractions dissuade a lot of people from even a first visit. But the faithful who do come here find those very features to be assets, not detractions.

Overnighters, for instance, can relax in beautiful surroundings without distractions in one of the few state-park campgrounds that rarely fills up. The 85 sites, all with electrical hookups and access to modern restrooms, are divided into two unequal sections. Most are spread over the top of a bluff under a dense canopy of virgin white pines and hardwoods that both dwarf and almost perpetually shade tents, trailers, and motor homes. The stand of trees plus the rolling terrain create adequate privacy, and needles and leaves carpet the roomy sites. At the bottom of the bluff, edging the rocky shore of Black Lake is the smaller camping unit. Cedars, pines and hardwoods crowd the lots there, which are slightly smaller than above and either back up to the lake or nestle against the steep-sided bluff.

A playground area separates the campground from the swimming beach, such as it is. The lakeshore bordering entire the park is very rocky, and the "beach" was created simply by pushing aside rocks in a postage-stamp-size area, then covering it with hauled-in sand. (While not so good for swimmers, the lake bottom and nearly one mile of park shoreline is a fossil hunter's treasure trove.)

An old, rustic-looking picnic pavilion overlooks the swimming area, and tables and grills nearby are wedged into small clearings in a stand of cedar so thick your nose will swear you're eating lunch in a cedar closet.

At the extreme eastern end of the park another picnic area is nestled among the cedar, red pines and hardwoods close to the rocky shoreline.

Black Lake, 6 miles long and 3 miles wide, is not only the eighth-largest in Michigan, but also one of the state's 10 best for walleye fishing, according to the DNR. Good catches of smallmouth bass and muskies are also pulled from its waters, and from all reports it's worth dropping a line for perch and pike. Fishermen and other boaters can launch at a ramp with skid pier and a parking lot for cars and boat trailers on the west side of the day-use area.

Wildflowers and morel mushrooms, in season, fill the wooded park. A 3-mile long nature trail winds through the park's deep woods, and even better hiking opportunities come at Ocqueoc Falls Bicentennial Pathway, 10 miles east of the village of Onaway on highway M-68. There, in addition to 3-, 4-, and 6.5-mile loops through a beautiful forest, you can also soak your feet in the tumbling waters of the Lower Peninsula's only "major" waterfall.

Other facilities/attractions

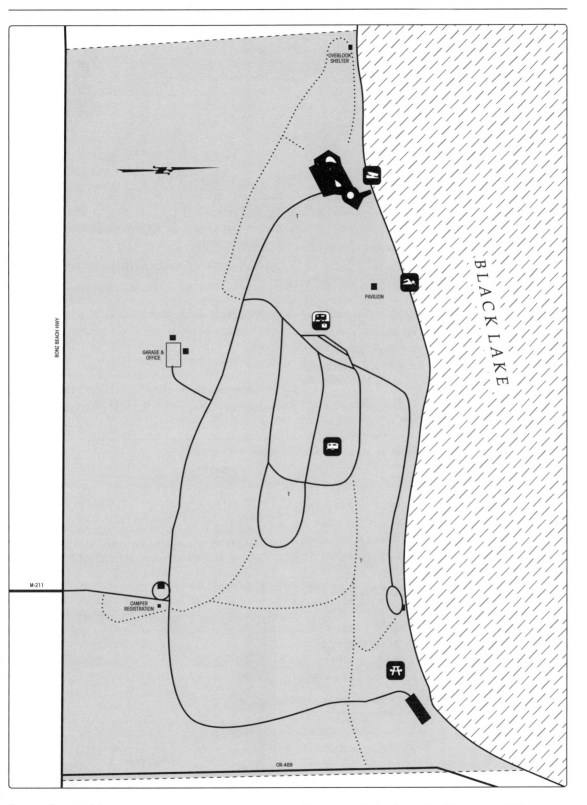

BLACK LAKE

OVERLOOK SHELTER

PAVILION

GARAGE & OFFICE

CAMPER REGISTRATION

BONZ BEACH HWY

M-211

CR-489

COUNTY: Presque Isle

CITY: Onaway

CAMPING SITES: 85, all modern.

SCHEDULE: The park is open all year, but the campground is closed October 15 to May 15.

DIRECTIONS: Go 6 miles north of Onaway on M-211.

FURTHER INFORMATION: Onaway State Park, 3622 North M-211, Onaway, MI 49765; (989) 733-8279.

Aloha State Park

If you like water or water sports, there's plenty to do and plenty of room to do it at Aloha State Park. The park stretches along the east shore of 13-mile-long and up-to-5-mile-wide Mullett Lake, Michigan's fifth-largest. Mullett is also one of three lakes that, along with connecting rivers, make up the Inland Waterway, a 40-mile scenic, navigable route from Cheboygan on Lake Huron to Conway, only three miles from Lake Michigan.

Mullett Lake is consistently rated as one of the state's top-10 walleye holes, and anglers also have good luck going after pike, perch, rock bass, small and largemouth bass, bluegills, muskies, smelt, and brook, brown, rainbow and lake trout. In 1974 the largest fish ever caught by a recreational fisherman in Michigan waters — a monstrous 193-pound, 87-inch-long sturgeon — was *speared* through Mullett's ice.

Fishermen and other boaters can launch from a large concrete ramp in a protected basin that is sandwiched between two of the park's campground loops.

The camping area takes up most of the park's almost totally developed (with no room for nature areas or hiking trails) 106 acres. Campground use is heavy throughout the summer, filling to capacity almost every weekend, so it's best to book an advance reservation if you come in late June through August. You won't find many shaded or private sites, but all are level, grassy and spacious enough for even the largest trailer or motor home to pull in and out. All also have electrical hookups and access to modern restrooms. None of the 285 sites are far from the water, and all campers have access to a designated swimming beach.

A second sandy, sun-drenched beach at the day-use area fronts a spacious grass-covered picnic area, with tables and grills scattered among sheltering hardwoods and cedars and a large, grassy playground only a few steps away.

Other facilities/attractions

(For further details about the Inland Waterway, see Burt Lake State Park, p. 6).

COUNTY: Cheboygan

CITY: Cheboygan

CAMPING SITES: 285, all modern.

SCHEDULE: Facilities are open from May 1 to October 31.

DIRECTIONS: From I-75 take the Indian River exit (310) and drive east 9 miles on M-68 to M-33. Turn left (north) onto M-33 and go about 9 miles to M-212. Turn left (west) onto M-212 and go less than a mile.

FURTHER INFORMATION: Aloha State Park, 4347 Third St., Cheboygan, MI 49721; (231) 625-2522.

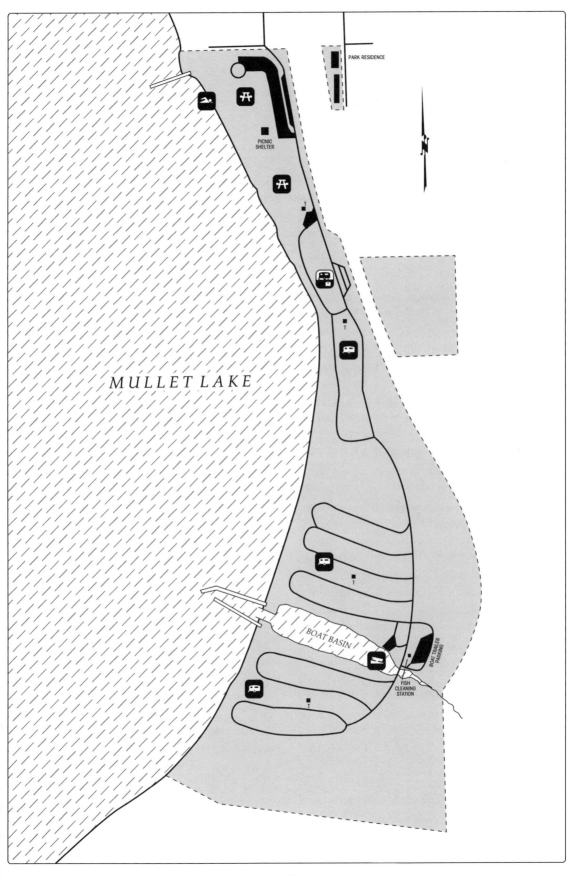

PARK RESIDENCE

PICNIC
SHELTER

MULLET LAKE

BOAT BASIN

BOAT TRAILER
PARKING

FISH
CLEANING
STATION

Cheboygan
State Park

Plenty of prime scenery; spacious, widely scattered facilities; and comparatively few people to share them with are the draws to Cheboygan State Park. Its 1,200 largely undeveloped acres, four miles of Lake Huron beach, six miles of hiking trails, cozy campground, three remote, rustic cabins and sandy beaches are used by only 60,000-plus people a year.

The park spreads over most of a narrow peninsula that is tipped by tiny Cheboygan and Lighthouse points. Near the peninsula's base on the west shore, the campground and day-use area are separated by a low, marshy area. The wetlands are created by the backwaters and many slow-moving channels of Little Billy Elliots Creek as it empties into shallow, protected Duncan Bay.

On the south side of the tree-ringed creekmouth, picnic tables and grills spread over an open area with fine views of a broad, sandy swimming beach, the bay and its wooded shoreline. Other facilities at the day-use area include a picnic shelter, playground equipment, and a bathhouse with modern restrooms and changing courts.

Only about a half mile north across the uncrossable marsh, four miles away by road, is the park's quiet, completely modern campground. All 75 lots are large and grassy with excellent privacy in the heavily wooded, out-of-the-way area. All overnighters are close to the beach and water, which are full of reeds and pebbles. With so few sites, in spite of the park's overall low use you will probably have difficulty finding a vacant spot on most summer weekends.

An unusual overnight alternative is to bunk at one of the park's three, widely separated, beach-side cabins. Each of the rustic (no electricity or indoor plumbing) one-room accommodations sleeps eight, in four double bunks, and comes with a wood stove, table and chairs. You furnish the rest. Two of the cabins are near the ruins of the historic Cheboygan Point Lighthouse, built in 1851. You can rent the cabins for $45 a night year round, but often the only way to get to them in the winter is on cross-country skis. Contact the park manager in advance for rental details and reservations.

Six miles of hiking trails that network the park's undeveloped acreage follow or parallel the varied coastline (which promises good birdwatching opportunities) and cut inland through low dunes, marshes, interdunal ponds, and stretches of forest. An abundance of wildflowers includes several varieties of lilies and many rare species found only in this region of the state. The park is open in the winter for cross-country skiing.

The park's small boat launch handles only 14- to 16-foot craft, but fishermen with large boats can put in at a public launch at Cheboygan, less than four miles away, and go after northern pike, small and largemouth bass, and panfish on Duncan Bay. Little Billy Elliots Creek, which flows through the southern part of the park, is known for its brook trout.

Other facilities/attractions

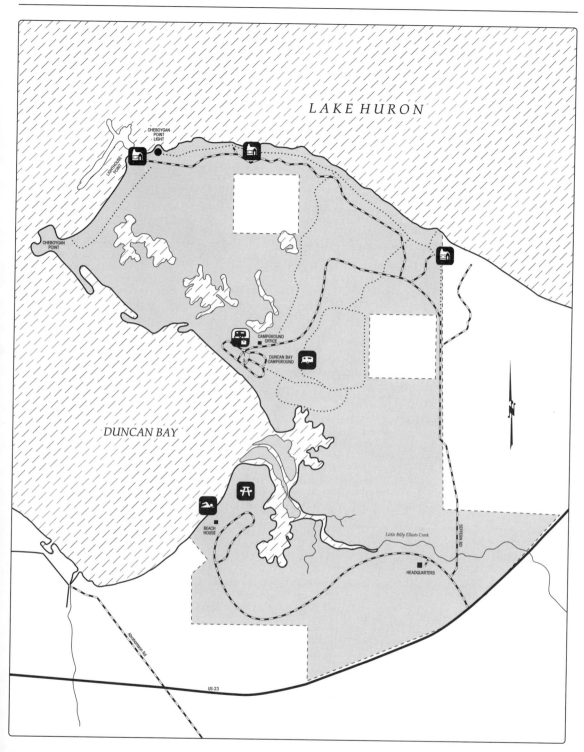

LAKE HURON

DUNCAN BAY

COUNTY: Cheboygan

CITY: Cheboygan

CAMPING SITES: 74, all modern, plus three frontier rental cabins, one rental tent, and one rental tipi.

DIRECTIONS: Go approximately 3.5 miles south of Cheboygan on US-23.

FURTHER INFORMATION: Cheboygan State Park, 4490 Beach Rd., Cheboygan, MI 49721; (231) 627-2811.

Mill Creek Historic State Park

Two centuries ago the blade of northern Michigan's first sawmill began spinning on the banks of a small creek just four miles south of the Straits of Mackinac. For the next 40 years the water-powered mill turned timber into planks and lumber for nearby Mackinac Island's building boom.

The mill ultimately fell into disuse, then disappeared from sight until 1972 when archaeologists, who had searched for years, finally discovered the remains. While the scientists meticulously excavated the area, historians pored over Revolutionary War-era books in a search for the construction and operating secrets of water-powered sawmills. The result of the years of work and research is an authentically reconstructed, working replica of an 18th-century sawmill that is the centerpiece of Mill Creek State Historic Park.

The rough-hewn, picturesque structure nearly straddles a small creek at the exact spot of the original mill. Every half hour inside, an operator throws a lever to open a gate, water flows over the power wheel, and the jumble of monstrous wood gears and other arcane paraphernalia roars to life.

Park guides detail the intricacies and history of the mill as well as demonstrate shingle making and some of the other operations that took place here, at northern Michigan's first industrial complex, 200 years ago. You can get more history plus a capsule look at the reconstruction of the mill by watching a multi-image slide show, run throughout the day inside a museum at the park entrance. Also inside are showcases that hold artifacts scientists have recovered during their excavations.

Building reconstruction with period tools and methods is an ongoing live interpretive demonstration. Re-creating the millwright's house is the current project, and you're welcome to ask questions of any of the workers. Though the mill complex is the main draw, you can easily spend as much time enjoying the natural setting (popular with birdwatchers) as its living history. The 625-acre park is nestled high above and several hundred yards back from Lake Huron amidst low hills that seem to almost cup the complex. Spectacular views of the lake and the Straits area come from two scenic overlooks on either side of the mill pond, and three miles of self-guiding nature trails wind through the wildflower-filled hills. A 15-minute walk along one of the paths ends at a beaver dam and pond.

The park's small picnic area overlooks the sawmill, and a nearby concession stand sells lunch, soft drinks and snacks.

COUNTY: Cheboygan

CITY: Mackinaw City

CAMPING SITES: None

SCHEDULE: The park is open May 7-October 14.

    The mill is operated every half hour June 15 through Labor Day and every hour during other times.

ADMISSION: Adults, $6.75; Children 6-12, $4; Children 5 and under, free.

DIRECTIONS: Go four miles east of Mackinaw City on US-23.

FURTHER INFORMATION: Mill Creek State Historic Park, c/o Mackinac State Historic Parks, Box 873, Mackinaw City, MI 49701; (231) 436-5563.

Colonial Michilimackinac

HISTORIC STATE PARK

The Straits of Mackinac area vibrates, not from the endless line of cars and trucks crossing the Mackinac Bridge, but with history. Centuries ago, native Americans, explorers, soldiers and fur traders all passed through this crossroads of the Great Lakes. When you stand on the wave-lapped shore today, it's not hard to imagine Indians pulling fishnets made of twisted-bark rope, French *voyageurs* paddling by in huge canoes piled with furs, Father Marquette (see p. 152) setting out on one of his explorations, or soldiers standing lonely vigils over the frontier's northernmost outpost.

H Fortunately, you don't have to depend entirely on your imagination. A piece of the romantic Straits area history is kept very much alive at the tip of the Lower Peninsula inside Colonial Michilimackinac State Historic Park.

The French constructed the fort on the site in 1715 to replace a crude palisades on the north side of the Straits. For the next several decades, explorers set out from the outpost to penetrate the unknown continent, and military expeditions were dispatched to fight in several wars. By 1761, when the British took over, Fort Michilimackinac also controlled a vast Northwest fur trading empire. Two years later Indians nearly wiped out the garrison in one of the most famous massacres in Michigan history. The British returned until 1781, when they moved to a new, more easily defensible installation on Mackinac Island and abandoned Fort Michilimackinac to the shifting sand and creeping vegetation.

When the village of Mackinaw City was laid out in the 1850s, the fort site was designated as a city park, and in 1904 that piece of land became our second state park. During the 1930s workmen discovered the remains of the palisades and rebuilt the fort walls, but it wasn't until 1959 that archaeologists began serious excavations.

Their years of painstaking work have resulted in the fort being rebuilt to look exactly as it did at the height of its power and influence in the 1770s. The reconstruction is so authentic that Fort Michilimackinac has been designated as a National Historic Landmark. Inside the wood gates, the Church of St. Anne, the row houses, the blacksmith shop and other reproductions all stand on the exact location of the originals. Several of the larger structures enclose displays and exhibits of some of the more than one million artifacts that archaeologists have discovered in the half of the fort area they have unearthed to date. If you visit between June 15 and Labor Day you can watch archaeological digs in progress.

This is truly living history. When you look into many of the buildings, you get the eerie feeling that the original inhabitants must have left just minutes before. In others people in authentic period-dress practice crafts of the 1770s. Booms from cannons, cracks of muskets and special events such as the re-enactment of the 1763 massacre add more realism and color.

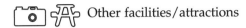 Other facilities/attractions

---

COUNTY: Emmet

CITY: Mackinaw City

CAMPING SITES: None

SCHEDULE: Open May 7 to October 14.

ADMISSION: Adults, $8; children 6-12, $5; children 5 and under, free.

DIRECTIONS: Take the last exit from I-75 before the Mackinac Bridge and follow the signs.

FURTHER INFORMATION: Colonial Michilimackinac, P.O. Box 873, Mackinaw City, MI 49701; (231) 436-5563.

Father Marquette
NATIONAL MEMORIAL

One of *the* finest views of the Mackinac Bridge comes from near a circular open-air building atop a high bluff on the St. Ignace side of the Straits. The simple stone-and-wood structure is dedicated to a Jesuit priest who, in nine short years, made a lasting impact on Michigan and Americ — Father Jacques Marquette.

In 1666 the Catholic Church sent the 29-year-old priest to New France, as Canada was then called, to bring Christianity to North American Indians. Considering that most of the continent was uncharted wilderness at the time, Fr. Marquette was as much an explorer as soul saver. He blazed his way from Canada to the rapids of the St. Mary's River, where in 1668 he established an Indian mission and Michigan's first permanent settlement, Sault Ste. Marie. Three years later he made his way to the north side of the Straits, where he founded St. Ignace. In May 1673 he, another Jesuit, and several voyageurs set out west from St. Ignace in bark canoes. They crossed Lake Michigan, then paddled and portaged across Wisconsin until they reached their goal—the legendary "Great River" that flowed north and south. Marquette and his group had discovered the Mississippi. Just two years later, Father Marquette died of an illness near the present site of Ludington.

Appropriately, the state park that commemorates the remarkable clergyman overlooks the Straits he paddled so often to and from his many expeditions. A paved path leads from a parking lot, which is bordered by a small, tree-shaded picnic area, to the modest circular memorial. A museum that was located a few yards farther unfortunately was destroyed by fire in March 2000. Plans call for reconstruction, but a schedule has not been set.

The Father Marquette Memorial is staffed with an interpreter, and two evening programs are scheduled each week throughout the summer.

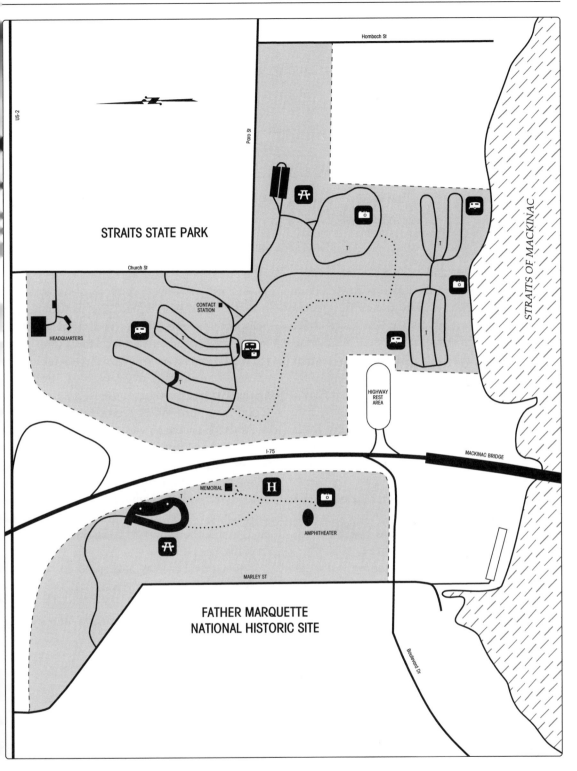

STRAITS STATE PARK

FATHER MARQUETTE
NATIONAL HISTORIC SITE

Hombach St

Paro St

US-2

Church St

HEADQUARTERS

CONTACT
STATION

T

T

T

T

T

HIGHWAY
REST
AREA

I-75

MACKINAC BRIDGE

STRAITS OF MACKINAC

MEMORIAL

H

AMPHITHEATER

MARLEY ST

T

Boulevard Dr

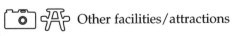 Other facilities/attractions

COUNTY: Mackinac
CITY: St. Ignace
CAMPING SITES: None

SCHEDULE: Open Memorial Day through Labor Day, 8 a.m. to 10 p.m. daily.

DIRECTIONS: From the intersection of US-2 and I-75 go less than half a mile west on US-2 to Marly Street. Turn left (south) onto Marly and go about three blocks.

FURTHER INFORMATION: Father Marquette National Memorial, 720 Church St., St. Ignace, MI 49781; (906) 643-8620.

153

S *traits* STATE PARK

A DNR brochure says that the Straits Area State Park is a "convenient campover on a high bluff overlooking the Mackinac Bridge." That somewhat antiseptic description is correct ... as far as it goes. The large campground is a great place to stay, and you do get a view of the bridge — a magnificent view, in fact, especially at night.

But left unsaid, and perhaps more important, is that this park also makes an excellent base from which to explore the entire greater Straits area. Less than two miles away at St. Ignace you can board a ferry to Mackinac Island (p. 155); the Father Marquette National Memorial (p. 152) is just across I-75; and Fort Michilimackinac (p. 150) and Mackinaw City's excess of tacky to tasteful souvenir and gift shops are five miles south across the Big Mac. Farther afield, the Seney National Wildlife Refuge, Tahquamenon Falls (p. 160) and the Soo Locks are each about an hour's drive away.

Most campers, evidently, opt for the one-night stand, because daily turnover is high. As a result, even though the campground is heavily used, you can almost always find an empty spot.

The 275 completely modern sites are divided into two distinctly different units. Camping sites in the park's original campground are closest to the beach and are shaded by a stand of cedar, birch and mixed hardwoods so thick that the trees screen not only views of your neighbors but also of the bridge and Straits. This lower campground used to hold 150 sites, but many of the smaller sites have been combined to make for more roomier and comfortable camping on 103 sites.

The 172 lots in the upper campground feature large, open, sunny sites located on high ground well back from the beach. Campers with big rigs will favor the easy-in, easy-out parking at the upper campground. The 18l-acre park's only trail descends from the west side of that camping area about a half mile to a scenic

overlook of the bridge and Straits.

A paved road also loops to the overlook, and the picture-perfect perspective of the bridge and Straits from there make the park a great place to take a break from driving or have lunch. A few tables are scattered around the overlook area, itself, and an even-larger picnic grounds is set among the woods just north of the scenic-loop drive.

Another excellent view of the span, plus a front-row seat for all the Straits boat traffic, comes from the park beach. After dark, campers gather on the shore for a hypnotizing light show put on, seemingly overhead, by the thousands of colored bulbs strung on the bridge and the moving headlights of vehicles crossing over it.

The sandy beach is also good for daytime walking or stretching out in the sun, but swimming is poor because the uncomfortably rocky lake bottom begins right at the water's edge. (Map, p. 153)

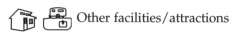 Other facilities/attractions

---

COUNTY: Mackinac

CITY: St. Ignace

CAMPING SITES: 275, all modern, plus two mini-cabins.

DIRECTIONS: From the intersection of I-75 and US-2 go less than a half mile east on US-2 to Church Street. Turn right (south) onto Church and go about three blocks.

FURTHER INFORMATION: Straits State Park, 720 Church St., St. Ignace, MI 49781; (906) 643-8620.

Mackinac Island
State Park

Mackinac Island State Park is one of the *world's* most unique and popular vacation spots and has been for more than 100 years. After just one visit you'll know why, and even after 20 visits you'll still want to come back for more of the crisp air, scenic beauty, vivid history, and cheerfully crass commercialism, all time-warped into a quaint Victorian atmosphere.

The state park takes up about 80 percent of the 2-mile-wide, 3-mile-long island, but you really can't separate what is and isn't park. There's no reason to try. Everybody who boards a ferry from the mainland gets the whole package.

When you step ashore, a short walk down the pier takes you right into another century. Huron Street, which parallels the harbor, seems, except for its asphalt, to have been lifted totally intact out of the late 1800s and deposited on the island. A steady stream of bicycles and horse-drawn carriages, dray wagons and taxis passes in front of clapboard-sided Victorian buildings that line both sides of the street. Motorized vehicles are prohibited on the island. The only traffic noise here is the clip-clop of hooves and the creak of harnesses, and the only polluting emissions — the odiferous leavings of the horses.

Many of the grand, old buildings now house shops at which you can buy everything from fine art, gifts and clothes to tacky souvenirs and that well-known Mackinac Island institution — fudge. So if you love to shop you may never see more of the island than the few square blocks that border the harbor.

You should, especially if you like history, scenery or, more often than not, both combined.

Like a time traveler, wherever you go you pass in and out of segments of three centuries, your journey marked by ubiquitous green historical markers. Just a block north of Huron, the island's "Main Street," for instance, are warehouses, offices and shops along Market Street, once the nerve center for a North American fur-trading empire.

At its east end is the site of a shooting that made medical history. In 1822 Dr. William Beaumont was summoned to the American Fur Trade Co. store to treat a young trapper who had suffered a severe gunshot wound to his abdomen. The man recovered, but the outside of the wound never healed. As a result Dr. Beaumont was able to peer inside the man's body and study the process of human digestion firsthand.

Around the corner from the tavern, on Fort Street, is the McGulpin house, the oldest known residence in Michigan.

Up the hill on Fort Street, you can take in one of the most beautiful panoramas in the state — a view of the Straits over the harbor and downtown area from Fort Mackinac 150 feet above. It's easy to see why the British picked the commanding, easily defensible site to construct the 2½- to 8-foot thick, white stone walls into and atop the high bluff in 1780. Today, you can walk through the restored barracks, officers' quarters and 12 other buildings while, outside, authentically costumed guides perform rifle drills, fire cannon, and otherwise act out military life as it was lived during the 1880s.

At the base of the fort across Huron Street is a state-park visitor center, which is a good place to get a good overall orientation to the island as well as purchase combination tickets to many of the major historical attractions.

After the military and fur-trading significance of the island faded, its importance as a summer-vacation spot grew. When railroad money built the Grand Hotel in 1886-87, Mackinac Island was already firmly established as a premier summer retreat of the world's wealthy. The pinnacle of high society also built enormous summer homes, leaving what today, on the south third of the island, must be one of the highest concentrations of Victorian buildings anywhere in the United States. Most still serve as palatial summer getaways for today's wealthy and powerful, but some have been turned into restaurants, businesses, living quarters for summer help, resort hotels, and bed-and-breakfast inns. The Grand itself, of course, is still one of the world's bastions of elegant, gracious and expensive 19th-century hospitality. You can get within a few yards of the Grand's 700-foot-long pillared porch by walking up Cadotte Street, but to look inside you have to pay an admission fee.

Some people are surprised to find that half of the island's 2,200 acres are essentially undeveloped, quiet woods edged by sand and rock beach. The quickest and most popular way to take in a lot of the scenery — including arch rock, a unique geological formation on the east side, plus nearly infinite perspectives of Lake Huron, the Mackinac Bridge and the Straits area — is on a bike. You can bring your own across on the ferry or rent one near the island ferry docks. You can pedal on any of the paved and gravel roads that thickly web the hilly interior. But the most traveled route is the 8-mile, nearly perfectly flat tour around the island's perimeter on M-185, the only Michigan state highway that bans automobile traffic.

You can also hop aboard a horse-drawn-carriage group tour, or rent a two-person horse and buggy and take the reins yourself. If you have the time and energy, you can walk any or all of the island's 70 miles of roads, trails and paths, including several remote interpretive nature trails.

Most people come just for the day, but those who stay overnight at one of the many fine

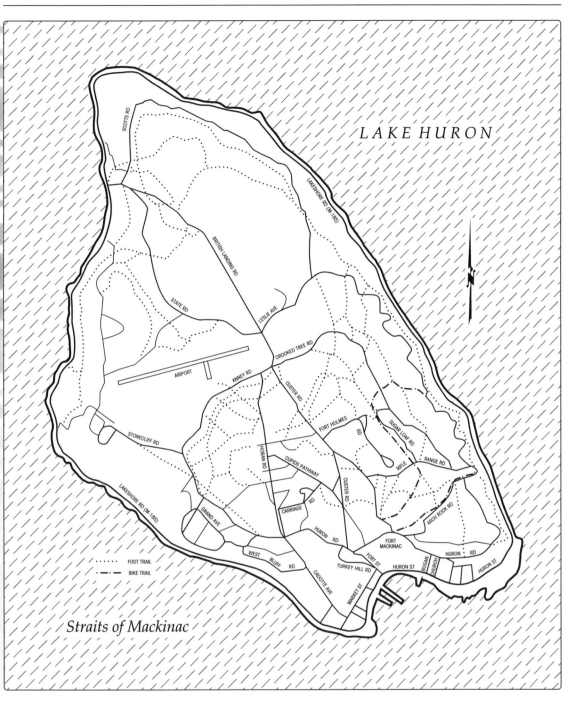

LAKE HURON

Straits of Mackinac

····· FOOT TRAIL
─·─· BIKE TRAIL

hotels or bed-and-breakfast inns, see the island take on a whole new character. After all the "fudgies," as day visitors are called, have departed, what was busy and crowded becomes eerily quiet as the streets empty and the lights of the Mackinac Bridge and passing freighters reflect and dance across the waters.

 Other facilities/attractions

COUNTY: Mackinac

CITY: Mackinac Island

CAMPING SITES: None

SCHEDULE: The park is open May 7-October 14.

ENTRANCE RATES TO FORT MACKINAC: Adults, $8; Children, $5.

DIRECTIONS: Ferry service departs from either Mackinaw City or St. Ignace approximately every 30 minutes during the peak summer months.

FURTHER INFORMATION: Mackinac Island State Park, P.O. Box 370, Mackinac Island, MI 49757; (906) 847-3328.

B rimley STATE PARK

To enjoy Lake Superior, there's no better Michigan state park than Brimley.

Oh granted, if you just want to *look* at the world's largest freshwater lake you can probably get more scenic perspectives from other parks. The views from Brimley, however, sure aren't bad. Across Whitefish Bay, the Canadian highlands darken the horizon, and a continuously passing show of ore carriers and ocean-going freighters head into and out of the nearby Soo Locks. If you want to get *onto* Superior, Brimley's boat-launching ramp (large enough to accommodate most boats towed by a vehicle) gives access to some of the most sheltered waters along its entire shoreline.

And best of all, from the shore here you can jump *into* the warmest waters — by Superior standards — anywhere on the lake. A wide strip of sand fronts the entire park, and the water is fairly shallow many yards out into the bay, which makes for about as fine a beach as you can find anywhere on this deep, rocky Great Lake.

Back from the beach on the park's east side, a completely modern campground is laid out like a small subdivision, in regularly spaced loops that parallel the shoreline. All 270

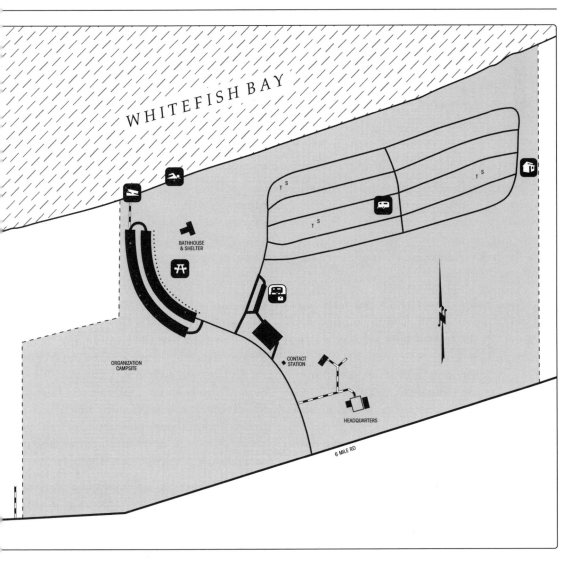

WHITEFISH BAY

BATHHOUSE & SHELTER

ORGANIZATION CAMPSITE

CONTACT STATION

HEADQUARTERS

6 MILE RD

sites are level, most are grass covered and roomy, and about half are well shaded. Lowest-numbered lots are farthest from the beach and least shaded, while the highest-numbered lots (220-271) line both sides of the road closest to the beach. Park officials report that the campground is heavily used during the summer months and recommend reservations for weekends.

At the west-side day-use area, a wide, grassy lawn separates a narrow strip of sand from a bathhouse and picnic shelter. Behind the rough wood structures, a large, open, grassy picnic area extends well inland.

At the extreme west edge of the beach, fishermen launch at the park's boat ramp and go after Whitefish Bay's pike, perch, bass, trout and walleye.

Hunters take deer, grouse, rabbit and squirrel from the large parcel of forested park land across the road from the developed facilities.

 Other facilities/attractions

---

County: Chippewa

City: Brimley

Camping Sites: 270, all modern, including a mini-cabin and a rustic cabin.

Directions: From I-75 about 8 miles south of Sault Ste. Marie, exit onto M-28 and drive west about 7 miles to M-221. Turn right (north) onto M-221 and go 3 miles to 6 mile Road in Brimley. Turn (right) east and go one mile.

Further Information: Brimley State Park, 9200 W. 6 Mile Rd., Brimley, MI 49715; (906) 248-3422.

T*ahquamenon Falls*
STATE PARK

Nineteen miles from where its empties into Lake Superior, the Tahquamenon River is abruptly, momentarily and dramatically freed from its rocky 200-foot-wide streambed. With a thunderous roar, 50,000 gallons a second of the tea-colored water plunges 50 feet over a sharp ledge into a foam-flecked pool. The spectacle, Upper Tahquamenon Falls, is the largest waterfall in Michigan and the third-largest east of the Mississippi.

Four miles downstream the river presents an encore, this time splitting and dropping 23 feet around both sides of a large midstream island. The water here doesn't ever become airborne long. Rather, in tumultuous cascades it crashes into rocks and boulders as it hurdles over a succession of small, closely spaced ledges and steps.

The Upper and Lower falls are the heart of Tahquamenon Falls State Park. Each year, nearly half a million visitors from around the country come to see them and for good reason. Not only are they stunningly beautiful, they're also easy to get to. The paved path to the Upper Falls cuts through a beautiful stand of hardwoods about a quarter of a mile to the lip of the canyon through which the river flows. From there, one asphalt trail heads about 200 yards upstream, another about the same distance downstream. The upstream path

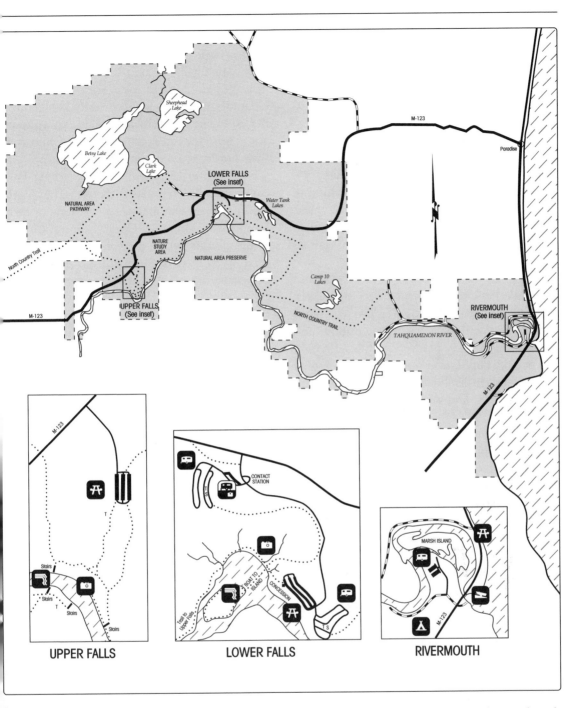

UPPER FALLS

LOWER FALLS

RIVERMOUTH

borders the edge of the gorge, with several fine views of the falls coming along the way. The route ends by descending nearly 100 wood stairs to a platform that hangs — seemingly almost within touching distance — out over the top of the falls. An even-longer series of steps at the end of the downstream path drops to sweeping river-level views through the canyon back to the falls.

A head-on panorama of the Lower Falls is even easier to get to. A 100-yard paved path from the Lower Falls parking lot gently rises to a prime viewing area above where the two channels rejoin at the base of the falls. To get within inches of the white water that drops through the north channel, take a 15-minute walk along a trail that follows the riverbank from the main overlook. Or for unique close-up views of both channels' cascades, rent a boat at a concession below the overlook, row a few hundred yards to the midstream island, and walk the trails that circle its shoreline.

Facilities at both Upper and Lower falls day-use areas include large parking lots, tree-shaded picnic grounds, souvenir shops and food-concession areas.

Though a day visit to the falls is the main draw, there are also good reasons to stay overnight at the park, which many do. The park's four campgrounds, with a total of approximately 330 sites, are heavily used. Though there are occasional vacancies, even on weekends, if the park is your vacation destination, it's best to make a reservation.

Two of the campgrounds, Rivers Bend and Overlook, flank the Lower Falls on high bluffs back from the river. All 183 sites are well worn and shaded and have electrical outlets and access to completely modern facilities. Privacy, however, is only fair at both areas. The lots at Rivers Bend closely border the edge of the bluff below the falls, and a few have good views of the river.

Overlooks' larger and a bit-more-private lots are cut out of a heavily wooded area north of and well back from the falls. Bring plenty of insect repellent to ward off the reason why the park's staff sometimes works with netting over their heads here — hordes of black flies.

Miles away, either by river or car, the park's other two campgrounds are tucked into the last long, lazy loops the Tahquamenon makes just before emptying into Lake Superior's Whitefish Bay. The Rivermouth Campground's completely modern unit occupies a narrow peninsula formed by the river, and all of the camping sites are hardly more than a stone's throw from the Tahquamenon.

The 60-site rustic unit lies further from M-123 and hugs the south side of the river.

Across M-123 from the Rivermouth Campground, a picnic area lines the bay north of the river's outlet. Canoers put in here, as do fishermen and boaters at the park's only boat launching ramp, then set out to fish or explore almost 14 miles of river, plus the open, sometimes treacherous waters of Lake Superior.

More than 25 miles of foot trails cut through the heart of the 33,733-acre state park, Michigan's second-largest. Much of that mileage is along a portion of the North Country Trail — which ultimately will connect the Appalachian Trail in Maine to the Lewis and Clark Trail in North Dakota — that runs from border to border in the park. One popular section is the 15 miles from the Lower Falls campgrounds to Lake Superior. The North Country trail also makes up portions of three loops that begin at the Upper Falls parking lot. Those circuits, which range from 3.7 to 13 miles long, head over old Indian trails and logging railroad grades into a backcountry world of pine, muskeg and picturesque bog lakes. Backcountry camping is not permitted.

Hunting is also allowed on much of the park acreage, with deer, grouse and woodcock the most-abundant game.

Though not many do it, winter is an especially good time to visit Tahquamenon Falls State Park. Blue-tinted ice sculptures frame the falls then, and cross-country skiers have four miles and snowmobilers 16 miles of trails to set tracks on.

 Other facilities/attractions

---

COUNTY: Chippewa

CITY: Paradise

CAMPING SITES: 330 (270 modern, 60 rustic).

SCHEDULE: The park and campgrounds are open year round, but modern restrooms are closed from October 15 to May 15.

DIRECTIONS: The entrance to the Lower Falls day-use area and campgrounds is 10 miles west of Paradise on M-123. The Upper Falls entrance is 4 miles farther west. To get to the Rivermouth Unit, go 5 miles south of Paradise on M-123.

FURTHER INFORMATION: Tahquamenon Falls State Park, 41382 West M-123, Paradise, MI 49768; (906) 492-3415.

Muskallonge Lake
STATE PARK

Most state parks are near someplace or on the way to somewhere. Not so with Muskallonge Lake State Park. About the only reason to drive 20-some miles up County Road H-37 from Newberry is to visit the narrow strip of state-owned property that separates Lake Superior from Muskallonge Lake. More than 60,000 people a year think it's worth the trip.

At the north edge of the more-than-mile-long park, you can spend hours searching for odd-shaped pieces of driftwood or colorful stones and agates on rocky portions of the Lake Superior shore. Or on the alternating patches of sand, you can spend the same amount of time stretched out, hypnotized by the pounding surf. And many visitors make annual trips here in July and August to pick the plentiful wild blueberries and strawberries found in the area.

Only a thousand to 2,000 yards away from the Great Lake, the park's developed facilities line a section of the north shore of Muskallonge Lake. Centering the area is a completely modern campground with 179 sites arranged in seven short loops whose tips all point at the water. All lots are large, level, grass covered and close to the water and a sandy campers-only swimming beach at the end of the easternmost loop. Lofty hardwoods shade and partially hide lots 1-150. For the most privacy and seclusion try for lots 151-179, which are screened by dense shrubs and trees. You don't often need it, however. The campground isn't exactly overrun. Park officials say the only heavy use comes from July 15 through late August, but even then i

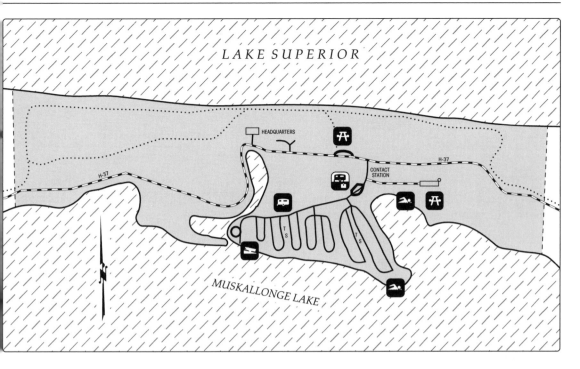

LAKE SUPERIOR

MUSKALLONGE LAKE

rarely fills.

At a shaded, grassy day-use area east of the campground, the varnish on picnic tables still shines and not many footprints mark the beach sand that gradually slides into the water. Few people come to this out-of-the-way park just for a day visit.

A boat ramp west of the campground is well used, however, and almost totally by fishermen. Unlike at many downstate park lakes, anglers here don't have to worry much about speedboats interrupting their quiet sport. In 1987 walleyes were introduced in Muskallonge Lake, already known for its fine northern-pike and perch fishing, and smallmouth bass and a remnant muskie population also provide some action. Rental fishing boats are available at two stores near the park. Many excellent trout-fishing streams, including the legendary Two Hearted River, flow through areas surrounding the park.

Hikers have the opportunity to wear down plenty of boot leather here. The park itself has only a single 1.5-mile trail, which closely follows the Superior shoreline. But it connects with the North Country Trail, which when completed will cross the entire Upper Peninsula as part of a system that will connect the Appalachian Trail in Maine to the Lewis and Clark Trail in North Dakota. Today, from Muskallonge State Park you can hike west approximately 20 miles to, then through, the Pictured Rocks National Lakeshore (see p. 205). But you don't have to go that far. A Lake Superior State Forest campground just five miles west along the route makes for a pleasant day-long round trip along the Superior shoreline. To the east on the North Country Trail, you can walk some 40 miles to the mouth of the Tahquamenon River (see p. 160) on Whitefish Bay. Many backpackers, however, opt for a shorter, but still-strenuous, two-day, 20-mile round trip to a state-forest campground at the mouth of the Two Hearted River.

Other facilities/attractions

COUNTY: Luce

CITY: Newberry

CAMPING SITES: 179, all modern.

SCHEDULE: The park is open year round and the campground is open from April 15 through November, but modern toilets are not available the first and last months.

DIRECTIONS: Go 28 miles north of Newberry on County Road H-37.

FURTHER INFORMATION: Muskallonge Lake State Park, Route 1, Box 245, Newberry, MI 49868; (906) 658-3338.

Wagner Falls
Scenic Site

You'll be glad you spent the few minutes and few steps it takes to see Wagner Falls, described by the Penrose family in their *Guide to 199 Michigan Waterfalls* as "a roaring, powerful example of one of Michigan's small waterfalls."

An 800-foot-long trail climbs alongside Wagner Creek, and just a few feet away from your car on the path you can hear the falls barreling over the rocks. A few steps farther and the exuberant cascade comes into view. Frothy, white water tumbles over several rocky ledges, its path to the valley floor obstructed by a jumble of large boulders and tree trunks that look like they've been tossed in a game of pick-up sticks by giants. Downstream, trees, flowers and shrubs crowd the small, sharp-sided valley.

Only 22 acres of state land surround the falls, making this site Michigan's smallest state park. It's also the least developed. The only "facilities" are a small roadside parking area, an identifying sign, and a gravel trail and boardwalk to the falls

COUNTY: Alger

CITY: Munising

CAMPING SITES: None

DIRECTIONS: From the intersection of M-94 and M-28, one mile south of Munising, drive west on M-94 approximately 0.5 miles to the parking area, on the south side of the road.

FURTHER INFORMATION: Wagner Falls Scenic Site, c/o Indian Lake State Park, Rt. 2, Box 2500, Manistique, MI 49854; (906) 341-2355.

Laughing Whitefish Falls
SCENIC SITE

Near Sundell, a ¾-mile woodchip-covered path tunnels through hardwood forest to one of only two* official Scenic Sites in the state-park system — Laughing Whitefish Falls. The designation is well deserved. The falls, which drops almost 100 feet into a deep, steep-sided gorge, is both spectacular and delicately beautiful .

From the top of a high, layered limestone wall, a small stream free-falls in thin ribbons about 10 feet before splashing onto a bulging dome of rock that curves out and down to the bottom of the gorge. In a beautiful counterpoint to its reckless start, the falls finishes its descent to a small

pool by spreading into a thin, glistening film that barely dampens the rock dome. It's hard, in fact, to detect any movement of water over the shimmering, sparkling rock.

The best view comes at about the midpoint of a very long flight of stairs that drops alongside the falls and sheer rock wall to the bottom of the gorge. At the top of the stairs, a wood observation deck overlooks the lip of the falls.

The walk to the falls can be either a cool 15-minute stroll or a much-shorter vigorous aerobic hike when black flies are out in force. Even if you douse yourself with an entire bottle of insect repellent then, you'll still have to frantically wave your arms and swat to keep the flies at a respectful distance.

Minimal facilities include pit toilets and a couple of picnic tables, all located near the gravel parking lot.

---

*The other is Wagner Falls.

COUNTY: Alger

CITY: Sundell

CAMPING SITES: None

DIRECTIONS: From M-94 in Sundell drive approximately 2 miles north, continuing straight when it turns to gravel.

FURTHER INFORMATION: Laughing Whitefish Falls Scenic Site, Wells Management Unit, N7670 Hwy. M-35, Cedar River, MI 49813; (906) 863-9747.

Van Riper
STATE PARK

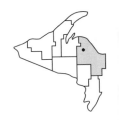

Located in the heart of the western Upper Peninsula, Van Riper State Park is surrounded by almost-limitless forest and near-trackless wilderness. This is a very special region, as you will discover when you see the first of many signs that read, "Moose Crossing Area." Only nine miles north of the park is the release point where the majestic animals were reintroduced into the Upper Peninsula. A slow drive on the surrounding gravel roads, especially the ones that cut through the wilderness to the north of the park, in search of moose is a must for overnight park visitors. Chances are small of spotting a moose, but for the lucky few who do, the rest of the trip could be a vacation from hell and still be remembered with fondness.

You can also use Van Riper as a base to head off into the wilderness in a four-wheel-drive vehicle on faint two-tracks, in your car or RV along miles of good dirt roads, or on foot over scenic backcountry trails. Or you can stick close to Lake Michigamme and stroll the sandy beach, swim, fish, or just relax and enjoy the panoramic view.

US-41/M-28 bisects the park, and most of the developed facilities are south of the highway in a parcel that wraps around the eastern end of Lake Michigamme. Punctuating the very tip of the lake is a long, wide beach, backed by a modern bathhouse/restroom. There's plenty of room to spread blankets and beach towels on the open, sunny strip of sand, and you can take lengthy strolls along the shore in either direction. Spread over a low hill in a grove of large white pine back from the water are a picnic shelter, grills and tables, with glimpses of the lake coming from most sites. From almost anywhere else in this section of the park you get sweeping views of the large lake and the green, tree-clad hills that ring it.

Just south of the picnic area, the stand of mature white pine shelters a 150-site modern campground. The lots are exceptionally clean and well kept, and the imposing trees plus low shrubs combine to shade and screen many sites. None of the lots are directly on the water, but the lake and swimming beach are only a short walk away. You can almost always find a vacant spot here, even on summer weekends.

An even more quiet, secluded overnight alternative is the park's 40-site rustic campground, on the banks of a creek and the shore of Lake Michigamme in the southwest section of the park. The campground is accessible via a separate paved road.

Pleasure boaters and fishermen also use the road to launch from a ramp near the rustic campground. Walleyes, bass, muskellunge, and perch are the fish most often pulled from the nearly 7-mile-long lake.

The park's north section is nearly undeveloped. There, the Peshekee River, in its last rush to Lake Michigamme cuts through the rolling, forested hills that make up the majority of the park's 1,044 acres. Four miles of hiking trails lead to abandoned mine shafts, pass through deep woods and along the banks of the river, and rise to high, panoramic overlooks.

 Other facilities/attractions

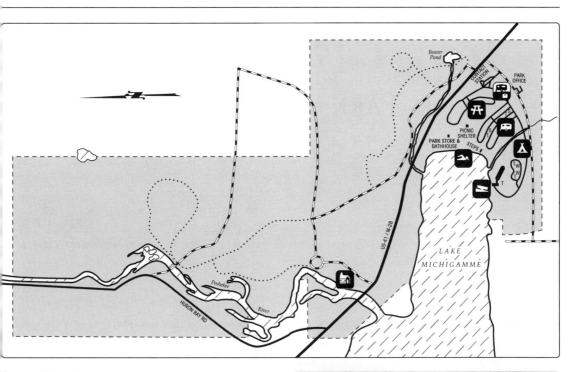

COUNTY: Marquette

CITY: Champion

CAMPING SITES: 190 sites (150 modern, 40 rustic), including a rustic cabin and two mini-cabins.

SCHEDULE: The park is open all year, but the campground is closed from October 15 to May 15.

DIRECTIONS: Go 1.5 miles west of Champion on US-41/M-28.

FURTHER INFORMATION: Van Riper State Park, P.O, Box 88, Champion, MI 49814; (906) 339-4461.

Craig Lake
STATE PARK

Craig Lake is about as primitive and off-the-beaten-track a park as you can find in Michigan's state-run system. Not only do most maps of the state omit the road leading to the park, they also don't usually even show the park itself. When you do pinpoint its location, you quickly see that Craig Lake is at the edge of the largest roadless area in the state.

Even calling the route into the park a "road" is being very charitable. Park officials warn that you should attempt the rock-, boulder- and pothole-strewn path only in a vehicle with high ground clearance and, preferably, four-wheel drive. And before you do, check on its condition with officials at Van Riper State Park (p. 168), 10 miles east on US-41/M-28.

Craig Lake State Park is the doorway to some of the most rugged, primitive and wild country in the entire state, and backpackers, hikers and fishermen who enjoy roughing it can do so here with little if any company. The only developed facilities are two rustic frontier rental cabins, and the only marked hiking trails are eight-plus miles that circle Craig Lake plus follow a section of the North Country Trail that passes through the park. But there's almost unlimited room for off-trail bushwhacking, and you can low-impact backcountry camp anywhere in the park except within 150 feet of water.

Teddy and Craig lakes are only short walks from roadside parking lots. With Keewaydin Lake Road ending at a parking lot/boat-launching area on Keewaydin Lake, it wins the award for being the most easily accessed body of water in the park. It is also the only lake where motors are allowed. But given the fact that park officials warn that the road to the park "is very rough and cars are not recommended," anglers will probably find it not worth the wear and tear to trailer a boat to

Keewaydin.

Three lakes — Clair, Craig, and Crooked — are linked by short portages.

Canoeists, shorefishermen, and sportsmen who carry in small boats on their shoulders all toss lures into Craig Lake, the park's best for angling. The response is excellent from bass, muskellunge, and northern pike and good from walleyes and perch. Special regulations, such as catch-and-release fishing (except for walleye and panfish) are in effect throughout the park. You can get a copy of the rules at either Van Riper State Park or directly from the DNR in Lansing.

Craig Lake State Park's 6,983 acres make up part of the area where moose were recently reintroduced in the Upper Peninsula, and several of the great animals have been spotted in the park.

Other facilities/attractions

COUNTY: Baraga

CITY: Champion

CAMPING SITES: Two frontier cabins. Backcountry camping is permitted from May 15 to October 15.

DIRECTIONS: From US-41/M-28 approximately 6 miles west of Champion, turn north onto Keewaydin Lake Road. To get to Craig Lake, go 12 miles, taking the left fork at about 5 miles.

FURTHER INFORMATION: Craig Lake State Park, c/o Van Riper State Park, P.O. Box 88, Champion, MI 49814; (906) 339-4461.

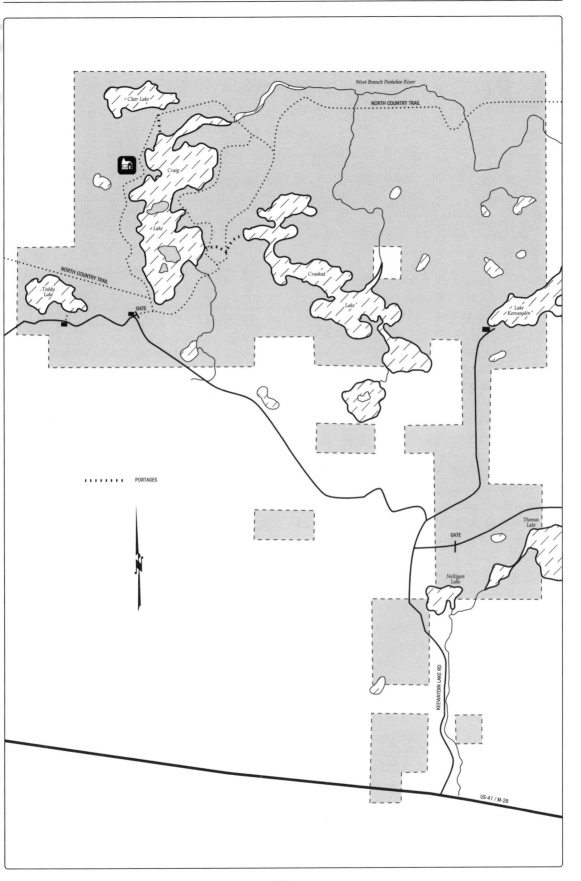

West Branch Peshekee River

NORTH COUNTRY TRAIL

Clair Lake

Craig

Lake

Crooked

Lake

Lake
Keewaydin

NORTH COUNTRY TRAIL

Teddy
Lake

GATE

PORTAGES

N

Thomas
Lake

GATE

Nelligan
Lake

KEEWAYDIN LAKE RD

US-41 / M-28

Baraga
STATE PARK

Rising from the shoreline almost at the very tip of Keweenaw Bay, Baraga State Park makes either a convenient base camp or a welcome stopover during Keweenaw Peninsula or western U.P. vacations.

US-41 separates the park's day-use area from the campground, which usually has vacancies even on summer weekends if you arrive early in the day. All 118 sites are shaded, grass covered, and exceptionally clean, and all have magnificent views of the bay. There's little or no privacy and highway noise can be intrusive, but those are small tradeoffs. All campers have easy access to modern restrooms with flush toilets and showers, but 10 sites have no electrical hookups.

It's just a short walk across US-41 to the open, grassy picnic area and small, sandy beach that are squeezed between the highway and Keweenaw Bay. The water here, at the foot of the bay, is as warm as any spot on Lake Superior, but that's still pretty cold.

Fishermen, who launch onto the bay's sheltered waters from a ramp at the south end of the beach, get plenty of action from the big lake's salmon, lake trout, whitefish, pike and herring. Others drop hooks for largemouth bass, walleye, pike perch and bluegill in several nearby inland lakes.

There's not a lot of room to roam in the 56-acre park, but the lone trail that does loop from the back of the campground is first class. The ¾-mile self-guiding (brochure available at park headquarters) route circles the top of glacial deposits and includes good looks at examples of area flora, several interesting natural features, and the bay and surrounding area.

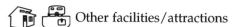 Other facilities/attractions

COUNTY: Baraga

CITY: Baraga

CAMPING SITES: 118 (108 fully modern, 10 semi modern), and a mini-cabin.

SCHEDULE: The park and campground are open all year, but the modern restroom facilities are closed from December 1 to May 10th.

DIRECTIONS: Go one mile south of Baraga on US-41.

FURTHER INFORMATION: Baraga State Park, 1300 US-41 South, Baraga, MI 49908; (906) 353-6558.

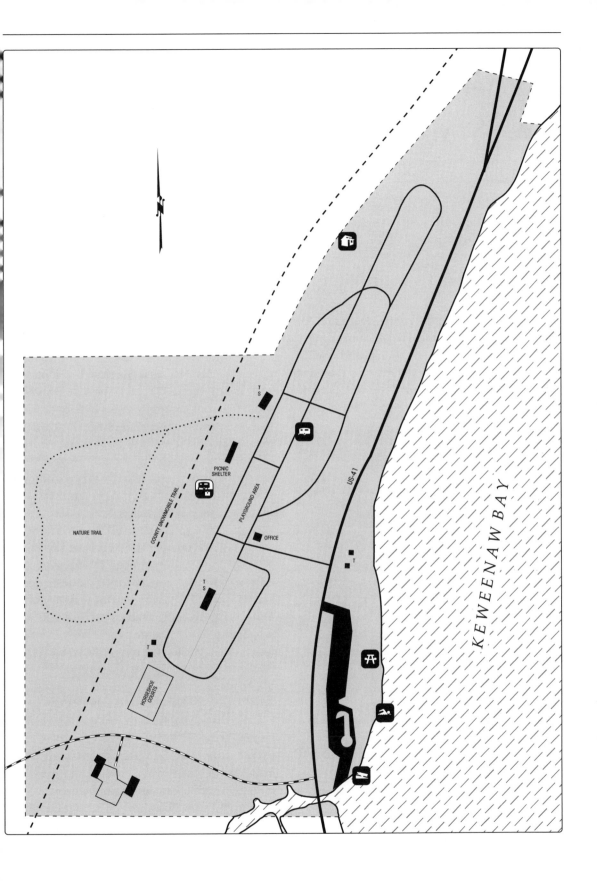

KEWEENAW BAY

NATURE TRAIL

COUNTY SNOWMOBILE TRAIL

PICNIC SHELTER

PLAYGROUND AREA

US-41

OFFICE

HORSESHOE COURTS

Twin Lakes
STATE PARK

Conspired against by location, Twin Lakes is the least-visited state park in Michigan for which the DNR keeps records. While vacationers pass through most state-park entrances by the hundreds of thousands each year, this 175-acre parcel, hidden away at the base of the Keweenaw Peninsula, is all but ignored. Only 30,000 visitors each year bother to search it out.

Many of those who do, return again and for good reason — quiet, uncrowded camping and near-ideal boating, water skiing and swimming at one of the Upper Peninsula's warmest inland lakes. Another plus: Twin Lakes State Park makes an excellent base camp for exploring surrounding Copper Country attractions.

M-26 splits the park into developed and undeveloped sections. To the east, between the blacktop and the shores of Lake Roland, is one of the Upper Peninsula's smallest, most-pleasant campgrounds. Twenty of the 62 spacious, grass-covered lots nearly touch the lake, but even the farthest from shore is only an Al Kaline toss from the water. The completely modern campground usually fills on July and August weekends, but you can almost always find a vacancy at any other time.

A short walk north from the campground ends at the park's 500-foot-long swimming beach. The sand strip, only a few feet wide at its broadest, gently slopes into the clear, warm water. Stately, mature hardwoods shade much of the area, which includes a change court, two picnic shelters, tables, grills, and playground equipment scattered over a large expanse of grass back of the beach.

Near the park boundary at the north end of the beach is a launch ramp, with it's own access road, used by pleasure boaters, water skiers, and fishermen, who toss lures for tiger muskies, bluegills, perch, bass and rainbow trout.

On the west side of M-26 a 1.5-mile hiking trail tunnels through the almost totally undeveloped woodland that makes up the vast majority of park property. On a clear day from two scenic overlooks along the loop, you can see Lake Superior shimmering on the horizon

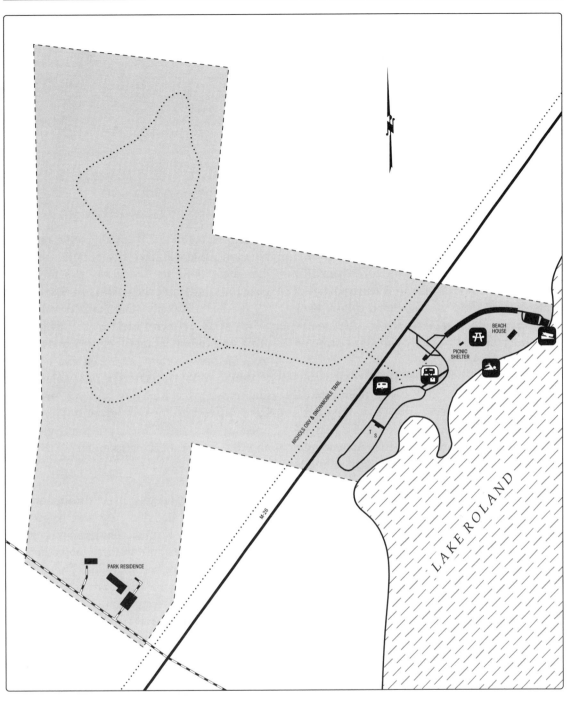

nearly 10 miles away. The forest and lakeshore both shelter a wide variety of birds and wildflowers.

 In the winter five miles of cross-country ski trails lace the park.

  Other facilities/attractions

COUNTY: Houghton

CITY: Twin Lakes

CAMPING SITES: 61, all modern and a mini-cabin.

SCHEDULE: Modern restroom facilities are closed from October 15 to May 15, and the entire park is closed December 1 to April 1.

DIRECTIONS: Go 28 miles south of Houghton on M-26.

FURTHER INFORMATION: Twin Lakes State Park, Twin Lakes 6204 Poyhonen Rd., Toivola, MI 49965; (906) 288 3321 [4/1-11/30] and (906) 482-0278 [12/1-3/31].

FJ *McLain* STATE PARK

Rangers and other employees at McLain State Park like to boast that they work at one of the prettiest state parks in Michigan. They don't often get an argument.

The scenic magnet here is two miles of magnificent Lake Superior coastline, which varies from wave-eroded ledges that drop straight into the lake to wide expanses of water-lapped sand to steep-sided dunes. Back from shore, a thick mixed hardwood/pine forest is interrupted by large, open areas carpeted with lush grass.

One broad sweep of lawn, which runs down to the water's edge from a parking lot near the entrance, makes up the park's large picnic grounds. Tables and grills are generously scattered around the spacious area, and scenic views of the world's largest freshwater lake come from almost any spot. Playground equipment is set up near the water, and on the west side, huge, old birches provide some shade as well as shelter from cool onshore breezes.

A wide strip of sand edges the water from the picnic grounds more than a half mile downshore to the park's extreme southwest corner. There, one arm of a seawall that forms the mouth of the Portage Lake Ship Canal protects a large "swimming" beach. Well back from shore on top of a low, wooded dune is a combination bathhouse, concession stand, pavilion, restroom building. The open, sandy shore is great for sunbathing on hot days, and you can roll up your pant legs and wade the fringes until your feet go numb. But you have to be hardy or foolhardy to take more than a brief dip in the frigid water.

Back from and paralleling the sandy shore in this section of the park are low, wooded dunes. Several unmarked paths wind through the area, and a posted hiking trail connects the swimming beach and the main picnic area. The pleasant walk will have hikers both searching the forest floor for wildflowers lifting their gaze for memorable views of Lake Superior.

The only other marked path in the 417-acre park is the Bear Lake Trail. The mile-plus loop begins across M-203 from the park entrance, cuts east through deep woods to follow a section of Bear Lake shoreline, crosses the highway and returns along Lake Superior to the campground. This trail is open in the winter for cross-country skiing, and the entire park is popular with snow shoers.

McLain State Park's 103 modern campsites are heavily used throughout the summer, filling daily in July and August, so reservations are a must. The spacious, grass-covered lots spread out in three loops that border the Lake Superior shoreline. The water is only a few steps away from any lot, and every evening campers congregate along the low dunes and bluffs to watch the sun set over Lake Superior. The park's rustic cabin sits off by itself on the east end of the campground.

Hunting is allowed in the park, with deer, bear, rabbit, squirrel, and ruffed grouse the most sought-after game.

 Other facilities/attractions

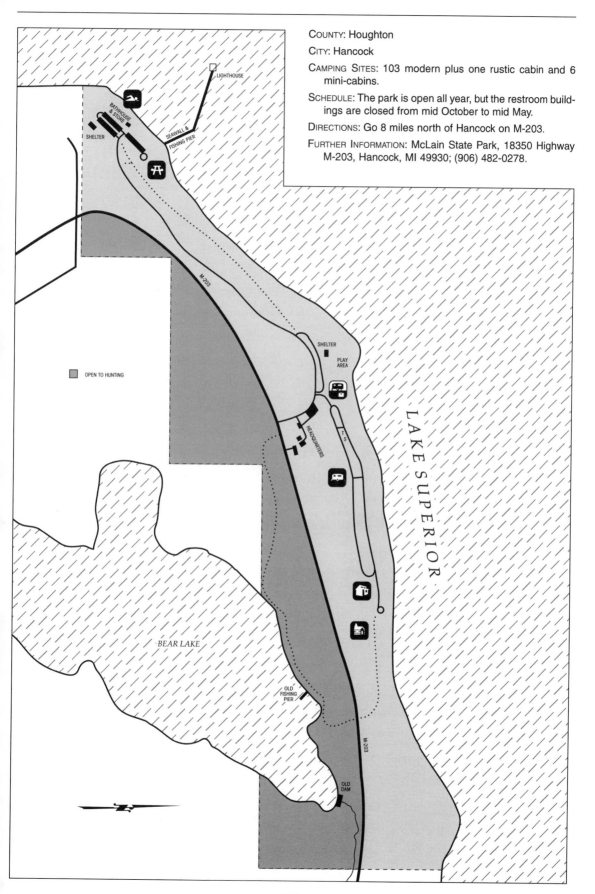

COUNTY: Houghton

CITY: Hancock

CAMPING SITES: 103 modern plus one rustic cabin and 6 mini-cabins.

SCHEDULE: The park is open all year, but the restroom buildings are closed from mid October to mid May.

DIRECTIONS: Go 8 miles north of Hancock on M-203.

FURTHER INFORMATION: McLain State Park, 18350 Highway M-203, Hancock, MI 49930; (906) 482-0278.

LIGHTHOUSE

BATHHOUSE & STORE

SHELTER

SEAWALL & FISHING PIER

M-203

OPEN TO HUNTING

SHELTER

PLAY AREA

HEADQUARTERS

LAKE SUPERIOR

BEAR LAKE

OLD FISHING PIER

M-203

OLD DAM

McLain State Park

Fort Wilkins Historic
State Park

Dark, mysterious Lake Fanny Hooe; rugged, rock-bound Lake Superior coast; a picturesque, historic lighthouse; and a superbly restored 150-year-old fort make Michigan's northernmost state park easy to enjoy and hard to forget.

The long, narrow park is squeezed between Lake Superior and Lake Fanny Hooe just a mile east of Copper Harbor, near the tip of the Keweenaw Peninsula. The Lake Superior coastline here is as scenic as any stretch of shoreline in the state. Looking north, a string of islands and a peninsula tipped by an antique lighthouse mark the boundary between deep-blue Copper Harbor and the open waters of the Great Lake. Huge rock slabs and boulders litter the harbor shore, and here and there stunted evergreens cling for life to fissures in the stone. Back from the edge of the exposed bedrock, mature pines carpet the ground with their needles and permeate the air

with their thick scent.

Just a few hundred yards inland the pines, now mixed with cedars, spread to the dark, still waters of Lake Fanny Hooe. The trees ring the lake, growing right to the water's edge and even leaning precariously out over it. Opposite the park, steep, tree-covered hills rise from the south shore. When summer fog shrouds the scene, as it often does, it's easy to feel like you're looking at a fjord half a world away.

Facing Lake Fanny Hooe from its north shore is the park's picturesque centerpiece — Fort Wilkins. Built at the beginning of the copper rush in 1844 to guard miners from the Indians, it ended up guarding the Indians from the miners and the miners from each other. When the Mexican War broke out two years later, the troops were sent south, and the fort did not hold a garrison again until after the Civil War, when it was only briefly occupied. Because it was used a grand total of only about five years, there were very few additions or alterations to its original construction. As a result, the complex is one of the few classic examples of the wood forts that sprouted up along the American frontier during the mid-1800s. Eighteen of the buildings have been completely and meticulously restored, and costumed interpreters explain and act out what mid-l9th century military and family life was like at this remote outpost.

Just east of the fort, picnic tables and playground equipment are scattered over the grass in a grove of stately, old pines. From this day-use area you can catch glimpses

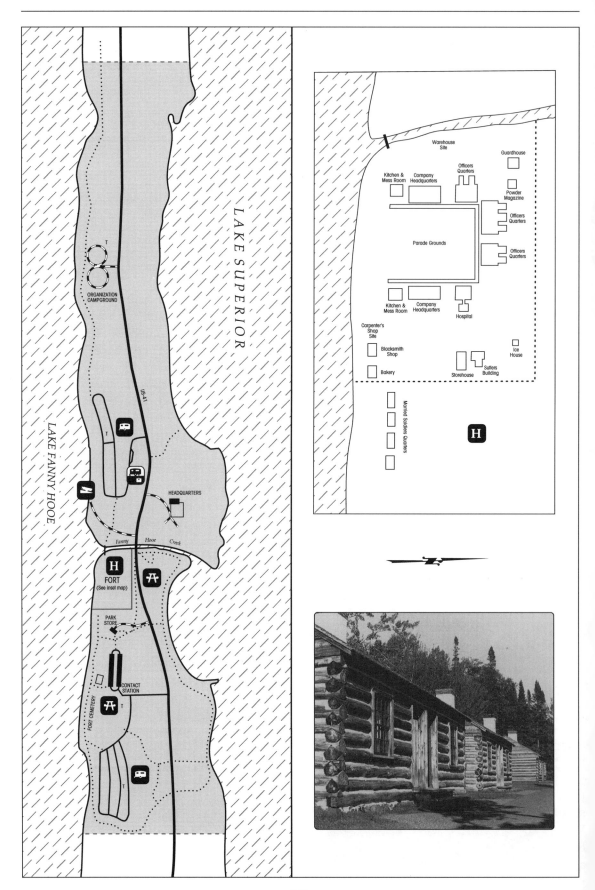

LAKE SUPERIOR

LAKE FANNY HOOE

US-41

ORGANIZATION
CAMPGROUND

HEADQUARTERS

Fanny Hooe Creek

H
FORT
(See inset map)

PARK
STORE

CONTACT
STATION

FORT CEMETERY

Warehouse
Site

Kitchen &
Mess Room

Company
Headquarters

Officers
Quarters

Guardhouse

Powder
Magazine

Officers
Quarters

Officers
Quarters

Parade Grounds

Kitchen &
Mess Room

Company
Headquarters

Hospital

Carpenter's
Shop
Site

Blacksmith
Shop

Bakery

Storehouse

Sutlers
Building

Ice
House

Married Soldiers Quarters

H

of Lake Fanny Hooe through the trees, but there is no swimming beach here or elsewhere in the park.

The park's 165 completely modern camping sites are divided between two wings, one west across Fanny Hooe Creek from the fort and the other just east of the day-use area. The most privacy and seclusion come from the west unit's lots, almost all of which are screened by brush and trees. Lots 143, 145, 155, 156, 158, 161, 162, 184, plus odd-numbered lots 163-183 and even-numbered lots 146-152 are either right on the shore of Lake Fanny Hooe or have no other sites between them and the water.

Sites at the east unit, the older of the two wings, also overlook the lake but from a low hill. Mature evergreens shelter the small, worn lots, but the trees don't create much privacy. The restroom in this wing has a coin-operated laundry, and campers here are closest to the bike and canoe rental concession plus the park store, although they won't find much more than pop, ice cream and lots of copper souvenirs. Near the store you can peer down into the open pits of an early copper mine.

Reservations are recommended during July and August, and all 165 lots are just a short walk from the shore of both lakes as well as the main attraction. Twilight is an especially appealing time to wander through the fort, and campers then pretty much have the proud, old buildings to themselves. Nights are always cool, daytime temperatures rarely exceed the 70s, and the campground is heavily shaded, so bring sweaters or jackets. And because bears frequently wander through the campground, don't cook or keep food in your tent, if that's what you're camping in.

Exhibits inside several of the fort buildings list all of the area's wildlife as well as give some good instruction on the 700-acre park's natural setting and geography. To apply what you've learned, walk the two miles of park trails that cut through the forest and follow the shores of both Lake Superior and Fanny Hooe. Wildflowers abound in the area as do thimbleberries, blueberries and square-twig bilberries, a remnant species, in Michigan found only in

this area. The Keweenaw Peninsula is well known to birdwatchers, who come during spring migrations to watch great numbers of birds of prey funnel up to its tip.

If you like to fish, you can get plenty of action, too. You can launch near the campground's west wing onto Lake Fanny Hooe and go after rainbow trout, smallmouth bass, perch, and walleye. Or from the Copper Harbor Marina you can launch onto Lake Superior and drop lures for lake trout, splake and coho.

At that state-owned and -operated marina, you can also hop aboard a tour boat, which leaves several times a day in the summer, for a ride across the water to a small peninsula tipped by the Copper Harbor Lighthouse. A beacon has guided ships into the shelter of the harbor from the site, now park property, since 1848. The current structure — almost fully restored and filled with displays — replaced the original lighthouse during the 1860s.

During the winter, cross-country skiers can use four miles of trails in the park plus several more miles at nearby Copper Harbor Pathway.

Fort Wilkins State Park makes an excellent base from which to explore the Keweenaw Peninsula's abandoned copper mines, ghost towns, waterfalls, beautiful coastline and small, quaint villages. Two don't-miss-'ems, both only a couple of miles from the park, are Estivant Pines, a stand of virgin white pine, and Brockway Mountain Drive, the highest above-sea-level road between the Alleghenies and the Rockies.

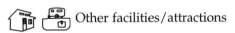 Other facilities/attractions

COUNTY: Keweenaw

CITY: Copper Harbor

CAMPING SITES: 165, all modern and a mini-cabin.

SCHEDULE: The park is open mid-May to mid-October. The Fort buildings are open daily from 8 a.m. to dusk.

DIRECTIONS: Go one mile east of Copper Harbor on US-41.

FURTHER INFORMATION: Fort Wilkins State Park, P.O. Box 71, Copper Harbor, MI 49918; (906) 289-4215.

Porcupine Mountains Wilderness State Park

Peace and solitude are not only just about guaranteed in Michigan's largest state park, they're almost hard to avoid. Its 60,000 acres of untamed rivers, spectacular waterfalls, crystal-clear lakes, miles of rugged Lake Superior coastline, ancient mountains, and the Midwest's largest virgin hemlock/northern hardwood forest seem to swallow up anyone who ventures from the few developed areas.

Since there's so much to see, begin your trip to the Porkies at the Visitor Center, near the junction of South Boundary Road and M-107. A multi-media show, exhibits and displays tell the story of the Porcupine Mountains, you can pick up the latest maps, and there is always a park ranger on duty to answer questions.

Then set out to see the Porkies the one best and basic way — on foot. Easy walks to breathtaking scenery, rugged multi-day backpacks deep into one of the last large wilderness areas in the Midwest, and just about every kind of hiking experience in between are all available along the 90 miles of trails that network Michigan's premier state park.

A short, paved path from a parking lot at the end of M-107, for instance, gently rises to the rim of a vertical cliff and the park's easiest-to-reach, most-famous attraction: a bird's-eye view of Lake of the Clouds. From the overlook you can take a strenuous one-hour hike down a steep trail to the lake and back up. Or you can just stay atop your perch near the park's center and enjoy the views of white clouds mirrored on the glassy, blue water and the miles of pristine wilderness that stretch out from it. It's tempting to imagine it was the view from here that inspired early Indians to give the area its name. In fact, it was the birch-bark canoeists' view of the high, thickly forested hills from Union Bay that reminded them of crouching porcupines.

The Summit Peak Tower Trail, accessible

from the South Boundary Road, may soon rival Lake of the Clouds in popularity. From the parking lot a half-mile route rises to Summit Peak, at 1,958 feet, the highest point in the park. Crowning the peak is a 40-foot-tall observation tower. The gasps from those who climb the tower are not only the result of slogging up the trail and climbing the structure but also from the stunning view that encompasses the park and distant views of Wisconsin, Minnesota and the Apostle Islands. A memorable view of the Little Carp River Valley comes from a deck on the trail to the summit.

At the east end of the park, the Union Mine Trail meanders through second-growth pine/hardwood forest and alongside the Little Union River on its way to the ruins of the area's first copper mine, dug in 1845. Access to the one-mile path comes two miles south of M-107 on South Boundary Road.

At the opposite end of the park is one of the most memorable one-mile stretches of river anywhere in the Midwest. During its final rush to join Lake Superior, the Presque Isle River drops 125 feet through a gorge in a roar of rapids and three stunning waterfalls. You can get good views from a boardwalk and trail that lead upstream from the rivermouth picnic area.

The elaborate network of interconnecting longer trails that lace Porcupine Mountains makes it *the* finest hiking and backpacking state park in Michigan. You can step into the wilderness from any of several access points and hike the rugged, wild interior for several days without retracing your steps. Before heading into the backcountry, however, you must register at the visitor center. You can also pick up a detailed trail map there, which is absolutely essential to finding your way through the intricate maze. Most trails are rugged, with many unbridged stream crossings and very little level walking. When you carry a fully loaded backpack, figure on covering about a mile an hour.

You can backcountry camp anywhere in the park except within a quarter mile of roads, designated scenic areas, shelters or cabins. Several small campsites are scattered throughout the backcountry. A few, usually those near trail intersections, are furnished with dry tent pads, campfire rings and pit toilets. Others are slated to be equipped with "bear poles" and simple box-style toilets.

The next step up the ladder in backpacking luxury are three roofed Adirondack-type shelters (with bunks) that are spaced through the deep interior. The rustic camping areas and Adirondack shelters are available on a first-come, first-served basis. This is black-bear country, so hang all food and scented items, such as toothpaste and deodorant, at least 10 feet off the ground, 150 feet from any campsite.

The ultimate in rustic living comes at 16 one-room cabins set amid some of the park's most secluded, scenic beauty. Each is furnished with a cupboard, a table, benches, a wash basin, pots and pans, tableware, a coffee pot, a broom, a mop, a rake, a water bucket, a wood stove, an axe, a saw, and two to eight bunks with mattresses. Outside are pit toilets and downed wood, which you can pick up and cut to size if you want a fire in the stove. Anything else you consider essential you have to haul in on your back, from one to four miles.

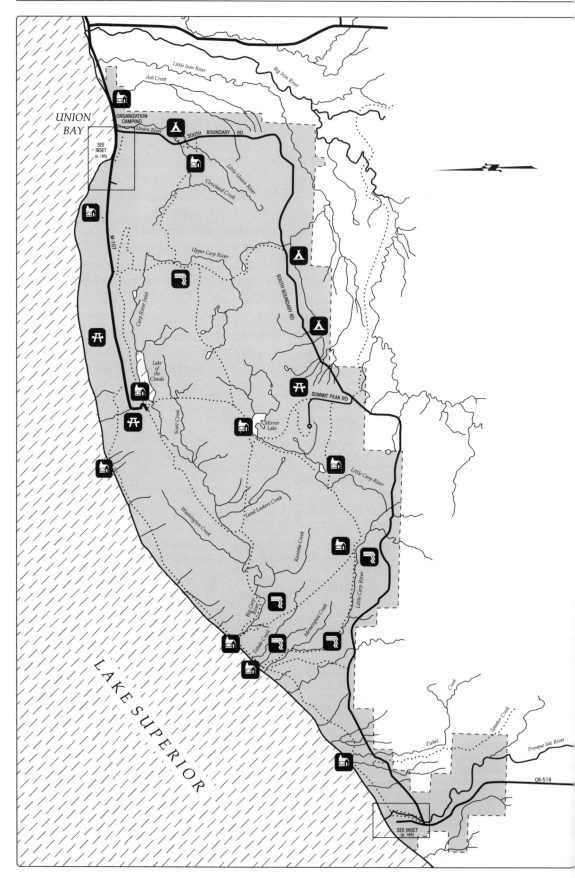

UNION
BAY

Little Iron River

Ash Creek

Big Iron River

ORGANIZATION
CAMPING

SEE
INSET
(p. 185)

Union River

SOUTH BOUNDARY RD

Little Union River

Cleveland Creek

M-107

Upper Carp River

Carp River Inlet

SOUTH BOUNDARY RD

Lake of the Clouds

Mirror Lake

SUMMIT PEAK RD

Scott Creek

Little Carp River

Washington Creek

Land Lookers Creek

Little Carp River

Korituka Creek

Big Carp River

Memengwa Creek

Toledak Creek

LAKE SUPERIOR

Creek

Speaker Creek

Tiebel

Presque Isle River

CR-519

SEE INSET
(p. 185)

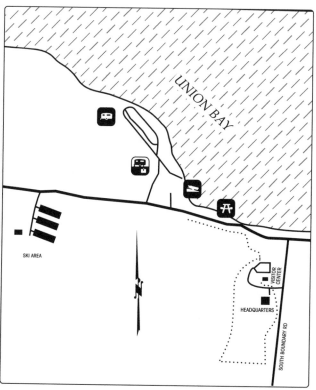

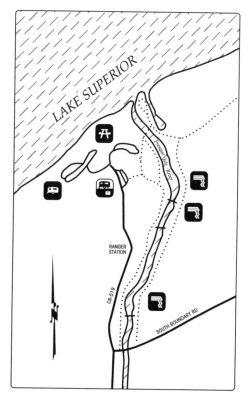

The unique accommodations are very popular, so if you want to try the pioneer living, make reservations with the park well in advance.

Still rustic, but a little closer to civilization are three designated camping areas strung out along South Boundary Road.

 Modern campgrounds are located at both the east and west ends of the park. Union Bay Campground, on the east, is conveniently close to grocery stores, the visitors center, Lake of the Clouds and numerous trailheads. One hundred large, completely modern sites loop around an open, grassy shelf that overlooks Lake Superior. Views of great slabs of bedrock that line the shore, plus the vast expanse of the greatest of the Great Lakes come from almost every lot. Also overlooking Superior, but from a high bluff at the west end of the park, is Presque Isle Campground. Eighty-eight semi-modern (flush toilets and showers but no electricity) sites there are spread in loops over a grassy clearing. Trees shade most lots, but they also obstruct views of the lake. The Presque Isle River and its beautiful waterfalls are just a short walk away.

You can often find a vacancy, even on summer weekends, at the Presque Isle Campground, but Union Bay fills almost every night from July through mid-August. Nights can be cool with an offshore breeze, so bring a jacket and long pants. In late May and early June, you may also want to bring a "bug-net" hat and carry a supply of industrial-strength insect repellent. There are enough black flies, then, to carry away a small dog.

Because of a steady offshore breeze, the flies probably won't interrupt your lunch at any of several picnic areas scattered throughout the park. But the views might. You can't go wrong hauling coolers to the tables right at the edge of Union Bay near the campground or alongside the Presque Isle River on the west side. And the panoramas from two small areas off M-107 just before you reach the Lake of the Clouds overlook are just about guaranteed to make you miss your mouth with your sandwich. From the tables there, you look down upon a green blanket of treetops that rolls away to the shoreline, sometimes a half mile distant, where water then spreads to merge with sky.

Not surprisingly, this vast, undeveloped tract shelters a long list of wildlife. Even coyotes have been sighted, occasionally within 100 yards of the visitors center. And you can

practically wear out your binoculars and the pages of your bird books here — 194 species have been spotted in the park. Another added plus: Wildflowers, including several species found in few other areas in the Midwest, carpet the forest floor.

Most of the park's vast acreage is open to hunters in season. Bear is near the top of the list of popular game, and during the past few years, bird hunting has also been good, particularly for ruffed grouse. Every deer-hunting season, the trailside cabins are in such demand that reservations are often filled up to two years in advance on a first-come, first-served basis .

The same is true during the first week of brook-trout season, when fly fishermen go after "brookies" in the park's several inland streams, some only yards from the cabins. Fishermen with boats launch them down a ramp near the Union Bay Campground, then troll for lake trout in the bay and surrounding Superior waters. Park rangers say that there's also "a notable steel-head run in spring and salmon runs in the fall."

When the snow flies, Porcupine Mountains is transformed into a major winter recreation area that includes the largest ski complex in any Michigan state park. A triple chairlift, a double chairlift, a T-bar and a handle-tow transport downhill skiers to 11 miles of Alpine trails that drop 641 vertical feet.

Cross-country skiers, too, can ride to the top then head off on 42 kilometers of power-tilled, double-track- set trails.

And snowmobilers can make tracks on their own 25 miles of trails, which inter-connect with hundreds of miles of other trails throughout Upper Michigan.

Other facilities/attractions

COUNTY: Ontonagon

CITY: Ontonagon

CAMPING SITES: 188 (100 completely modern, 88 without electrical hookups).

Sixteen trailside cabins are available for rent from April 1 through November 30, plus three of them are open all year. Reservations are accepted on a calendar-year-plus-one basis.

SCHEDULE: The park is open year round, but the camp-grounds are closed from December 1 through April 30.

DIRECTIONS: Go 17 miles west of Ontonagon on M-107.

FURTHER INFORMATION: Porcupine Mountains Wilderness State Park, 412 South Boundary Rd., Ontonagon MI 49953; (906) 885-5275.

Lake Gogebic STATE PARK

Great walleye fishing, swimming, a fine campground and 361 beautiful acres with frontage on the western shore of the Upper Peninsula's largest lake are reasons to spend time at Lake Gogebic State Park. You won't have a lot of company either. Only 52,000 campers and day users go out of their way to come here each year.

The park's focal point is long, narrow and shallow Lake Gogebic, which spreads out in front of the developed facilities like a giant front porch. The campground and day-use area are strung down a thin strip of land squeezed between the lake and M-64. One hundred twenty-seven spacious, grass-covered, fairly shaded campsites are arranged in several rows that parallel the lake. Almost a fourth of the lots directly front the shore, but you're within sight of and a short walk to the lake from any campsite. Twenty-two of the lots have no electrical hookups, but all campers have access to modern restrooms with flush toilets and showers. As you would expect from the park's low attendance figures, camping sites are almost always available.

On the south end of the developed area is a boat-launch ramp that is heavily used by walleye fishermen. Daily limits are the rule rather than the exception here, and the DNR annually uses walleye eggs from Lake Gogebic to stock other western U.P. lakes. Bass, perch and northern pike are also hooked, but it's the walleyes that bring fishermen back year after year. Rental boats are available at nearby private liveries.

North of the boat ramp, a sandy swimming beach lines a small cove. Lake Gogebic's shallow water (maximum depth 37 feet) warms by early summer, so swimming is excellent. A picnic shelter, with change courts and restrooms, plus a large playground area back the beach, and nearby, stately trees shade and shelter a large, grass-cov-

ered picnic area that overlooks the lake.

A 3-mile-long nature trail begins at the day-use parking lot (or at the north end of the campground), crosses M-64, then circles through the wild, undisturbed backcountry that makes up the vast majority of park land.

Cross-country skiers set tracks on the trail during the winter. You can't snowmobile within park boundaries, but hundreds of miles of trails crisscross the vast wilderness areas surrounding the park.

Hunting is not allowed in the park, but surrounding parcels of the Ottawa State Forest yield deer, partridge, rabbit and bear.

Other facilities/attractions

COUNTY: Gogebic

CITY: Marenisco

CAMPING SITES: 127 (105 completely modern, 22 lack electrical hookups).

SCHEDULE: The park and campground are open April 15 to October 30, but the modern restrooms are only open from May to the second week of October.

DIRECTIONS: Go 10 miles north on M-64 from the intersection of US-2, or drive 8 miles south on M-64 from the intersection of M-28.

FURTHER INFORMATION: Lake Gogebic State Park, N9995 State Hwy. M-64, Marenisco, MI 49947. From May to October call (906) 842-3341; the rest of the year call (906) 885-5275.

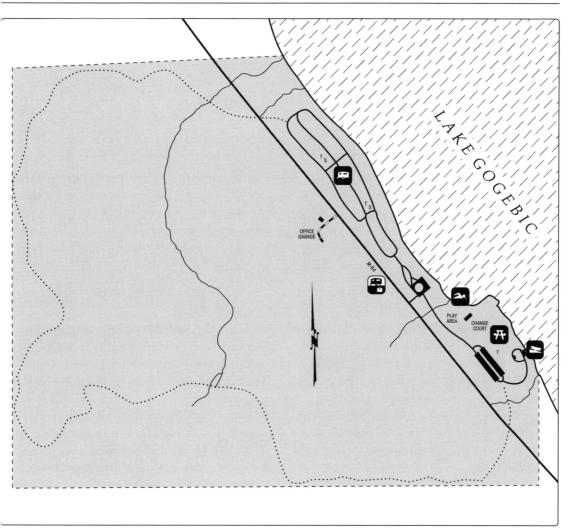

LAKE GOGEBIC

OFFICE
GARAGE

M-64

PLAY
AREA

CHANGE
COURT

Bewabic STATE PARK

If you're looking for gift shops, fast-food restaurants and glitzy tourist attractions don't come anywhere near Bewabic State Park. If you like the feeling of camping, swimming and fishing in the middle of nowhere, then this is the place for you. All that interrupts the unspoiled scenery for hundreds of miles in just about any direction is an occasional turn-of-the-century mining town. The surrounding sharply rising hills and thousands of acres of dense forest seem almost more appropriate for West Virginia than western Michigan.

Yet almost surrealistically plunked down in the middle of the park are two tennis courts. Bewabic, about as remote from any population center as you can get, is the only state park in Michigan where you can play tennis.

Carved out of the dense forest that covers most of the park's 315 hilly acres is a completely modern campground, with 144 sites widely dispersed over three large loops. Stands of trees and heavy undergrowth surround and separate most lots to the point that on some you feel like you're camping alone in the vast northern forest. Only lots 130-144, in an open, almost-treeless meadow, get full sun. The campground is only moderately used, and you can usually find a vacant lot any day of the week.

Just a few minutes' walk from the campground's north loop is the park's day-use area. Towering pines and hardwoods there tower over picnic tables and grills that spread over a large, grassy knoll. The

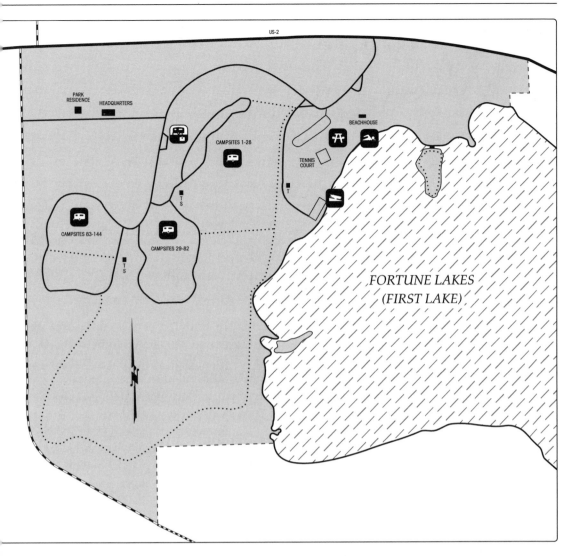

...bank falls away past a large picnic shelter, the tennis courts, and a bathhouse to the swimming beach. The sandy strip takes up just a tiny fraction of the park's forest-fringed shoreline along the first in a string of four interconnected lakes all named "Fortune" (1 through 4).

For some scenic views of the lake and park, walk a little way north of the beach and cross a footbridge to a short trail that circles a small, tree-clad island. Another path loops for two miles, briefly touching Fortune 1's shore, through the park's undeveloped southern section. Benches are scattered along the route, which is open in the winter to cross-country skiers.

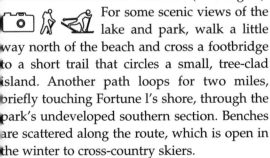

Canoeists put in at the park and paddle south on day trips through the beautiful, relatively undisturbed chain of lakes. Fishermen, who launch at the park's ramp, go after the lakes' walleyes, perch, northern pike and bass. Rental boats are available at a nearby livery.

 Other facilities/attractions

---

COUNTY: Iron

CITY: Crystal Falls

CAMPING SITES: 144, all modern.

SCHEDULE: The park and campground are open April 15 to November 30, but the modern restrooms in the campgrounds are only open May 15 to October 15.

DIRECTIONS: Go 4 miles west of Crystal Falls on US-2.

FURTHER INFORMATION: Bewabic State Park, 120 Idlewild Rd., Crystal Falls, MI 49920; (906) 875-3324.

JW *Wells* STATE PARK

At J.W. Wells State Park, natural beauty comes at almost every turn. Like a long, green ribbon, quiet forest — carpeted with ferns and wildflowers — covers the park's developed area, a narrow 3-mile-long strip between M-35 and Green Bay. East across the blue water, Wisconsin's Door Peninsula and Washington Island smudge the distant horizon. And inland, across the highway, not even a trail penetrates a deer-filled, undeveloped tract of old-growth pine, maples, beech, cedar, spruce and elm.

Four marked trails, ranging from 1.1 to 3 miles long, trace the shoreline, wind through peaceful woods, and probe the remote corners of the developed parcel. Three roofed trailside shelters are used more by cross-country skiers than hikers.

Skiers also make good winter use of six rental cabins, which line the shore only yards from the bay at the north end of the park. The one-room cabins, located at the end of a gravel road that tunnels through the dense woods, are secluded and rustic. Bunk beds, a wood stove for heat, firewood, and a table and chairs are the only standard furnishings. Pit toilets and drinking water are within a hundred-yard walk. You have to supply any other amenities.

Also hugging the rocky shore, but far removed from the cabins, is the park's 150-site completely modern campground. All lots are large, level, grassy, and open but with some shade. Many of the lots directly edge the bay, and you get good looks at the water from most of the other sites. You can usually find an empty spot, except on peak summer weekends, if you arrive early in the day.

The park's large, sandy, swimming beach dips into the bay just south of the campground. A bathhouse overlooks the sand and water, and there's plenty of playground equipment for young children. Farther downshore, picnic tables and grills are scattered over a grassy area under a dense canopy of stately, old hardwoods. A picnic shelter there, like the campground and most of the other facilities in the park, was constructed in the 1930s and '40s by Civilian Conservation Corps workers.

Smallmouth bass fishing in the Cedar River is good all year, and just after ice out, usually in early April, action for brown trout along the bay shore is as good as it gets anywhere in Michigan. Park rangers say that salmon, pike, perch and walleyes are also caught in area waters. You can't launch from the park, but a ramp is available in Cedar River, less than a mile north.

Hunting is not allowed in the park either, but the bordering Escanaba River State Forest is some of the finest deer-hunting country in the state. Sportsmen who go after grouse, pheasant, rabbit, and waterfowl there also report good luck.

  Other facilities/attractions

COUNTY: Menominee

CITY: Cedar River

CAMPING SITES: 150, all modern, plus six rustic rental cabins (two sleep up to 12, four sleep up to eight).

DIRECTIONS: On M-35 go 30 miles south of Escanaba or 25 miles north of Menominee.

FURTHER INFORMATION: J. W. Wells State Park, N7670 Hwy M-35, Cedar River, MI 49813; (906) 863-9747.

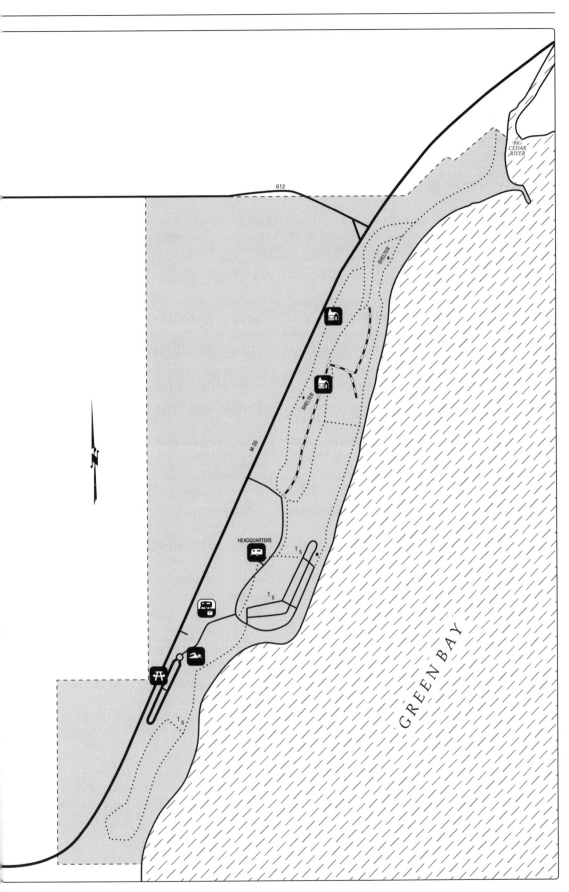

BIG
CEDAR
RIVER

G12

SHELTER

SHELTER

M-35

HEADQUARTERS

T S

T S

T S

GREEN BAY

Fayette Historic
STATE PARK

Fayette's natural scenery rivals that in almost any other Michigan state park. Part of it's mile-plus of Garden Peninsula shoreline is made up of 90-foot-high limestone cliffs that wrap around one of Lake Michigan's most-photographic harbors. A magnificent white-sand swimming beach also lines the waters of Big Bay De Noc, and deep, lush hardwood forests cover nearly 700 inland acres.

H But what draws most visitors to the park is the haunting beauty of its centerpiece — the almost-totally intact, carefully restored company town of Fayette. The village spreads over a fishhook-shaped finger of land that curls out into Big Bay de Noc to form Snail Shell Harbor. Perpendicular, white limestone walls; thick, green trees; the partially restored stacks of 100-year-old blast furnaces; and dozens of old, gray buildings almost totally enclose the small harbor's clear, blue water.

The setting, the scene, is near perfect. Fayette, without a doubt, is *the* most-picturesque village, deserted or inhabited, in Michigan.

Fayette began life in the 1860s with only one purpose: to process Upper Peninsula ore into pig iron for the Jackson Iron Company. The plentiful hardwood forests in the area yielded all the charcoal needed, and the outcroppings

that overlooked the company town provided the other essential ingredient, lime. At its peak during the 1870s the bustling industrial village was home and workplace to nearly 500 people. But just 20 years later, new smelting processes in the East rendered Fayette's blast furnaces obsolete, and the entire town picked up and left. The shells of the wood buildings and huge stone blast-furnace complex stood a lonely vigil over the picturesque harbor, then began crumbling into ruin until the 1960s, when the spot was resurrected as a state park.

More than 20 of the original buildings — including the opera house, hotel, doctor's office, superintendent's home, and company office — today stand as they did 100 years ago. Some have been fully restored and furnished to look exactly as they might have in the 1870s. Others serve as museums that illustrate daily life in the village as well as the history and industrial development of the town. Self-guided tour maps of the village are available at the visitor center, and guided tours run regularly during the summer.

The museum village, alone, is definitely worth a day trip. But you should also consider staying at the park's campground and enjoying the other fine facilities and attractions in this off-the-beaten track area away from crowds, traffic and tourist traps. A half mile south of the townsite, 61 fair-size, semi-modern (electrical hookups but no modern restrooms) sites are nestled in a stand of hardwoods several hundred feet back from the

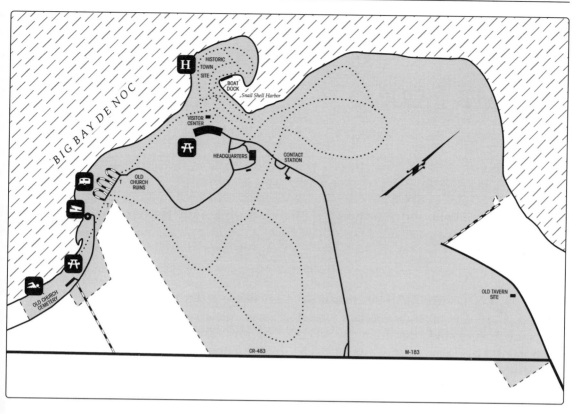

water. The tall trees are good for both shade and privacy, but they also completely screen any views of the bay. Overnighters only moderately use the area, and you can almost always find a vacancy during the week. Reservations are recommended for summer weekends.

Boat camping is allowed in Snail Shell Harbor, but there are few spaces and they are allotted on a first-come, first-served basis.

The park's 2,000-foot-long white-sand beach, backed by low dunes, is just a quarter-mile walk (or a two-mile-plus round-about drive) down the shore from the campground. Facilities there include a large picnic area, vault toilets, a water fountain and a picnic shelter.

Fishermen can launch at a ramp between the campground and beach, then go after perch and smallmouth bass in the bay's many hot spots, including Snail Shell Harbor.

And there is more than fishing action under the waters of Snail Shell Harbor; scuba diving is allowed during certain times of the day. A fee and use permit are required, and divers must leave all submerged artifacts in place.

Much of Fayette is open to hunters, who take squirrel, ruffed grouse, deer and bear both in and around the park.

 Some of the best opportunities for spectacular photographs come along more than five miles of well-marked hiking trails that loop through the 711-acre park. Some routes edge the limestone cliffs above Big Bay De Noc; one winds through deep woods in the backcountry.

Cross-country skiers can use the trails in the winter.

Other facilities/attractions

COUNTY: Delta

CITY: Garden

CAMPING SITES: 61, semi-modern.

SCHEDULE: The park is open May 15 to October 15. Village hours are—Spring & fall, 9 a.m.-5 p.m.; Summer, 9 a.m.-8 p.m.

DIRECTIONS: Approximately 15 miles west of Manistique on US-2, turn south onto M-183 and drive 17 miles.

FURTHER INFORMATION: Fayette State Park, 13700 13.25 Lane, Garden, MI 49835; (906) 644-2603.

Indian Lake
State Park

Two ... no, actually three for one is what you get at Indian Lake. The popular park itself is composed of two distinctly different, widely separated units, both with frontage on the Upper Peninsula's fourth-largest lake. And while at either, you should make the very short trip north to Palms Book State Park (p. 198) for a raft ride across Michigan's largest spring.

The 567 acres that make up Indian Lake's largest unit sprawl along and back from the lake's south shore. A large day-use area and a 158-site completely modern campground with two mini-cabins are fronted by more than a mile of sandy beach. You'll probably get tired of wading before you even reach waist-deep water, however, because the 4.5-mile-long, 3-mile-wide lake is an immense, shallow saucer. Ninety percent of its 8,000-plus acres is less than 15 feet deep, and its maximum depth is only 18 feet. This is one of the safest places in the state to turn small children loose in the water.

In the eastern half of the unit, the grass-covered campground stretches along the shoreline in a long loop. All lots are generally roomy, and a tree or two on most provides some shade but little privacy. Nearly forty of the lots are directly on the water, and the rest all have views of the lake.

West of the campground, picnic tables, grills a stately, old log-and-limestone pavilion, and a handicap-accessible trail line the shore.

Pleasure boaters and fishermen all put in at a launch ramp, which marks the westernmost of the unit's developed facilities. Indian Lake is rated as one of the best walleye holes in the state, but perch, pike, muskies, bass and bluegills also provide plenty of action. Rental boats and canoes are available at the beach.

Two marked hiking trails loop through this south-shore unit. The longest, a mile circuit, follows the shore from the picnic area, cuts inland along a creek, then winds through dense forest to the entrance road. Another path, the Chippewa Trail, though only a few hundred feet long can take more than an hour to walk.

Numbered posts along the route, which loops from and to the day-use area's easternmost parking lot, correspond to numbered paragraphs in a brochure, available at the trailhead. It's easy to get immersed in learning how early Indians used the variety of plants and trees that grow along the trail for medicine, food and tools.

Nearly three miles up the shore from the south unit is the park's much-smaller west-shore unit. That area features a small picnic area, playground and swimming beach , and its campground is completely different in layout and atmosphere than the south unit. The 144 sites are clustered in small cul-de-sacs at the ends of short roads that radiate out, like the spokes of a wheel. Thick woods shade all lots, and from any site you can see only a few other lots through the deep foliage. Each site has electricity, but there are no modern restroom facilities only vault toilets. It's a quarter- to half-mile walk from the sites to a campers-only beach that, while nice, doesn't rival the shoreline a the south unit. Overnighters here also have access to their own boat-launch ramp.

You can often find a vacancy at the west unit, but if you want to camp in the south unit, make reservations, as it usually fills first.

 Hunting is allowed in the fall at the west-shore unit, with partridge and other small game the most pursued. In addition to Indian Lake, anglers will find good fishing in other small lakes nearby. And just a few miles away on Lake Michigan, especially at the mouths of Thompson Creek and Manistique River, fishermen pull out good catches of coho and steelhead in season.

Other facilities/attractions

COUNTY: Schoolcraft

CITY: Manistique

CAMPING SITES: 302 (158 modern, 144 semi-modern), one rental tent and two mini-cabins.

SCHEDULE: The park and campgrounds are open year round, but the modern restrooms are closed from mid-October to mid-April.

DIRECTIONS: Go 5 miles west of Manistique on County Road 442.

FURTHER INFORMATION: Indian Lake State Park, Route 2, Box 2500, Manistique, MI 49854; (906) 341-2355.

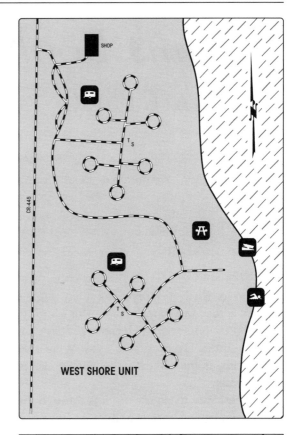

WEST SHORE UNIT

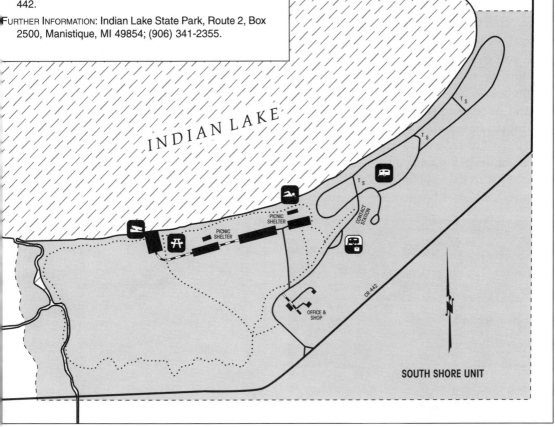

INDIAN LAKE

SOUTH SHORE UNIT

Palms Book
STATE PARK

Sparkling like a precious jewel mounted in a Sherwood green setting of thick cedar and pine in Palms Book State Park is *Kitch-iti-kipi*, Indian for "big cold water" or "big spring." Kitch-iti-kipi is, in fact, *the* biggest freshwater spring in Michigan, and the deep, nearly round pool is one of the most unusually beautiful sights in the state.

It's not its sheer size that is so impressive. Kitch-iti-kipi is definitely big — 200 feet across and 40 feet deep — for a spring, but even from its shore you can take it in with a single quick sweep of the eyes. What's so captivating is the almost-unbelievable clarity of the water.

The best way to experience it is through the two large viewing portals or over the edge of a 15-foot-square raft that one (or more) of 30-40 passengers pull along a cable from shore to shore. From the edges of the pond, submerged, mineral-encrusted fallen tree trunks seem to hang suspended in space, their tapered ends pointing to the magic taking place in the depths below. The bottom moves slowly by — colorful patterns of sand, moss and algae are interrupted by several roiling inlets that pump in 10,000 gallons of water a minute. Even at the center, the deepest point, you get a near-perfect view down to the bubbling cauldron of gray-white sand 40 feet below. Slowly cruising in

and out of the picture are 16- to 18-inch brown trout, magnified to look even larger by the water. The scene is one of few in Michigan where you become absorbed in, rather than overpowered by, the great natural beauty.

A 50-yard paved path connects the raft loading dock around the north edge of the spring to the parking lot. Facilities at this day-use-only park, all within a few yards of the parking area, include a small, grassy, shaded picnic area, restrooms and a concession stand/gift shop.

COUNTY: Schoolcraft

CITY: Manistique

CAMPING SITES: None

DIRECTIONS: From US-2 in Thompson, about 5 miles west of Manistique, turn north onto M-149 and follow it about 10 miles to the park.

FURTHER INFORMATION: Palms Book State Park, c/o Indian Lake State Park, Route 2, Box 2500, Manistique, MI 49854; (906) 341-2355.

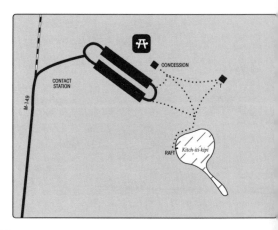

198

National
PARKS

Sleeping Bear Dunes
NATIONAL LAKESHORE

The beautiful sand-swept beach — often backed by striking dunes, and always flanked by the glorious blue-green waters of Lake Michigan — that runs nearly uninterrupted from the Indiana/Michigan border to the Straits of Mackinac is a unique state treasure.

The 40 miles between Platte and Good Harbor bays, where the coastline reaches its high point of dramatic natural beauty, has been declared a keepsake of the entire *country* as the Sleeping Bear Dunes National Lakeshore. There, massive headlands, some that rear up more than 400 feet, shoulder their way out into and over the lake. Frozen waves of sand top the towering bluffs and, below, march away from the glistening Lake Michigan beaches. Offshore, two beautiful wilderness island retreats stand guard, and inland, sand mixes with forest to form white-and-green necklaces around some of the world's most beautiful small lakes .

There's so much scenery, so much space, and so much to do that you can't possibly take in all of this vast natural area in just one day. The best way to enjoy the sprawling park is a section at a time. Conveniently, both nature and man have divided the national lakeshore land into four distinct parcels, separated either by private property or the waters of Lake Michigan.

CRYSTAL LAKE TO EMPIRE

Most of the action and scenery in this southern section of park land, which drops from high bluffs near Empire to low coastal plains around the mouth of the Platte River, comes on foot.

---

* Numbers in parentheses in text correspond to numbered hiking trailheads on map.

A short trail (3*), for instance, leads from just south of Empire to a breathtaking overlook of Lake Michigan from Empire Bluff, a popular hang-gliding spot. Farther south, between Otter Creek and the Platte River, a network of old logging roads and the abandoned grade of a narrow-gauge railroad make up most of the 15 miles of hiking and backpacking paths of the Platte Plains Trail (2). The system winds to several scenic overlooks of Lake Michigan, past a ghost town, and along the crests of ancient dunal ridges created during much higher water levels shortly after the retreat of glaciers.

In the heart of the Platte Plains Trail system, near the shore of Platte Bay, are a limited number of rustic backcountry sites at the White Pine campground, reached only on foot.

Just a mile south of White Pine, and connected by the trail (2) system, is the park's largest camping area, the Platte River Campground. The 171 modern sites there are widely spaced on tree-covered, low, rolling dunes just north, across a road, from the river. Overnighters at this busy area are only about two miles by car and four miles by river from Lake Michigan.

The Platte River dominates the southern quarter of the park as it flows out of Platte Lake and makes its way in lazy S's to Lake Michigan. The stream is popular with tube rafters, canoers, and especially anglers when king and coho salmon cause a

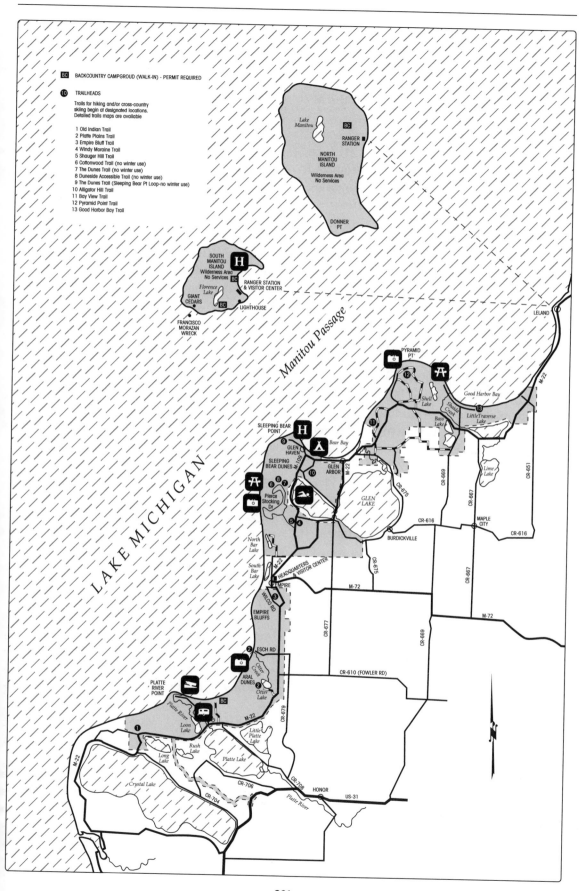

BC BACKCOUNTRY CAMPGROUD (WALK-IN) - PERMIT REQUIRED

10 TRAILHEADS

Trails for hiking and/or cross-country
skiing begin at designated locations.
Detailed trails maps are avaiable

1 Old Indian Trail
2 Platte Plains Trail
3 Empire Bluff Trail
4 Windy Moraine Trail
5 Shauger Hill Trail
6 Cottonwood Trail (no winter use)
7 The Dunes Trail (no winter use)
8 Duneside Accessible Trail (no winter use)
9 The Dunes Trail (Sleeping Bear Pt Loop-no winter use)
10 Alligator Hill Trail
11 Bay View Trail
12 Pyramid Point Trail
13 Good Harbor Bay Trail

fishing frenzy here in the fall. Boat access to Lake Michigan comes from a ramp at the river-mouth, but the outlet can run very shallow across shifting sand bars. To get to Platte Lake, 🚶 📷 use a ramp onto the river at the M-22 bridge.

Near the southern tip of the park, two 2.2-mile loops of the Old Indian Hiking Trail **(1)** both lead to a scenic overlook of Lake Michigan and the Platte Plains Dunes. As the name implies, the paths follow parts of an old Indian route.

EMPIRE TO GLEN ARBOR

The park's most strenuous (and rewarding) walks, one of the state's most beautiful picnic areas, one of the nation's most scenic drives, and the world's most famous sand dune are packed into this, the heart of the national lakeshore area.

Starting point for all the activity is the Visitors Interpretive Center, in Empire, where you can pick up self-guiding brochures, detailed maps to the extensive trail system, 🚲 📷 and loads of other information about the park.

About three miles north of the Center, Pierce Stocking Drive, one of the most scenic paved roads in the country, leaves M-109 to loop for 7.6 miles around the top of forested dunes. (If you want to mix beauty with strenuous exercise, pedal the bordering bike path.) Panoramic views along the one-way route come from three observation platforms constructed at the very edge of the cliffs, where sand and gravel fall sharply to the shore below. The most stunning is a look at Lake Michigan from the 450-foot-high crest of the park's largest dune.

🏕️ Tucked into a shaded, sheltered, grass-covered area 400 feet atop another area of the gigantic dune, is one of the Midwest's most picturesque picnic areas.

🚶 You can explore on foot from any of the stops, and you may be tempted to skid down the dunes' faces to the narrow strip of beach. Though it looks inviting, remember, it's a long, tough climb back to the top.

🚶 📷 At its northernmost point, the road rises to skirt the edge of the world's most famous sand dune, from which the park takes it's name — Sleeping Bear (itself so named by Indians who thought that the trees that then covered the bluff looked like a sleeping bear). North of Pierce Stocking Drive, from a parking area off M-109, you can climb 150 feet up a wall of sand to the summit of Sleeping Bear and good views of the surrounding countryside including Glen Lake and the Manitou islands. From the top, nine miles of trails **(6, 7 and 8)** mark the broad plateau's four square miles of sun-baked sand and alien landscape. Unfortunately, the shortest route to Lake Michigan is two miles — one way. Trail conditions here are hot and dry, reasons the park service advises that you carry water and wear a hat, shoes and suntan lotion.

🏊 🏕️ 🚶 After the strenuous Dune Climb and hikes, if you take them, you can cool off by crossing the highway and jumping into a beach at shallow, sandy Glen Lake. From the few picnic tables there, you can keep one eye on your children in the water and the other on the struggling dune climbers. From the highway just up from the beach, side roads lead to the start of several long trails **(10)** that loop through the land north of Glen Lake.

ⓗ 🚶 From M-109 farther north, Michigan's shortest state highway, M-209, leads to Glen Haven, and from there a gravel road ends at the Sleeping Bear Point Coast Guard Station and Maritime Museum. U.S. Life Saving Ser-vice displays there include a fully restored rescue-boat house, a crew bunkhouse, and a ship pilot house. Trails **(9)** that begin nearby head south into sandy wasteland, with the shortest loop to Sleeping Bear measuring nearly 6.5 miles.

⛺ 🏊 East of Glen Haven, nestled in low, wooded dunes along Sleeping Bear Bay, are 80 large, well-shaded lots at the D.H. Day Campground. The rustic sites are well spaced, private, and only a short distance from a fine swimming beach. Campground use is heavy throughout the summer, but since reservations are not accepted, you can often find a vacancy, especially in midweek.

GLEN ARBOR TO GOOD HARBOR BAY

In this northernmost mainland unit, you can enjoy the same striking scenery as in the rest of the park but without the crowds. Basch and Point Oneida roads both lead to the head of massive Pyramid Point and the start of several hiking trails. A quarter-mile-long branch from one, the 2.5-mile Pyramid Point Trail **(12)**, climbs steeply up the back of the bluff that marks the end of the blunt peninsula. From the top come spectacular views of the Manitou islands, Lake Michigan and on a clear day the Fox Islands, more than 25 miles to the north. You might be in the company of hang gliders who launch from the spot, but you can walk along the crest of the bluff in either direction with little chance of meeting the crowds found in other areas of the park.

From M-22 farther east, County Road 669 ends at miles of beautiful, seldom-used beach that edges Good Harbor Bay. A sand road leads east a few hundred yards farther to a picnic area and the start of another 2.5 miles of hiking trails **(13)**.

MANITOU ISLANDS

Least-accessible, yet near-irresistible, are North and South Manitou islands, the cubs, according to Indian legend, of the sleeping mother bear on the mainland.

You can cross the seven miles to South Manitou Island on a walk-on ferry, which makes one daily trip from Leland. Trouble is, the boat returns to the mainland after only three hours, but there's more than a day's worth of things to see and do. The only sure way to take in everything in that short time — albeit, cursorily — is to ride the motor tour.

To see less, but at a more leisurely pace, hike the many old roads that crisscross the island. And be sure to pack a lunch; there are no restaurants or stores on the island.

If you want to fully experience South Manitou, stay overnight at one of three primitive campgrounds scattered over its 5,000 acres. You have to backpack in (the closest is a few hundred yards from the boat dock) and low-impact camping methods are a must. You have access to pit toilets and potable water, but no other supplies are available.

H The island is packed with both natural and man-made attractions. You can walk through a lighthouse, built in 1871, and the island post office, which has been turned into a museum. Old deserted farms dot the interior, and off the southern shore the wreck of the *Francisco Morazan* a freighter that ran aground in 1961, juts from the water as mute testimony to the dangers of the coast. Tucked away in the southwest corner is the Valley of the Giants, a grove of towering virgin white cedar that includes the world's largest specimen.

While South Manitou has minimal facilities, North Manitou has none — no supplies and, away from the reception area, no toilets or potable water. It is 15,000 acres of wilderness about as remote as you can find in the Lower Peninsula. The only way to the island is on the walk-on ferry from Leland. Once there, you can wilderness camp at the single designated campground, near the ranger station, or anywhere else on the heavily wooded island you feel like setting up.

The ferry also takes hunters to North Manitou in season to thin the overpopulated deer herd that was introduced on the island in 1927 and managed for a time as a private hunting-preserve herd. The rest of the park is also open to hunting, with deer rabbit,

squirrel, ruffed grouse and waterfowl all successfully taken.

During the summer, park rangers conduct interpretive programs at the park's campgrounds and other locations.

 During the winter, many of the trails are open to cross country skiers and snowshoers.

Other facilities/attractions

COUNTIES: Benzie and Leelanau

CITY: Empire

CAMPING SITES: 251 (171 modern, 80 rustic). Reservations are accepted.

DIRECTIONS: Highways M-22 and M-109 run through the park from Frankfort to Leland.

FURTHER INFORMATION: Sleeping Bear Dunes National Lakeshore, 9922 Front St., Empire, MI 49630; (231) 326-5134.

Pictured Rocks
National Lakeshore

Even if you can only spend a couple of hours in the Pictured Rocks National Lakeshore, do it. Though you'll barely get a peek at this varied, spectacularly beautiful stretch of Lake Superior coastline, you'll still take home some unforgettable memories.

The next-best way to sample the waterfalls, inland lakes, streams, 300-foot-high Grand Sable Banks, mountainous sand dunes, vast beaches and near-vertical cliffs is to spend an entire day driving and walking. Even better, stay a night or two at one of the park's three secluded campgrounds.

And the ultimate? Plunge into the heart of the park on a week-long backpacking expedition.

Pictured Rocks Cruises photo

Nature has divided the 3-mile-wide, 40-mile-long park into three distinct sections. Dominating the west end are 15 miles of sheer cliffs that rise 50-200 feet directly from the lapping waves. Wind and water have carved the rock into pillars, arches, caves and other formations with such distinct character that they have acquired names such as Grand Portal Point, Miners Castle, Chapel Rock, and Indianhead. The faint, earthy pastels of a variety of minerals color the cliffs, and as sunlight plays across their face, the delicate greens, reds and browns continuously shift in shade and mood.

There's only one road in the park that goes out to the shoreline in this section — Miners Castle Road, which leads to viewing decks near the top of the turret-shaped sandstone pillar named Miners Castle. But the best you can say about the views of the cliffs from there is that they're easy to reach. An easier way to appreciate both the size and colors of the stretch of coastline that gives the park its name is from a privately operated boat tour that runs out of Munising.

The middle stretch of the lakeshore is a broad, seemingly endless straight stretch of sand and pebbles known as Twelvemile Beach. Beachcombers love the unbroken expanse, and indecisive sunbathers may spend an entire day

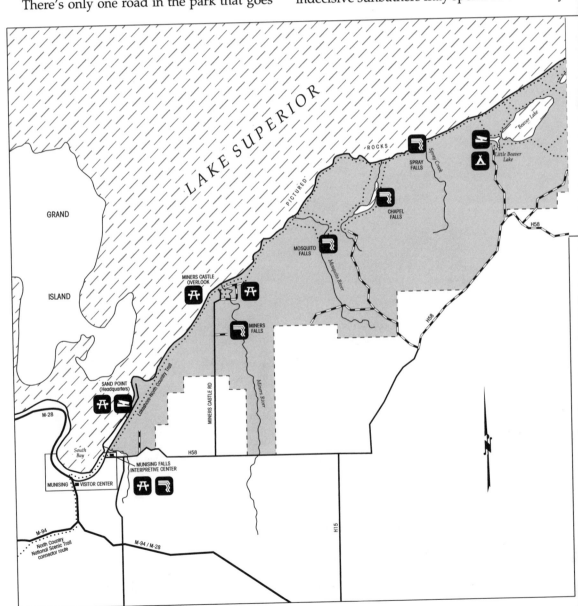

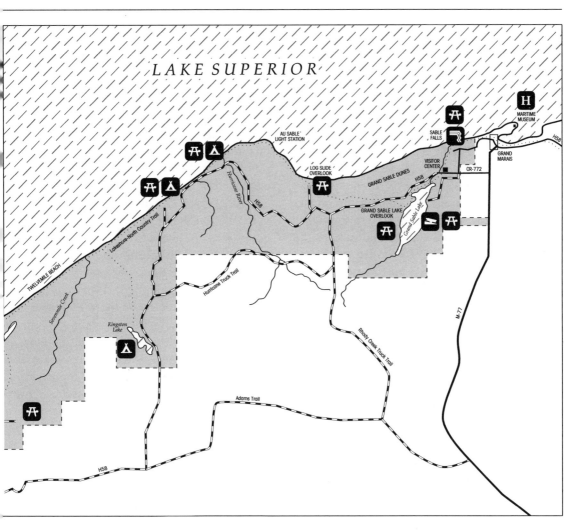

wandering from perfect spot to perfect spot. To take a dip here, however, nearly requires membership in the Polar Bear Club. Warmer swimming comes at Grand Sable Lake.

That lake is cut off from Superior by acres of sand in the park's third and easternmost section, from Au Sable Point to near Grand Marais. The main attraction in that five miles of park coastline is the Grand Sable Banks, monstrous piles of gravelly debris left by receding glaciers. The banks rise from the water at an angle of 35 degrees to a height of 275 feet in some places. On their tops at the east edge, four square miles of constantly shifting white sand known as the Grand Sable Dunes reach another 80 feet into the sky.

Eight waterfalls add exclamation marks along the park's entire length. Spray Falls plummets from the lip of the cliffs directly into Superior, while Bridal Veil Falls cascades down the rocky face of the cliff into the big lake.

Two of the most beautiful falls, Munising and Sable, are also the most accessible, almost serving as official greeters at the park entrances. From the west visitors center, a less-than-five-minute walk along a paved path ends at a platform with a head-on look at where Munising Creek drops like a plumb line for 50 feet from a large, rocky overhang.

At the opposite end of the park, tucked into a secluded, wooded setting just inside the Grand Marais entrance point, is Sable Falls. Sable Creek, in its last rush to the world's largest freshwater lake, tumultuously tumbles through a narrow, steep-sided gorge over a series of rock terraces. To get to the top of the falls, take an easy-to-walk quarter-mile path from a parking area off H-58 just north of the visitors center. At the falls itself, great views and photos come from a long series of steps that parallels the stream. At the bottom, another path ends at one of the best agate beaches in Michigan.

Other short to moderate walks, many self-guided by interpretive brochures, end at still-more waterfalls, rise to panoramic views from the top of Grand Sable Banks and Dunes, circle inland lakes, lead to a lighthouse, and pass shipwreck remains.

Many of those trails are a part of or connect to the backbone of the park's 80-mile system — the Lakeshore Trail, which follows the Lake Superior coast the park's entire 42.8-mile length. Hiking all or even part of the route is well worth the effort, and you'll take in a variety of stunning scenes available nowhere else in the state or even the country. There are several access points for day hikes along County Road H-58, which runs the length of the park.

Backpackers who make the several-day trek along the entire trail stay at 13 small camping areas scattered at 2- to 5-mile intervals. You must get a permit at one of the two visitor centers to backcountry camp or have advance reservations. Demand is heavy for the three to 10 sites at each area in July and August. A privately operated shuttle bus service relieves hikers of the necessity of either making a round trip or hitchhiking back to their car after an extended trek. The shuttle bus makes pick-ups at the visitor center and drop offs at either the other end of the park or at a point down the trail where you can then hike back to your car.

If you want to camp within sight of your vehicle, you have three areas within park boundaries to choose from. Twenty-two sites at the Hurricane River unit are nestled in deep woods bordering the lakeshore. Not far down the coast, strung along a bluff overlooking Twelvemile Beach are 37 more lots, and near the center of the park an eight-site unit is tucked into the heavily wooded shoreline of Little Beaver Lake. But with that grand total of only 67 sites, none reserveable, "choose from" becomes "try your luck getting a spot at," especially in July and August.

All three campgrounds are secluded, scenic and rustic, with water, picnic tables, and pit

toilets but no electricity. There is a fee for camping, and rangers conduct interpretive programs in July and August.

Hunting is allowed in the park, but from all reports is poor except for ruffed grouse.

Fishermen pull northern pike out of the park's several small inland lakes, and you can launch onto Grand Sable Lake and go after its panfish. This area of Lake Superior is also known for good spring runs of steelhead, trout and salmon. For small boats, access to Munising Bay and the open waters comes from a ramp at Sand Point. Larger boats can be floated from a City of Munising ramp near the southwest corner of the bay.

When the annual 200-inch-plus snowfall blankets the park, cross-country skiers glide over 16 miles of groomed trails or set out on more off-trail opportunities than you can shake a ski pole at. Several other trails at both ends of the park are reserved for snowshoers, and several unplowed roads may be used by snowmobilers.

COUNTY: Alger

CITY: Munising

CAMPING SITES: 67, all primitive.

SCHEDULE: The park is open all year, but the campgrounds are closed from November 1 to May 9.

DIRECTIONS: Take County Road H-58 east from Munising or west from Grand Marais.

FURTHER INFORMATION: Pictured Rocks National Lakeshore, P.O. Box 40, Munising, MI 49862-0040; (906) 387-2607 or 387-3700.

Keewenaw

NATIONAL HISTORIC PARK

The site of America's first mining rush has been designated as Michigan's newest national park.

In the 1840s the Keweenaw Peninsula's rich copper-bearing rock drew thousands of miners, prospectors, con artists, dance hall girls, soldiers, and even the likes of Horace Greeley (of "Go West, young man" fame) to this rockbound finger of land jutting into the icy waters of Lake Superior. Most who came here never got rich, but many ended up clawing a living out of the world's richest copper deposits. Eventually, more than 400 mines honeycombed the peninsula, and by 1910 Calumet, the queen of the copper towns, supported a population of over 30,000.

By the end of World War I, however, all the petals on the copper rose had fallen as the area's mines closed one by one. Today, only 7,000 people call Calumet home, and the Keweenaw economy has skimped along almost solely on the tourist trade.

The potential for increased tourism got an immense boost on October 27, 1992, when the Keweenaw National Historical Park was established "to commemorate the heritage of copper mining on the Keweenaw Peninsula — its mines, its machinery and its people." The park is only the second in the national system created to tell the history of an industry. Historic buildings will be preserved, and museums and exhibits will help tell the dramatic and colorful history of the area.

Fittingly, the entire village of Calumet will be included in one of the park's two units. The boundaries of the second unit will encompass the Quincy Mine, near Houghton-Hancock. Development will not begin soon, however. It will be several years, at best, before extensive visitor services, operated by the National Park Service, will be built.

But you don't have to wait to sample the unique atmosphere and history of the area. Many of the historic attractions that will be a part of the park are currently either governmentally or privately owned and are open to the public. Better yet, some of the most striking attractions are the small villages and towns of the Keweenaw Peninsula that are, in themselves, living museums of the copper era.

Calumet's downtown business district is already a virtual time capsule holding the glory of the old boom town. Red brick and sandstone buildings line the main street and wow visitors with their ornate cornices, bays, terra-cotta reliefs and stone trim. The jewel of the city is the Calumet Theater, built in 1900 and now listed as a National Historic Monument. Counter-pointing the historic business district of Calumet is the residential district of Laurium, just a few miles east. Think of Laurium as Calumet's Grosse Point. It was here that the men who made small fortunes from the mines built grand Victorian homes in which to relax after a hard day at the bank or mine office. Many of the magnificent old homes are beautifully restored, and a walk through the area takes you back to the turn of the century. Detailed brochures of walking tours for both areas are available.

Another leading attraction is the Quincy Mine, which has been designated a National Historic Site. Perched on a high hill overlooking Houghton-Hancock, the mine boasts the world's largest steam hoist, which during boom times raised 10 tons of copper at a time from depths of 9,000 feet. During guided tours you can stand next to the huge machine, but the high point of the visit is actually the low point — when you're taken down into the mine to experience, first-hand, the world of a Keweenaw copper miner. Farther to the north on the Keweenaw Peninsula, you can also take an underground tour of the Delaware Copper Mine, one of the oldest copper mines on the peninsula.

Other historical attractions in the area include a restored Finnish homestead, several fascinating museums, and the community of Old Victoria, which preserves small log homes that used to house miners.

The Keweenaw Tourism Council, on the corner of US-41 and M-26, has a wealth of guides and pamphlets directing you to and explaining all the attractions. You can also pick up most of the same literature in virtually any business in Calumet or by mail from the addresses in FURTHER INFORMATION.

Calumet Theatre

COUNTY: Keweenaw

CITY: Calumet

CAMPING SITES: None

DIRECTIONS: Begin by writing or phoning ahead or picking up guides in Calumet.

FURTHER INFORMATION: Keweenaw Tourism Council, P.O. Box 336, Houghton, MI 49931: (906) 337-4579 and Keweenaw National Historical Park, P.O. Box 471, Calumet, MI 49913: (906) 337-3168.

Isle Royale
National Park

Isle Royale isn't a park. It's paradise.

This remarkable 210-square-mile oasis, surrounded by the cold waters of Lake Superior, is uniquely wild and beautiful. The narrow, rocky inlets, sharp promontories and dozens of small offshore islands that form the coastline are more remindful of Maine than Michigan. Inland, 42 quiet lakes are tucked into thick pine, spruce and cedar forests pierced by long, rocky ridges. The sight and sounds of the island's wildlife, including the well-known moose and wolf population, are a variety and mix like nowhere else in the world.

And it's remote. The Michigan mainland is 56 miles away, at its closest, and the only way in and out is by seaplane or boat. Even so, park attendance has mushroomed in recent years, and Isle Royale currently ranks 12th among all national parks in backcountry use. People come not only for the remoteness and spectacular beauty but also because no drive-through gawkers litter the place with fast-food containers and aluminum cans, no loud radios squawk, no human herds trample the trails into muddy goo, and you never have to shoulder your way through a crowd of picture-snappers to get a glimpse of the scenery. Even at relatively developed Rock Harbor and the usually crowded backcountry campgrounds you can walk a few hundred yards from the boat dock, lodge, or camping site and enter as close to a primeval forest as you will find in Michigan and be lost to the sight and sound of civilization.

Few people come here on a whim. Experienced backpackers, canoeists, fishermen, and those who prefer the comfort of Rock Harbor's lodge complex almost all plan their Isle Royale trip in advance, sometimes years in advance. And they don't spend the time (average stay is 3.5 days), effort and money it takes to get here for the opportunity just to *see* the staggering beauty. They come to be immersed in it.

The unique combination of geologic, ecologic and environmental forces that have molded Isle Royale's character began eons ago when immense lava flows oozed over the region. During the following millenniums the center of the huge lava plate settled into the earth, creating a bowl that now holds Lake Superior. Today, pieces of the bowl's rim stick out of the water as the Keweenaw Peninsula and Isle Royale. The edge of this bowl is not smooth and polished. The distinct surface of Isle Royale, in fact, looks like someone stood parallel rows of gigantic rock slabs on end, then toppled them over like dominoes. The edges of those bedrock ridges are still wrinkled and cracked, but over the centuries, glaciers and erosion have deepened and rounded the valleys between.

Indians were early visitors, and trappers, miners and fishermen later worked the island, with a few families staying here year round during the late 1800s. From the turn of the century until it became a national park in 1940, Isle Royale was an expensive and popular summer resort spot.

Isle Royale's most-famous inhabitants, moose, arrived shortly after the turn of the century, probably by swimming from the Canadian mainland. In the near-ideal environment their numbers rapidly increased to the point that the herd nearly wiped out its food supply and itself during a period of mass starvation. When wolves arrived via an ice bridge from the mainland in the winter of 1948-49 they helped stabilize the herd's population. The study of how the wolves influence moose numbers and vice versa is one of the longest research projects of its kind in the world.

The moose and just about all other park wildlife share a striking characteristic: They are not intimidated by us humans. They almost seem to deliberately let us know that it's *their* island, not ours. Moose would just as soon walk through a campground as around it, and if you meet one on a trail there is no question who will step aside for whom. The majestic but comical animals have even been known to peer into the lodge restaurant windows to check out what's for breakfast. Fox constantly prowl campsites waiting to dart in and nab some food. And around Rock Harbor Lodge they walk the paved paths, often passing within

inches of incredulous visitors who have just stepped off the boat. Wolves are the only bashful animals and usually only make their presence known by isolated howls at night.

Because of most animals' apparent tameness, visitors need to be reminded to neither feed nor crowd the wildlife. And never forget, advise park rangers, that the animals have the right-of-way.

There's plenty of action below the surface, too — of Isle Royale's waters, that is. The island's many inland lakes and streams are only poor to average yielders (artificial lures only) of fish, but the waters of Lake Superior are another matter altogether. The brook and rainbow trout and northern pike that move through the island's many Lake Superior inlets and harbors leave fishermen dreaming about a return visit and wetting a line on the big waters. Monster lake trout await offshore, and if you want to go after the "big lakers" you can hop aboard a fishing charter at Rock Harbor or bring your own craft over on

the *Ranger III* (see DIRECTIONS). A Michigan fishing license is required for dipping a line into Lake Superior, but no license is needed on any of the islands, inland lakes or streams, although limits and other regulations do apply.

There's an awful lot to see and do, and there are many ways to take it all in. The best is to settle a backpack on your shoulders, cinch up its waist strap and strike off on the 165-mile trail system. You can literally spend weeks on the trails, which range from a one-mile walk to the 45-mile-long Greenstone Ridge Trail, without ever crossing your own tracks. Most of the 36 campgrounds are conveniently spaced at about full-day walks along the routes. If you want to see a lot of the island without trudging *every* step of the way, you can become a commuter on either a water taxi or a small passenger ferry that regularly drops off and picks up hikers at stops around the island.

All of the trails are accessible from either of the park's two entry points — Windigo, on the island's west end, and Rock Harbor, on the east. All routes are beautiful and all are rugged. Experienced backpackers say that they come here for R & R — roots and rocks. Trails are liberally laced with both kinds of toe-stubbers, and the only dead-level walking on the whole island comes on the sometimes-lengthy stretches of planks that cross marshy areas.

Don't take on Isle Royale without first-rate equipment that you've broken in, along with yourself, on training hikes on the mainland. Good sturdy hiking boots are a must, and you should carry rain gear, insect repellent, a first-aid kit, and a 0.4-micron water filter. (Tapeworm eggs contaminate all surface water, so it must be boiled for at least two minutes or filtered before drinking.)

Take your time to both enjoy the scenery and avoid becoming exhausted. An injured, sick, or sick-at-heart backpacker deep in the interior, can be days away from help. Any time you do need a dose of civilization, you can come out of the woods at Rock Harbor. The campground there has showers, and at a nearby restaurant you can put something into your stomach other than freeze-dried preparations.

Camping areas at the heart of the island are usually just clearings in the forest, but many along the coastline are furnished with roofed, three-sided, 8- by 12-foot wood shel-

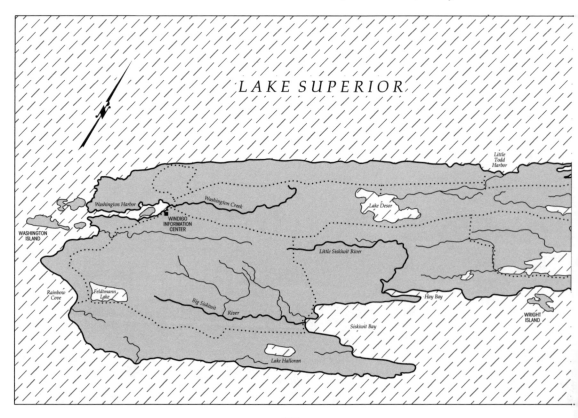

ters. You can use them to get out of the elements and escape the potentially murderous mosquitoes and black flies. Most of the 253 campsites have an occupancy limit of one, two, three or five days, and you must get a permit at one of the two park entry points. Because of the park's growing popularity it is almost a given that you will have to double up on camping sites from late June through late August. Bring a backpacker's stove (ground fires are prohibited at most areas) and plan to carry out everything you carried in, including garbage.

Both the shelters and tent sites are limited to a maximum of 6 campers. There are a limited number of group campsites that can accommodate 7-10 people. Groups larger than 10 are not permitted.

Another great way to see the island — and it seems to be a well-kept secret — is by canoe or kayak. Paddlers, who rent canoes at Rock Harbor or bring their own on any of the ferry boats, are the only ones who can reach campgrounds that are located on several small inland lakes. Portages that connect sheltered harbors and long, narrow inlets on opposite

sides of the island via inland lakes make for an outstanding circle canoe tour of the northern half of the island. That expedition also includes the only intimate looks at the jumble of odd-shaped peninsulas, islands, and long, narrow bays that shape, like the pieces of an unfinished jigsaw puzzle, the exceptionally scenic northwest end.

Not everybody who comes to Isle Royale sleeps in a tent or shelter, or under the stars. Many stay at motel-like units that line the edge of Rock Harbor or, on the opposite side of a narrow peninsula, in cottages that overlook Tobin Harbor. All rooms at Rock Harbor are furnished with spectacular views of Lake Superior, and the one-room cottages on Tobin Harbor, while not the lap of luxury, do come with bunk and rollaway beds, a kitchenette and a table. Backpackers who come out of the wilds join lodge and cottage residents at a sit-down restaurant that serves breakfast, lunch and dinner, including their specialty, fresh-caught lake trout. You can also get hamburgers, ice cream, soft drinks and other take-out foods at a concession area attached to the restaurant.

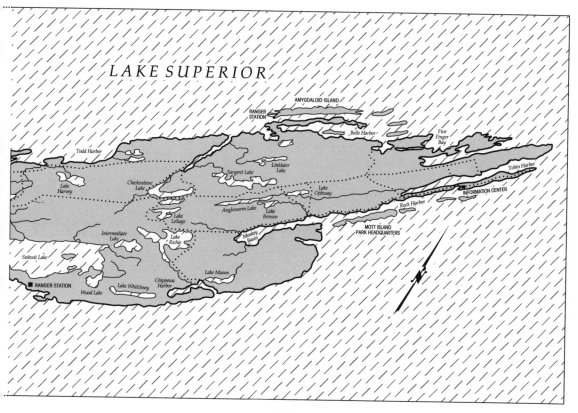

From Rock Harbor, you can set out on a number of half-day and day-long hikes. You can also rent canoes or small boats with motors and paddle or cruise for a few hours, an entire day, or even combine the craft with hikes for overnight excursions. The most-popular boat trip is an organized twilight cruise aboard the 45-foot *Sandy*. The two-hour-plus group outing, guided by a park ranger, starts with a skip across Rock Harbor to Raspberry Island for a mile hike through a spruce bog, which is followed by a voyage around the northern tip of Isle Royale to watch the sun set over Lake Superior.

Other regularly scheduled, guided day trips combine lengthy cruises on the *Sandy* with brisk hikes to abandoned copper mines, old fisheries and the Rock Harbor Lighthouse. Closer to the lodge, rangers conduct interpretive walks and also nightly programs in an auditorium.

COUNTY: Keweenaw

CITY: Houghton

CAMPING SITES: 253, all primitive. Groups of 7-10 campers must make advance reservations by calling (906) 482-0984.

SCHEDULE: Isle Royale is open April 16 to October 31. Full services—that is, concessions, lodge, restaurants and water taxi—are offered mid-June through Labor Day.

DIRECTIONS (from Michigan departure points): The 100-passenger Isle Royale Queen III makes daily round trips in August (4.5 hours one way) and less-frequent trips the rest of the summer from Copper Harbor.

The 165-foot government-operated Ranger III carries 125 passengers on a 6-hour crossing from Houghton to Rock Harbor. The Ranger departs from Houghton on Tuesdays and Fridays, overnights on the island, and returns to Houghton the following day.

Charter seaplane service out of Houghton makes 30- to 40-minute flights to either Rock Harbor or Windigo.

FURTHER INFORMATION: Isle Royale National Park, 800 E. Lakeshore Dr., Houghton, MI 49931; (906) 482-0984.

Isle Royale Seaplane Service, P.O. Box 366, Houghton, MI 49931.

Isle Royale Line, Box 24, Copper Harbor, MI 49918; (906) 289-4437.

Website: www.nps.gov/isro

email: isro_parkinfo@nps.gov

ALPHABETICAL LISTING OF
STATE AND NATIONAL PARKS

Parks with Hiking Trails

Parks with Historical Attractions

Parks with Cross-Country Ski Trails

Parks with Mini-Cabins
(see *Preface* for description)

Parks with Fishing Access Sites

Parks that Allow Snowmobiling

Parks that Allow Hunting

Algonac...113
Bald Mountain.....................................110
Bay City...88
Brighton...158
Brimley...146
Cheboygan...170
Craig Lake..42
Duck Lake...42
Fayette...194
Fisherman's Island.............................10
Fort Custer..66
Grand Mere...68
Hartwick Pines...................................20
Higgins Lake, South............................26
Highland...96
Hoeft...140
Holly...104
Indian Lake..196
Ionia...50
Island Lake..90
Lake Hudson..74
Leelanau...12
Ludington...32
McLain..176
Metamora-Hadley...............................108
Negwegon..135
Ortonville..106
Pictured Rocks....................................205
Pinckney...84
Pontiac Lake.......................................100
Porcupine Mountains..........................182
Port Crescent......................................120
Proud Lake...94
Rifle River..128
Seven Lakes...102
Silver Lake...36
Sleeper...122
Sleeping Bear Dunes..........................200
Sleepy Hollow.....................................53
Tahquamenon Falls.............................160
Thompson's Harbor.............................138
Van Buren...64
Van Riper..168
Warren Dunes......................................70
Waterloo...81
Wetzel..112
Wilderness..1
Yankee Springs....................................60

Parks Good for Birdwatching

Bald Mountain.....................................110
Bay City...124
Grand Mere...68
Hayes...78
Highland...96
Hoffmaster..46
Holly...104
Ionia...50
Island Lake..90
Leelanau...12
Mackinac Island..................................155
Mill Creek..148
Muskegon...43
Newaygo..40
Pontiac Lake.......................................100
Porcupine Mountains..........................182
Proud Lake...94
Seven Lakes...102
Sleepy Hollow.....................................53
Sterling..76
Tawas Point...130
Warren Woods.....................................72
Waterloo...81
Wilderness..1
Yankee Springs....................................60

Parks with Bridle Trails

Brighton...88
Fort Custer..66
Highland...96
Ionia...50
Maybury...92
Ortonville..106
Pinckney...84
Pontiac Lake.......................................100
Proud Lake...94
Van Buren...64
Waterloo...81
Yankee Springs....................................60

Parks with Rustic Cabins
(see *Preface* for description)

Parks with Mountain Bike Trails

Parks with Outstanding Scenic Attractions

Parks with Boat Launches

Parks with Shooting or Archery Ranges

Parks with Waterfalls

The Author

Tom Powers retired from the Flint Public Library in 1999, after 31 years of service, in order to devote the appropriate amount of time that writing, reading, traveling, and enjoying nature and hockey so richly deserve.

Power's first book, *Natural Michigan,* was published in 1987, and the first edition of *Michigan State and National Parks: A Complete Guide* appeared in 1989. His other books include *Michigan In Quotes, Audubon Guide to the National Wildlife Refuges: Northern Midwest,* and *Great Birding in the Great Lakes.* The last was published by Walloon Press, which the author and his wife founded in 1997.

Powers is the creator of the world's first Mime Radio Show and the Julia Moore Poetry Festival, which honors America's worst poet. The author continues to deny the Mime Radio Show had any part in the radio station's subsequent demise.

Barbara, his wife of 37 years; their two children and their spouses; and four grandchildren bring constant joy to his life.